THE VICTIMIZATION OF WOMEN

Sage Yearbooks in
WOMEN'S POLICY STUDIES

Series Editors

Jane Roberts Chapman and Margaret Gates
Center for Women Policy Studies
Washington, D.C.

Editorial Board

Volume 3
Sage Yearbooks in WOMEN'S POLICY STUDIES

THE VICTIMIZATION OF WOMEN

Edited by
JANE ROBERTS CHAPMAN
and
MARGARET GATES

SAGE Publications   Beverly Hills / London

For information address:

SAGE PUBLICATIONS, INC.
275 South Beverly Drive
Beverly Hills, California 90212

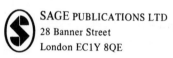

SAGE PUBLICATIONS LTD
28 Banner Street
London EC1Y 8QE

Printed in the United States of America

International Standard Book Number 0-8039-0923-3 (cloth)
International Standard Book Number 0-8039-0924-1 (paper)

Library of Congress Catalog Card No. 77-93701

SECOND PRINTING

CONTENTS

ADELE NICOLE SOLOMON
1954 - 1976

This book is dedicated to "Nicky" Solomon, a young woman, student, daughter, feminist, resident of our community, and victim. She died near the Center for Women Policy Studies, following an assault by a male stranger. Her death was one of the spurs that led to this volume on the victimization of women.

1

INTRODUCTION

MARGARET GATES

We have had the morality of submission, and the morality of chivalry and generosity; the time is now come for the morality of justice.

John Stuart Mill, 1869.

This is a book about violence, sex, and power. It tells of helpless women and female children who are beaten and sexually abused. And it is the story of a society that appears unable or unwilling to stop this victimization. This is the stuff of which millions of fantasy lives—and too many real ones—are made. We do not know why this is so. Some believe it is because of the illness or perversity of individuals, while others think that it is the natural result of a sexist social order.

The editors agree with the second point of view, and this chapter is intended to explain their opinion. However, the rest of the volume does not seek the root causes of female victimization, but suggests treatments for the symptoms of this social sickness. We aimed at collecting as much as is known about the extent of female victimization, treatment modalities, and prevention techniques. The contributors are practitioners, planners, and policy-oriented professionals. Although they recognize the importance of discovering and destroying the cause(s) of the various abuses of women described in this book, their own jobs are to treat the symptoms of these related societal illnesses until a cure can be found.

The reader might ask why we have constructed a book which addresses the victimization of a class of people (women) rather than the criminality of another class (men). In other words, why address the passive role rather than the aggressive one? One answer has already been suggested: in the short term, women victims need not only legal, medical, and social services, but psychological and emotional support so that they can help themselves and each other. These needs should be defined and legitimized so that they can be met. Second, unfortunately, there is a need to establish that women and children who are abused in the ways described in this book are "bona fide victims."

The Women's Movement has been attempting to validate the sexually assaulted woman and the battered woman as true victims. Despite an apparent rise in the consciousness of the general public with respect to these crimes, the victims continue to be subjected to a second "victimization" by the criminal justice system, the community, and sometimes their families, who suggest that the women contributed to their criminal victimization or even "deserved it." The objective of women's efforts to substantiate this double victimization is not so much to shift the blame from the victims to individual offenders, police officers, judges, and jurors, as to indict, instead, our value systems, social organization, and institutions.

In the academic realm, a similar phenomenon has been taking place. The study of victims has emerged as a recent development in the field of criminology, itself a discipline not more than a century old. The term "victimology," and therefore the parameters of the subject, are not yet well defined. One victimologist (Dadrian, 1976:42) has broadly described his field as "the study of the social processes through which individuals and groups are maltreated in such a way that social problems are created." This definition encompasses two areas of concern: "the social context in which victimization occurs, and the social consequences of such victimization." In this chapter we will look at the social context of female victimization; its social consequences will be discussed in the remainder of the book.

Organizing a discussion of the social context of female victimization is difficult because the problem has historical, cross-cultural, and interdisciplinary dimensions. Since none of these can be adequately developed here given the space limitations, we must deal in generalities and confine ourselves to the basic concepts.

The simplest explanation for maltreatment of women by men is the obvious fact that most men are physically stronger than most women, so that when it comes to fights, women are more often the losers. An extension of this observation is that most women anticipate their own defeat and are, therefore, intimidated by and make themselves subservient to men. This disparate power relationship has been recognized, sanctioned, and reinforced over time by all our social institutions.

In addition to their smaller stature and comparative weakness, women are made more vulnerable by their childbearing function. Not that pregnant women or nursing mothers are usually disabled, but their need for security is normally heightened. As important, their ability to produce offspring has made women valuable to the opposite sex and, at least in earlier eras, subject to being carried off like property to be used for breeding as well as for pleasure.

These same characteristics of women that make them so desirable to men that they are subject to capture and control, also make them likely pawns in power struggles between men. Thus men have protected their mothers, daughters, sisters, and wives in much the same way as their land and livestock. The price women paid for protection has been fidelity and obedience. From the earliest of times, this was thought of as "the natural order of things"—and in some cultures it still is.

But, as humankind grew civilized, men developed codes aimed at reducing war and hostility among themselves so that they could turn their attention to other matters such as commerce and the arts. To be sure, laws and treaties frequently broke down, but men have created civilizations in which brute force no longer prevails as a general practice in daily life.

Since men have learned to form systems through which to protect even the weakest male in the community and his property, it is surprising to find that women still need "protection" from individual men. Yet the legal institutions that deter men from taking advantage of each other do not welcome complaints by women who have been victimized by men. When the man accused is a stranger, their question is why the woman made herself vulnerable to attack by being without a protecting male. When it is the husband or lover who is expected to protect her but in fact abuses her, their question is whether she has paid the fidelity and obedience required by the protector for his services.

From this thumbnail sketch, the reader will have perceived that we are suggesting that victimization of women by men is a consequence of the disparate power relationship between these two classes of human beings.

The quotation with which this chapter began is from the 19th century essayist John Stuart Mill's work, "The Subjection of Women," and gives us a basis for further analysis. The quotation suggests that there was an ancient era in which the weak had a moral obligation to submit to power. This was replaced by an age in which morality dictated the right of the weak to the forbearance and protection of the strong. More than a hundred years ago, Mill saw that this code of "chivalry and generosity" of the powerful (men) toward the powerless (women) was not viable, and he predicted the coming of an age of justice based on equality between the sexes.

The chronological progression of moralities that Mill describes is not as clear-cut as he implies. As we shall see, there are still cultures in which females submit themselves or are subjected to having the status of property, with no guarantees of male "protection" of their rights as human beings. Overlapping stages are found in our own middle-class society, where the call for a constitutional amendment to guarantee equal rights for women is countered by the voices of women who want to maintain the status quo (dependency of the female on the male). Despite these imperfections, Mill's chronology serves as a three-stage framework for the discussion of the social context of female victimization.

THE MORALITY OF SUBMISSIVENESS

Women are not the only people in the history of humankind who, as a class, have been submissive. Slaves, serfs, and vanquished nations or tribes have adapted to subjugation in this way. Similarly, most of the major religions have required that their followers submit to the will of their deity whether this meant giving their own lives, sacrificing loved ones, or making war. Submission to the authority of God-ordained priests and kings followed from this principle.

Within the family, children are taught to submit to their parents, although in some cultures boys reach an age when they are ritualistically released from the obligation to obey the older women in the family and take a place in the "man's world," albeit beneath the station of their fathers. Of course, the families themselves are subject to ranking within society. In other words, in organized societies there is a pecking order that is determined in families largely by sex and age and in the larger community by race, religion, caste, economic status, occupation, and other variables. Admiration for individuals or families who attempt to rise above their assigned status is a relatively recent phenomenon and still far from universal.

On the contrary, submission to a societally validated superior has usually been considered virtuous. Certainly, within the Christian world, Jesus gave the example by submitting himself to die on the cross to fulfill the will of His Father. His followers have emulated him by taking vows of obedience and self-denial when they enter holy orders. Christian mystics have gone farther by completely nullifying their own wills to accomplish the union of their souls with God.

Submissiveness, then, is a personal quality which anyone, male or female, can develop in order to adjust to an inferior power relationship entered into by choice or by force. It is an adaptive behavior that is essentially neither "masculine" nor "feminine." If more women than men manifest this trait, that fact is owing to their lower rank.

In the traditional heterosexual relationship, the male has more power than the female—as Kate Millett (1970:343) has made clear: "sex role is sex rank" even in a homosexual relationship. Thus, femininity has become linked to submissiveness in sexual relationships, and gender identity has come to include power for men and powerlessness for women.

It should be acknowledged parenthetically that powerlessness can also lead to feelings of helplessness and horror. We have seen this played out in implicitly sexual terms on the covers of magazines and "comic" books where a terrified woman is being attacked by a madman or a monster. Submission is a way of coping with the reality of being overpowered—that is, it is an act of will over which the victim has control, a surrender.

In sexual terms, the surrender of one person to another can have widely varying results depending upon the response it receives. The mutual surrender of two lovers to each other is described by Robin Morgan (1977:237) as the feminist ideal of egalitarian give and take between partners:

> The possibility of their naked minds and bodies engaging one another—a joyous competition which must include any assumption of defeat as (1) temporary and (2) utterly lacking in humiliation; of any triumph as, obversely, impermanent and meaningless. The taking and giving of turns.

At the other end of the spectrum of response to surrender is the sadomasochism so well exemplified in Pauline Reage's *Story of O* (1965) which is alternatively described as pornography and a parable of Christian love. O is a woman who gives herself to her lover to be tortured and sexually abused by others for his sake. Significantly, this is accomplished in several institutions established to ritualistically train women to convert the pain of beatings, brandings, and sexual abuse into pleasure and love for their masters. The book is at once erotic and symbolic. Its relevance to our discussion is that it epitomizes social approval for the destruction by women of their own egos and their assent to objectification of their bodies—especially when these are characterized as acts of love.

Indeed, there has been so much written (mostly by men) of the desire of women to be humiliated and degraded that it is no wonder that literary figures of the magnitude of Jean Paul Sartre have been intrigued by the work of Jean Genet. Genet, a French orphan who spent virtually his whole life in reformatories and prisons, had a series of sexual identities which are described in his books and plays. Through his work one perceives how an all male prison population establishes rank based on "virility." The weaker, younger, or more vulnerable males are "feminized" and thereby stigmatized. Genet's reaction to his own feminization was a mixture of both hostility toward and desire for the supermales, and a kind of glorification of the female role. As Kate Millett (1970:344) said in her lengthy analysis of his writing:

> Through the miracle of Genet's prose the masochism consonant with their [feminized males] role as slaves is converted to the aura of sainthood. How else does the good woman traditionally excel except through suffering.

In his *Miracle of the Rose,* Genet (1966), gives us his interpretation of the mental processes of a fellow inmate who was subjected by older boys to a kind of initiation ritual. The victim was made to stand against a wall so that the others, lined up at a distance, could attempt to spit into his mouth. In order to ameliorate the humiliation inherent in this act, the boy imagined that what he was receiving in his mouth and over his body was not spit but roses, and that love rather than hate had propelled them. But as the assailants became excited by their game, the victim in his own mind carried one step further this transformation of hostility into love:

I was no longer the adulterous woman being stoned. I was the object of an amorous rite. I wanted them to spit more and thicker slime. Deloffre was the first to realize what was happening. He pointed to a part of my tight-fitting pants and cried out: "Hey! Look at his pussy! It's making him come, the bitch!" [Genet, 1966:316]

The significance of this bizarre anecdote is that although the victim is male, he reacts in the same way to degradation as do the female characters in the sadomasochistic relationships recounted or invented in other literature. It seems to suggest that masochism is not exclusively a component of female sexuality, as the Freudians would have us think, but is a possible adaption by either men or women to physical or sexual abuse from which the victim sees no escape.

We do not have to consider the difficult question of why some human beings (the true masochists) find pleasure in punishment, since such people cannot be categorized as victims for the purpose of our discussion. But we must acknowledge that it is a very common opinion that most women like to be overpowered and even abused by men. This belief has a self-fulfilling quality in that it encourages men to bully and brutalize women, and it may cause women to be more accepting of this behavior than they need be. People who say that rape victims should "relax and enjoy it" and who assume that battered women like being beaten are of this mind set.

The roots of the female masochism myth are difficult to trace. A large part of it may come from the failure to distinguish between actually experiencing pleasure from being hurt and the related phenomenon of fantasizing being sexually overpowered. Although most are reluctant to discuss it, many women seem to have indulged in such fantasies. The same women would never choose to act out these scenarios and, in fact, would likely be severely traumatized if their daydreams turned to reality.

A number of theories have been posited to explain the masochistic nature of such fantasies. A popular one is that young girls cannot amuse themselves by imagining a consensual sexual encounter without tainting their enjoyment with guilt. Since they are socialized to take responsibility for avoiding premarital lovemaking, the only context in which girls can enjoy guiltless fantasies is one in which control of the situation has been taken away from them by force or authority. Thus the girl who daydreams being gang-raped by the boys in her neighborhood may actually desire sexual contact with these boys on her own terms, which are apt to be quite romantic, but would be seriously injured psychically if even one of her neighbors forced her to have sexual relations with him.

Robin Morgan (1977) in her essay "Politics of Sado-Masochistic Fantasies" summarizes other explanations for masochistic fantasies, including the idea that they are self-punishing devices used by women who are ashamed of their own assertiveness, their sexuality, or their whole selves. Morgan sets out her own theory in a parable telling of woman's quest for understanding of and response to her sexuality by man. She says that "the sado-masochistic fantasies are themselves symbols for realities of dominance and submission, which are in themselves metaphors for power and powerlessness" (Morgan, 1977:236). Since in patriarchy men have power and women do not, woman has not succeeded in establishing sexual relationships on her own terms and is degraded by the realization that she has accepted what she and man both know is his pretense of complying with her wishes.

Of course, not all women consider themselves degraded by their submissive sex role. But the fact that they do not resent having to conform to the expectation of passivity does not prove that it is "natural" for them to be submissive. Women have been socialized to behave in a variety of ways in different cultures and different eras. To show that all these customs, however widely practiced, do not necessarily reflect natural behavior, we can point to one of the most bizarre—the self-mutilation of millions of Chinese women.

The morality of submissiveness is well exemplified by the so-called "art" of footbinding practiced by Chinese women for a thousand years. Female children of six or seven years of age were subjected to a process in which their toes were turned under toward the soles of their feet and bound that way until the flesh petrified, the toenails fell out, and the bone and muscle structure was completely deformed. A girl could scarcely move about on the tiny feet which were produced by this painful procedure, and the lines of her body became distorted by her efforts to walk.

Andrea Dworkin in her book *Woman Hating* (1974) tells how, in 1931, footbound women, captured in war because of their inability to flee, were tortured by their foreign captors who despised them for their disfigurement. Their own men, however, considered bound feet to be an essential component of female beauty and, furthermore, believed that the resulting posture of the pelvis created folds in the vagina which increased a woman's sexual urge and the pleasure of her partner.

Psychologically as well as physically, the footbound wife was satisfying to her husband. Dworkin quotes a Chinese man who admits to being a very ordinary person, "But to my footbound wife, confined for life to her house except when I bear her in my arms to her palanquin, my stride is heroic, my voice is that of a roaring lion, my wisdom is of the sages. To her I am the world; I am life itself" (Dworkin, 1974:108). As Dworkin remarks, "Chinese men, it is clear, stood tall and strong on women's tiny feet." Bear in mind that footbound women were not victims of isolated atrocities but represented a cultural pattern of self-inflicted disability affecting virtually all women of a huge nation for 10 centuries.

Chinese women have apparently made a great leap toward equality in this century, but other women are still subjected to inhuman practices. The popular press regularly informs us of the way women are treated in other cultures. Recently, a newspaper reported that one Somali tribe concluded a property settlement with another which included, along with livestock and farm implements, two young girls for brides. The article added that female circumcision without anesthesia or sterile implements is commonplace in Somali and that it "insures virginity until marriage" (*Washington Post,* 1977:A28). What is referred to as circumcision and is also known as "female castration" is actually a combination of procedures properly termed clitoridectomy (removal of the clitoris), excision (removal of all the genitalia except the *labia majora),* and infibulation (excision followed by the sewing of the genitals to prevent intercourse). According to testimony given at the International Tribunal on Crimes Against Women in Brussels in 1976 (Russell and Van de Ven, 1976), clitoridectomy is a common practice in Africa, and parts of the Near East, where it is considered an "initiation ceremony" for girls seven to 12 years old. A witness from Guinea said that 85% of the women in her country are excised. Infibulation which "insures virginity" can be reversed when the girl marries but if the husband so wishes, he can have her sewed up again to insure chastity while he is away from home.

Indeed, we do not have to go to another continent or another era for evidence of female submissiveness. In her book, *Fascinating Woman-hood,* announced on its cover as a "million-copy bestseller," Helen Andelin (1975) describes the feminine and masculine roles which she believes are typical and appropriate for today in the United States:

Femininity is a gentle, tender quality found in a woman's appearance, manner and actions. It is a sort of softness, delicateness, submissiveness, and dependency upon men for their masculine care and protection. More than anything else, it is a lack of masculine ability—a lack of male aggressiveness, competency, efficiency, fearlessness, strength, and "the ability to kill your own snake."

The important thing to remember is this: Men enjoy protecting women. Do not think, therefore, that it is an imposition on a man to protect a dependent, feminine woman. One of the most pleasant sensations a real man can experience is his consciousness of the power to give his manly care and protection. Rob him of this sensation, of superior strength and ability, and you rob him of his manliness. [Andelin, 1975:261]

THE MORALITY OF CHIVALRY

Andelin's descriptions of femininity and masculinity capture the essence of chivalry. The woman is delicate, soft, submissive, dependent, and virtuous, and the man is strong, competent, courageous, and protective toward her. These are the ladies and gentlemen whose lives in Victorian society provided the subject matter for John Stuart Mill's essay "The Subjection of Women." Mill recognized that chivalry and courtly love were ideals that had been glorified in literature but were faulty in practice.

In his famous essay he wrote of the way women's inferior legal and economic status made them helpless victims when their male protectors declined to be knights in shining armor. He said, "If ever any system of privilege and enforced subjection had its yoke tightly riveted on the necks of those who are kept down by it, this has." He pointed out that, "Until a late period in European history, the father had the power to dispose of his daughter in marriage at his own will and pleasure, without any regard to hers." Mill also acknowledged the possibility of rape in marriage: "However brutal a tyrant she may be chained to—though she may know that he hates her, though it may be his daily pleasure to torture her, and though she may feel it impossible not to loathe him—he can claim from her and enforce the lowest degradation of a human being, that of being made the instrument of an animal function contrary to her inclinations." And he recognized other forms of physical abuse of women in the home as commonplace: "When we consider how vast is the number of men, in any great country, who are little more than brutes, and that this never prevents them from being able, through the law of marriage, to obtain a victim, the breadth and depth of human misery caused in this shape alone by the abuse of the institution swells to something appalling" (Mill, 1970:30-36).

A hundred years later, American women are still in need of equal rights before the law, and it has been only in the very recent past that the availability of divorce and abortion have made it possible for some American women to free themselves from the brutality that Mill described. Poor women often cannot afford these means of escape.

The wives of middle-class American men are sometimes too "poor" to leave abusive husbands, and that is a reality which John Stuart Mill did not have the opportunity to observe. Andelin, on the other hand, seems to have ignored the unfortunate legal and economic position of most homemakers. What is the middle-class American woman to do if her "protector" refuses to support her or becomes abusive? Her dependency on him, which may have been feigned initially to gratify his ego, has probably become quite real as she has children and her ability to support herself diminishes. When she really wants to escape an abusive relationship, she may find that economically she is as effectively immobilized as the Chinese woman was by her bound feet.

We see then that the morality of submissiveness and that of chivalry differ only in that the latter places a moral obligation on the male to protect the female. The underlying power relationship between the sexes is the same, so that chivalry is merely a way of relating to women, which a man can adopt or reject with differing social consequences depending upon his class. As Kate Millett put it:

> While a palliative to the injustice of woman's social position, chivalry is also a technique for disguising it. One must acknowledge that the chivalrous stance is a game the master group plays in elevating its subject to the pedestal level. [1970:37]

Millett observes that, in addition to masking women's real powerlessness, the practice of chivalry exacerbated class and life-style differences among women, manipulating lower-class women into docility with the hope of becoming ladies while intimidating the "ladies" with the threat of being toppled from their pedestals. As she said:

> the Victorian doctrine of chivalrous protection and its familiar protesta-tions of respect, rests upon the tacit assumption, a cleverly expeditious bit of humbug, that all women were "ladies"—namely members of that

fraction of the upper classes and bourgeois which treated women to elaborate expressions of concern, while permitting them no legal or personal freedoms. [1970:73]

In Victorian England, being a lady did not guarantee a woman's safety or autonomy, but it did mean protection from hard and demeaning work. Ladies were cut off by class from household servants and by lack of physical proximity from female factory workers and prostitutes. Because solidarity among women in such differing economic circumstances was impossible, there was no political base from which to work against the patriarchal system.

The situation is not much changed in the United States today. The upper- and middle-class housewife, although she may work outside the home at times, maintains a ladylike self-image. Typically, she is dependent upon her husband, and he supports her. Her life-style is considered the norm, while the woman who is the only or primary wage earner for her family is considered unfortunate. Women who choose to have a career are viewed as unfeminine and a threat to the traditional organization of the nuclear family. Envy and insecurity operate to isolate these categories of women from each other so that they do not become natural allies in a struggle to improve the condition of women as a class.

Quite apart from the role of chivalry in disguising the true status of women and in reducing female solidarity, there are two other interrelated problems caused by the morality of chivalry. These stem from equating "manliness" with the ability to defend one's woman, as Andelin does in the passages quoted earlier. In the first place, it causes the woman to become a target of the man's enemies; hostility toward him can be displaced on her. Susan Brownmiller, in *Against Our Will: Men, Women and Rape* (1975), documents the fact that rape of women has been a commonplace, if not accepted, spoil of war.

On the personal political level, the principle operates in a similar way. Black activist and convicted rapist Eldridge Cleaver has offered this as his primary motivation for rape:

Rape was an insurrectionary act. It delighted me that I was defying and trampling upon the white man's law, upon his system of values, and that I was defiling his women—and this point, I believe, was the most satisfying to me because I was very resentful over the historical fact of how the white man has used the black woman. I felt I was getting revenge. [Cleaver, 1968:14]

Cleaver's admission also offers a second reason why "manliness"—or a man's worth—should not be defined by his ability to protect his woman. What has been the lasting imprint upon the black man in this country of the sexual abuse of the black woman by slaveholders? (Brownmiller, 1975). How has it affected his feelings for white men, white women, black women? How has this institutional assault on his "manliness" affected his collective self-image, and what sorts of social behaviors has this tended to produce?

There are still other reasons why it is not a good idea to socialize children to form submissive female/protective male dyads. What if they never find, or if they lose, the person with whom they want to play these complementary roles? Must they remain "incomplete," or should they develop the other role within their own personalities and become "complete" human beings, but less stereotypically male or female?

But clearly the most persuasive reason for women to abandon this "protection racket," which is still one of the foundations of marriage, has already been alluded to. That is, women have the same right as men to move about freely in society and to count on the maintenance of law and order. And when they are willfully injured by another, they should be no more blamed than a man would be in similar circumstances. When a charwoman who works at night is robbed on her way from work, she should not be made to feel ashamed for not having a male escort to protect her. And when a pretty coed is raped while hitchhiking, she should not be accused of "asking for it." Golda Meir had the right idea when she refused to place a curfew on Israeli women to reduce the number of crimes committed against them. She suggested instead a curfew for men since they, not the women, were the criminals.

It is often remarked, sometimes with regret, that chivalry is dead. But for many women the demise of chivalry has opened the doors to their gilded cages and helped them get down safely from their pedestals so that, like so many Sleeping Beauties released from an evil spell, they can return to their natural state—equality with men.

THE MORALITY OF JUSTICE

John Stuart Mill wrote in 1869 that "the true virtue of human beings is fitness to live together as equals" (Mill, 1970:44). He believed that Western society was progressing toward this ideal and that "Justice [would assert] its claim as the foundation of virtue" as it had in the republics of antiquity. When he speaks of the Morality of Justice, he refers to a state of equality between men and women "without power on one side or obedience on the other" (Mill, 1970:45).

Without doubt, the legal status of women has improved since Mill's day but, while the Morality of Justice receives lip service in some quarters, chivalry still appears to be the dominant morality. In other words, there is still pervasive resistance to the notion of equality between the sexes. One reason for this is that both men and women, for slightly different reasons, fear the equal distribution of power among men and women. Men are quite naturally reluctant to share their power pool, to relinquish control over their natural domain (women), and even to risk being overpowered by women.

In subtle ways we have all been socialized to accept not only the validity of the powerful male and the powerless female but also the notion that a powerful woman is unnatural, unfeminine, and inherently bad. Women as well as men view power and "femininity" as antithetical and usually choose to pursue the traditional role. There is evidence in our folklore and history, as well as in feminist political analysis, for this proposition.

Consider the male and female role models from familiar fairy tales. The man is Prince Charming who wins the favors of his Princess by protecting or rescuing her from some plight. She is the beautiful, victimized innocent—Cinderella, Snow White, and Sleeping Beauty. What American girl, under the influence of a Disney production of these stories, has not dreamed of being a pure, pretty, and pitiable victim?

Furthermore, it will be remembered that these role models were not gobbled up like Red Riding Hood by a wolf (evil man), but were plagued and paralyzed by evil women, often in the form of mother figures. These stepmothers, queens, and witches were not only evil but they were also powerful, and, in the context of our favorite fairy tales, these adjectives are too often synonymous when applied to women. More than one feminist author (Brownmiller, 1975; Dworkin, 1974) has suggested that such fables either create or chronicle in both male and female a fear of powerful women.

This fear has not been confined to the world of make-believe. If we had a tradition of "herstory" rather than history, we might know more about the fate of powerful women. But we do have one example of massive proportions, the burning of witches during the dark ages, which Dworkin describes in her book, *Woman Hating* (1974). Whether or not one accepts her estimate that nine million people, nearly all women, were put to death in a 300-year period, the data from which she extrapolated the figures are impressive. For example, 500 were executed in Geneva during a three-month period in 1515, and 1,000 in one year in one district of Switzerland.

Many of those women had rejected the Judeo-Christian teaching, which Dworkin (1974:137) labels "misogyny, patriarchy and sexist suppression, alternatively known as the Garden-of-Eden-Hype," in favor of the older totemic cults of Western Europe which centered on fertility rites and celebrated woman's role in the reproductive process. Witches knew the medicinal value of herbs, including mood controlling drugs, and they used hypnosis. They treated impotency and alleviated the pain of childbirth. For this last practice, they incurred the wrath of the Church which insisted that women suffer the pain of childbirth as punishment for Eve's sin. But, it was the combination of these magical powers with the carnality of witchcraft which led to allegations that witches stole semen from men in their sleep and cast "glamours" over their genitals causing them to disappear. According to Dworkin, such accusations evoked in men the primal dread of castration which finally impelled them to exterminate the witches and their art.

Brownmiller (1975) has another story of how women are punished by men for not maintaining their traditionally powerless and passive role, particularly where sexuality is concerned. She calls rape "the ultimate physical threat by which all men keep all women in a state of psychological intimidation," and likens it to the lynching of blacks by groups of whites as punishment for "uppity" behavior. She also believes that fear of an "open season of rape," and not a natural inclination toward monogamy and motherhood, caused the first subjugation of women into protective mating.

If Dworkin and Brownmiller are correct in what they say about the politics of female victimization, we see that men are so protective of their own sexuality that they will slaughter women (witches) who threaten their virility, and they will use their sexuality as a weapon (rape) against women who threaten their dominance. In her book, *Sexual Politics,* Kate Millett has drawn similar conclusions:

Patriarchial societies typically link feelings of cruelty with sexuality, the latter often equated both with evil and with power. This is apparent both in the sexual fantasy reported by psychoanalysis and that reported by pornography. The rule here associates sadism with the male ("the masculine role") and victimization with the female ("the feminine role"). Emotional response to violence against women in patriarchy is often curiously ambivalent. [1970:44]

This analysis suggests that violence between men and women not only results from polarized sex role stereotypes but is inextricably linked with sexuality. It runs counter to the conventional wisdom that opposites are attracted to each other and instead supposes that the contrary is true. It posits that male hostility and cruelty toward women bears a resemblance to the rationale used by nations at war that the enemy is an inferior type of human being, or not human at all. In other words, the fact that women are the "other" sex makes it easy for some men to dehumanize them—that is, their "otherness" permits them to be victimized. Traditionally, they are viewed not only as the "other" sex but as the "opposite" sex. For men who believe that "masculine" attributes are the epitome of human virtue, what can the worth of the "opposite" be? "Femininity" to them must be pitiable, even despicable, and deserving of violation.

The more usual point of view, that sexual opposites attract, is held by Eldridge Cleaver, but he acknowledges that despite this, male-female relationships are not normally harmonious. In his opinion, however, class structure rather than polarized sex roles is to blame. Up to this point, our discussion has been limited to sex roles in the dominant culture; some consideration of the interplay of race and class distinctions may be also appropriate. Cleaver (1968) argues in his essay "The Primeval Mitosis" that male and female in their primeval state are the two halves of the human sphere which have been pulled apart but exist in a "dynamic magnetism of opposites." They yearn to transcend this mitosis and achieve reunion in a Unitary Sexual Image. But this can happen only in a Unitary Society, and we are living instead in a Class Society.

According to Cleaver, in a Class Society the function of the dominant males is to rule, an essentially cerebral task. They leave to the lower-class male the body-associated functions such as labor and athletic prowess. The first male is referred to as the Omnipotent Administrator and the second, the Supermasculine Menial. The upper-class female must be defined as the Ultrafeminine to make her more feminine than her man. She, therefore, relinquishes her strength and her domestic functions to the woman beneath her who is called the Amazon. The sexuality of each of these classes follows their function in such a manner that there is both attraction and antagonism in the way that each relates to the other. This dynamic frustrates the drive toward a Unitary Sexual Image and creates conflict among all the groups. Using this theory, Cleaver explains why black men long for forbidden sexual contact with white women, why black women cannot respect black men, and why white men do not satisfy white women. The underlying reason, of course, is that when added to the sexual dichotomy, class structure further fragments the unity that all human beings have the potential· to achieve.

The difference between Cleaver's conceptualization and feminist theory is that Cleaver believes that wholeness is achieved through the fusion of the primeval (classless) male and female, who each now represent only half of human possibility. Many feminists, on the other hand, consider men and women to be alike except for the obvious biological distinctions and the artificial differences produced by the socialization process. Some propose that we move toward androgyny, the combination in every person of the best traits now attributed to each of the sexes.

People who do not want boys to exercise that part of their temperament which is sensitive, tender, and compassionate, or for girls to become brave, disciplined, and assertive, argue that diminishing the difference in the way that males and females behave will reduce the attraction between the sexes. But Simone de Beauvoir (1953:688) admonishes us to "not forget that our lack of imagination always depopulates the future; . . . New relations of flesh and sentiment of which we have no conception will arise between the sexes; already, indeed, there have appeared between men and women friendships, rivalries, complicities, comradeships—chaste or sensual— which past centuries could not have conceived."

Whether or not breaking down sex role stereotypes would reduce attraction between the sexes, there is some evidence that it would reduce hostility. For example, presumption of male superiority has been observed by Dr. Murray Straus to be a major mischief maker in the nuclear family. In "Sexual Inequality, Cultural Norms and Wife-Beating," Straus (1977:69) points out that when husbands fail to surpass their wives in personal "resources," such as intelligence, knowledge, occupational prestige, and income, they may fall back on the "ultimate resource" of physical force to maintain their superiority. Another example we must not overlook is the fact that role differentiation between male and female has always implied a double standard of sexual conduct. This was usually rationalized on the basis of the right of the man to know that the children his wife bears, and he must support, are his own. The availability of birth control methods, including sterilization and abortion, is said to be "liberating" women from the need to bear unwanted children. But it is less clear that woman's ability to control her reproductive capacity is "liberating" men from concern about their wives' fidelity.

This may be so because a man's desire for exclusive sexual access to his wife, whatever its origins, is now considered a manly prerogative—in fact, a kind of property right which he obtains in exchange for providing her a safe home. In other words, he protects her not only from abusive or assaultive men, but also from her own inclination to enter consensual relationships with other men. As Havelock Ellis (1969:63) put it, "Monogamy and the home, it was claimed, alike existed for the benefit and protection of women. It was not so often explained that they greatly benefited and protected men, with moreover this additional advantage: that while women were absolutely confined to the home, men were free to exercise their activities outside the home, even on the erotic side."

Enforcing this double standard has been a point of honor for men throughout history, as well as the occasion of many "crimes of passion." A recent police department study (Police Foundation, 1977) indicated that in 66 out of 90 family conflict homicides, one person (men more often than women) was defining another as an object of personal property and acting on that basis.

Perhaps, referring again to our chronology of moralities, we can interpret the apparent increase—or the increased appearance—of male violence against women as a transitional problem accompanying a change in women's status. As women become less submissive and dependent, they are receiving less protection and support. This would appear a reasonable road to the equality between the sexes that Mill anticipated. However, an equally plausible explanation for the violence is that women are being punished by men for attempting to revise the power relationship between them. If the second interpretation is valid, Mill's equality "without power on one side and obedience on the other" may never be attained.

Perhaps Mill and many of his successors have been naive in their hope that equality and justice for women can be reached without revising sex roles, restructuring the family, and reviewing the entire patriarchal system. Equality in legal rights and economic opportunity are important objectives, but men will resort to brute force to maintain power so long as the "protection racket" is allowed to operate with impunity.

To a large extent the remedy lies in the personal decisions of individual women to counter traditional sex role expectations. But what is also needed is a justice system that does not shrink from invading a man's castle to defend the women and children he is abusing, and that does not condone the victimization of women who have nontraditional life-styles. Other societal institutions must also respond to women victims to help them withstand the force of male resistance to the female quest for power. These are the matters to be discussed in the chapters that follow.

REFERENCES

ANDELIN, H. (1975). Fascinating womanhood. New York: Bantam.

BROWNMILLER, S. (1975). Against our will: Men, women and rape. New York: Simon and Schuster.

CLEAVER, E. (1968). Soul on ice. New York: Delta.

DADRIAN, V. (1976). "An attempt at defining victimology." Pp. 40-42 in E. Viano (ed.), Victims and society. Washington, D.C.: Visage Press.

De BEAUVOIR, S. (1953). The second sex. New York: Knopf.

DWORKIN, A. (1974). Woman hating. New York: E.P. Dutton.

ELLIS, H. (1969). "The love rights of women." Pp. 61-67 in B. Roszuk and T. Roszoch (eds.), Masculine/feminine. New York: Harper and Row.

GENET, J. (1966). Miracle of the rose. New York: Grove Press.

MILL, J.S. (1970). The subjection of women. Cambridge: MIT Press. Original edition, 1869. London: Longmann, Green, Reader, and Dyer.

MILLETT, K. (1970). Sexual politics. Garden City, N.Y.: Doubleday.

MORGAN, R. (1977). Going too far. New York: Random House.

Police Foundation (1977). Domestic violence and the police, studies in Detroit and Kansas City. Washington, D.C.: Police Foundation.

REAGE, P. (1965). Story of O. New York: Grove Press.

RUSSELL, D. and VAN De VEN, W. (1976). Crimes against women. Millbrae, Calif.: Les Femmes.

STRAUS, M. (1977). "Sexual inequality, cultural norms and wife beating." Pp. 45-57 in J.R. Chapman and M. Gates (eds.), Women into wives. Beverly Hills, Calif.: Sage.

Washington Post (1977). "Liberated women in Somalia—catalysts for development." September 1, A28.

2

MEN AND THE VICTIMIZATION OF WOMEN

JUDITH V. BECKER
GENE G. ABEL

A **variety** of social, economic, legal, and psychological forms of victimization are perpetrated by men on women. We live in a society in which men are in charge of the majority of institutions. Economically, women are discriminated against in the job market. Sex role stereotyping has victimized and "imprisoned" a number of women. Often women have been victimized by the institution of marriage, in which, although they are no longer identified as property, they are still repressed by implied and covert social-cultural practices. In some cases in the course of a marital relationship, women have been exploited physically, emotionally, and sexually by their husbands. Mental as well as physical "injury" has been inflicted on women by the health professions; until recently women did not have the right to decide whether they would continue a pregnancy or terminate it. Many women have suffered through months and years of psychotherapy by therapists whose attempts at being objective all too often fall short of that goal, resulting in the perpetuation of a value system that feeds the sexist social structure. Perhaps the most apparent indicator of the victimization of women is the fact that the Equal Rights Amendment remains unratified.

Victimization is tied to aggression, be it physical or verbal. Men are socialized to be aggressive and women to be victims. This paper

AUTHORS' NOTE: Preparation of this chapter was supported by the Center for the Prevention and Control of Rape, USPHS Grant MH-28051.

will attempt to examine the phenomenon of male victimization of females by (1) reviewing a sample of the theories and research to date in the area of human aggression and violence, (2) examining the differential impact of exposure to violence on males and females, (3) focusing on rape as a prototype of female victimization, and (4) describing a treatment program for sexually aggressive men.

Everyone in our society is familiar with aggression, either through the media, as a purveyor of violence, or as a victim of an aggressive act. For example, 34% of females in one New York area have been victims of serious crimes (Goldstein, 1975). How can such a high incidence of violence be explained? Are violent acts primarily a product of our instincts, and thus unlikely to be altered and changed, or is violence a learned behavior, a result of life's experiences, and thus a behavior that can be unlearned?

Support for the theory that aggressive behavior is instinctual comes from: (1) ethologists such as Desmond Morris, Conrad Lorenz, and Robert Ardrey; (2) research on electrical and chemical brain stimulation; and (3) psychoanalytic theory. The ethologists propose that our animal ancestors were instinctively violent beings and that our violent behaviors are products of these inherited instinctual drives. However, this is not always the case—some research (Binford, 1972) confirms that certain animals are not aggressive at all, and humans do not always pattern themselves on other primates' behavior because of their more complex nervous system.

Freud and his contemporaries held that aggression is instinctive. However, because of the presence of what Freud termed ego defense mechanisms, not all people express their aggressive instincts. For example, an individual with strong urges to inflict injury on others might maintain those urges but express them indirectly by becoming, for example, a surgeon. As a surgeon, he or she aggressively attacks another person's body with a surgical knife. In this manner, the person's violent tendencies to injure or destroy are channeled through socially acceptable pathways. Although there are elaborate theorizations, many such psychoanalytic hypotheses have yet to be validated (Berkowitz, 1970).

A more intriguing theory is that violence is not an instinctual behavior but a learned one, resulting from the same matrix whereby we learn to speak, dress, and socialize. The expression of such learned aggression may be as varied as the environments in which it is learned. For example, Eskimos learn that the direct expression of aggression in their culture is not acceptable. Instead, abusive songs are sung in public about the people with whom one is angry.

Goldstein (1975:19), viewing aggression as a learned behavior, breaks down the components necessary for the expression of aggressive behavior. He states,

> Aggression behavior is a complex act, based on a number of simultaneously acting factors. In order for aggression to occur, there must be some impetus to aggress, inhibitions against aggressing must be overcome, and the situation in terms of the opportunity and ability to aggress and the availability of the target must be appropriate.

Goldstein further proposes that there are long-term and situational factors that facilitate either aggressive or nonaggressive behavior. Long-term factors include the process of socialization we undergo as children; for example, the values, norms, attitudes, beliefs, and expectations that our parents, teachers, and peers instill and selectively reinforce. Situational factors facilitating aggression include familiar environments, the presence of alcohol, or the presence of relatives or peers with whom aggression is associated.

There are situations in which even the most violent people are nonaggressive, and vice versa. Therefore, what are the factors that facilitate nonaggression? Goldstein (1975) believes there are certain environments and individuals that do not elicit or facilitate aggression. Inappropriate locations for aggression include churches or theaters, and inappropriate targets are hypothesized to include children and the aged.

A large number of psychological experiments demonstrate that aggressive behavior is learned or acquired (Kagan and Moss, 1962; Loew, 1967). Interestingly, several of these studies find that males are more prone to aggression than females. Kagan and Moss (1962) found that aggressive behavior patterns learned in childhood persist through adulthood, especially for males. Loew (1967) and Green and Pigg (1970) found that if parents positively reinforce verbal or nonverbal aggressive responses in their children, they increase their children's use of aggressive behavior.

Sears, Maccoby, and Leven (1957) interviewed nearly 400 mothers of kindergarten age children in an attempt to examine child-rearing practices and their relationship to aggressive behaviors. The results indicate that the amount of aggression shown by the children was directly related to the physical punishment used by parents.

Bandura and his associates (1963, 1965) have demonstrated that children learned aggression not only by engaging in aggressive behaviors that are rewarded or punished by the environment, but they also learn aggression through observing aggressive acts. Children mimic the behavior of parents, who serve as important models for imparting values, attitudes, and behavior patterns to their children. Other models include peers, teachers, and characters with whom children come into contact on TV and in books. Society is only recently becoming aware that television is an important transmitter of social behavior to our children.

In one study, Bandura (1965) exposed three groups of 22 nursery school children to one of three, five-minute videotape scenes. The theme in all of these films involved an adult engaging in a series of verbal and physical attacks on a large, human-like doll. One group witnessed the adult receiving food reinforcement (candy and soft drinks) following the expression of aggression. The second group saw the adult punished by means of spanking and verbal rebuke for the aggression. A third group saw the adult receive no punishment or reward for the aggressive behavior. After viewing the film, the children were placed in a room with a variety of toys, including the plastic doll, where their free-play behavior was observed. After 10 minutes of free play, the children were told they would receive picture booklets and free fruit juice if they would imitate what they had just seen on TV. Two indices of aggression were thus observed: spontaneous aggression (observed during the free-play period), and learned aggression (where they were rewarded for imitating the models).

The results indicated that spontaneous aggression was greatest in the group that witnessed the adult receiving rewards for aggressive behavior. The least amount of spontaneous aggression was evidenced by the group that saw the adult punished, suggesting that punishment inhibits spontaneous aggression in children. All three groups of children were able to imitate the adult's aggressive behavior. Learning thus occurred irrespective of the consequences to the adult model for the aggressive behavior. Finally, Bandura found that both spontaneous and learned aggression were greatest in the male children.

The ramifications of this and similar studies are far-reaching. First, a child can acquire new behaviors only by observing a model. Second, children are more likely to spontaneously imitate aggressive behavior observed on TV when a model or the actors are not punished for such behavior. Last, by nursery school age, male children have already learned to behave in a more aggressive manner than female children.

DIFFERENTIAL EFFECTS OF AGGRESSION
ON MALES AND FEMALES

The effect of viewed aggression on children has become a focus of national concern. A recent article in Newsweek (Waters, 1977) reports that children under 5 years of age watch an average of 23.5 hours of television per week. Children are learning their values, morals, beliefs, and attitudes from TV as well as from their parents. What effect is TV having on male and female children? Cantor and Orwant (1977:19), in reviewing the "classic" studies on the effects of TV violence on children, report that most of the studies have used male rather than female children as subjects. Therefore, the bulk of the data can be generalized for only half of the population: "Girls have been systematically ignored, both in the data collection and in the data analysis."

In those studies that included females as subjects, a differential effect is found. Male children become more aggressive and violent after viewing a program in which violence was portrayed. This should not surprise us, as our culture reinforces acts of aggression in males and inhibits or punishes aggressive behavior in female children. Furthermore the perpetrators of aggression on TV are, in the majority of situations, male. Again, male children are reinforced for modeling adult male behaviors and roles. We are caught in a vicious circle. Our culture is sexist, the media industry is controlled by males, and the programming to which we and our children are exposed typically portrays aggressive males and passive-impotent females. Should we be surprised that boys imitate what they view on TV, that they do in fact act aggressively or violently after viewing violence? Furthermore, girls identify with the female actresses, who are almost universally victims. Cantor (1977:17) concludes, and we agree, "Sex role socialization and aggressive behavior are not separate problems but two sides of the same coin." Female children learn the role of victim and an acceptance of violence. Male children learn to aggress, and girls are likely targets for their aggression.

Frequently what is viewed on TV is reinforced in the home, where children are exposed to the victimization of women in the form of wife-beating. Straus (1977:59), in discussing sexual inequality, cultural norms, and wife-beating, reports:

> For many people a marriage license is a hitting license, that physical violence between family members is probably as common as love and

affection between family members, and that if one is truly concerned with the level of violence in America the place to look is in the home rather than on the streets.

Wives are more frequently the victims of violence than are husbands. Of 588 homicide victims, 40% of the women victims were killed by their husbands, whereas only 11% of the male victims were killed by their wives (Wolfgang, 1956). Straus (1977) contends that the police and courts legitimatize husband-wife violence in several ways; police and prosecutors are slow to respond to the wives' "call for help." In some jurisdictions, "spousal immunity" prohibits women from suing their spouses for aggressive acts committed against them.

Straus (1977) asserts that the reason for the high incidence of male violence is to provide "ultimate support for the existing power structure of the family." He lists nine specific ways in which the male-dominated social structure maintains a high level of violence in the family; they are: (1) defense of male authority—males have established themselves as being superior, they are however not superior in all realms, hence they fall back on physical force to maintain their status and position; (2) compulsive masculinity—male children are raised by females, yet the message they get is that it is not appropriate to be like a female or to emulate their mothers; therefore, they strive to be masculine; (3) economic constraints and discrimination—women are provided few alternatives with which to compete in the economic realm; (4) burdens of child care—insisting that women remain at home with the children keeps them out of the economic sphere and dependent on their husbands; (5) myth of the single parent—the hypothesis that children are harmed if they are raised by one parent implies that a woman with a child needs the support of a man; (6) prominence of the wife role for women—the message is that to be other than a wife and mother is to be inferior; (7) negative self-image—women do not receive positive reinforcement for achieving in other than domestic areas; (8) women are viewed as children who need the protection of a man; (9) the criminal justice system has a definite male orientation.

Brownmiller (1975) asserts that women learn to be victims. Just as women learn victim roles, males learn a different role—how to victimize women. In discussing rape victims, Brownmiller affirms that before female children learn to read, they acquire an acceptance of victimization. Fairy tales are filled with themes in which the helpless passive female is subdued, captured, or saved by a strong, male figure. For instance, the story of Red Riding Hood exemplifies a sweet, feminine character who is defenseless in the face of the male wolf's strength. It takes a male huntsman to extricate Red Riding Hood. Brownmiller asks us to compare Red Riding Hood with Peter and the Wolf and the tale of the Three Little (male) Pigs who were able to fight the wolf on their own. Unfortunately, Red Riding Hood is not so well blessed and must rely on the strength of a male to save her.

What do female children learn from these tales? They see that females are helpless, unassertive, and unable to protect themselves. What do male children learn from these same tales? That women are the appropriate targets of such aggression. That women cannot protect themselves. That women are victims.

The popular and classical literature and films young men and women read and see also reflect the theme that women are victims and males the evildoers or rescuers. Brownmiller cites, for example, the rape scenes in such films as "The Adventurers," "A Clockwork Orange," "Frenzy," "Straw Dogs," "Going Home," and "The Man Who Loved Cat Dancing," all of which glamorize rape in one manner or another. Similarly, literature is replete with rape scenes—such as those in "The Fountainhead," "Diary of a Rapist," and "Last Exit to Brooklyn"—in which rape is glorified or the victims misrepresented. Not only in the area of sexual assault are male/female interactions permeated by what Brownmiller has called the male "mass psychology of the conquerer" and the female "mass psychology of the conquered." Kate Millett (1970:168) similarly reflects the role of women in our society,

> All the mechanisms of human inequality arose out of the foundations of male supremacy and the subjugation of women, sexual politics serving historically as the foundation of all other social, political and economic structures . . . the subjugation of women (being) of course far more than an economic or even a political event, but a total social and psychological phenomenon, a way of life.

RAPE AS A PROTOTYPE OF VICTIMIZATION

The remainder of this chapter will focus on one form of female victimization, the crime of rape. This appears especially relevant since rape is one of the most rapidly increasing crimes of violence in this country, and scientific inquiry is beginning to make headway into our understanding of males' sexual assault on females.

Most studies of why rapists select their victims have found that victims are selected for their availability and vulnerability. Rape thus is a crime of opportunity. But not all men who are exposed to and reinforced for aggressive behavior victimize women. What then distinguishes males who rape from those who do not? One must first look at the male's attitude toward women in general.

Kanin (1970) interviewed 500 college females and 400 college males to determine the extent of sexual aggression in college men. He found that the types of force used on college campuses ranged from forcible kissing to forcible rape. Two thirds of the females involved in forced encounters responded by screaming, fighting, crying, and pleading, and the majority of them were able to deter the males from proceeding further. However, fewer than 1% of the females reported the aggressive encounter to legal or academic authorities.

These aggressive sexual exploitations were more prone to be directed toward females whose backgrounds were dissimilar to the men's, and women defined as undesirable by the males were more prone to be targets for such aggression. This was especially true for those males who had a double standard of sexual morality.

Sixty percent of the males who were aggressive in college were also aggressive in high school. They frequently duped their female partners by professing love or attempting to get them intoxicated.

Kanin reports, "The aggressives are immersed in a male subculture that stresses erotic accomplishment and offers prestige rewards for success" (Kanin, 1960:35). The greater the male affiliation with a stronghold of male subculture, such as a social fraternity, the greater the pressure to succeed sexually, to the point of using coercion if necessary.

The attitudes of these men toward women, including their relationships with their mothers and other women, were explored. Results indicated that 90% of the aggressive males and 61% of the nonaggressive males reported either not loving their mothers or having had painful experiences (rejection) with females they had dated. The aggressive males also scored higher on a general aggressiveness scale. Kanin concluded that aggressive tendencies in a male, paired with generalized hostilities toward women, would almost inevitably lead to sexual aggression upon a female.

Based upon the material reviewed to this point, it is apparent that sexually aggressive behavior will not be eliminated unless, first, the "masculine mystique" is eroded, and, second, those males who already act on their learned sexual aggressiveness can be taught new ways of socializing with females. *UNTIL ATTITUDES TOWARD WOMEN CHANGE*

To determine how ingrained certain values and attitudes are in a culture, one can look to its institutions, which often reflect the attitudes and mores of society. It should not be surprising that in a prison setting (1) rape occurs, and (2) when a male rapes another male in such an environment, the rapist describes his victim in feminine terms.

Scacco (1975:79) in his book, *Rape in Prisons,* discusses the inmates' view of women and how this affects sexual aggression:

> A significant portion of lower class males are raised in homes where a female is the predominant member since there is usually a consistent lack of a male or father image in the home situation. The result is that the males in this situation seek to express themselves in ways they consider to be masculine beyond question.

Behaviors through which men assert their masculinity include athletic prowess and the conceptualization of women as objects of conquest.

Eldridge Cleaver's (1968) autobiography exemplifies how anger actually directed toward the white man becomes redirected toward the white woman. His racial anger manifested itself as a sexual anger, an anger directed not at the white male, but the white female:

> Rape was an insurrectionary act. It delighted me that I was defying and trampling upon the white man's law, upon his system of values, and that I was defiling his women—and this point, I believe, was the most satisfying to me, how the white man has used the black woman. I feel I was getting revenge. [p. 14]

Cleaver points out that his rape of white women had nothing to do with the aesthetic attraction of the white women, but was motivated by a "bloody, hateful, bitter" anger toward white oppression.

Scacco (1975) asserts that black men are mimicking the behavior of white males who had raped their women and have dominated them for years. White males have made sexuality a political tool, and black males model that behavior. He further states that the heart of sexual domination in prison is not racism, but sexism; that is, male supremacy must be maintained at all costs.

If society were to nullify its gender role stereotypes, males would not have to validate their masculinity by such acts as raping females. People would be people. Proscribed role behaviors would not exist, and masculinity would not be assumed to be analogous with strength, aggression, and power over others. Likewise, femininity would not be typified by passivity, conformity, and the acceptance of the victim role.

If having to maintain a stereotype of masculinity is what is at the heart of assaults on women, then the prescription that our society needs is to eradicate social-sexual role stereotypes through male consciousness-raising groups, nonsexist children's literature, legislation such as the Equal Rights Amendment, and training of women to assert themselves with males so that their beliefs and wishes can be equally appreciated by all.

THE CLASSIFICATION OF SEXUALLY AGGRESSIVE BEHAVIORS

The rate of rape in the United States is 40 to 70 rapes per 100,000 women at risk per/year, with the actual number of rapes occurring but unreported being anywhere from 2.2 to 10 times this number. Since rape occurs at such a high frequency and because it is a clear example of men victimizing women, sexual assault will be explored in considerable detail from the psychoanalytic and behavioral viewpoint. The goal of such an exploration is to identify forces that lead to rape and those interventions that could prevent rape.

Cohen et al. (1971), working from a psychoanalytic model, have explored motivational factors that have led to men raping women. In those rapists who are not retarded or who have not raped because of an institutional setting (imprisonment), Cohen believes that rape behavior can be classified according to the rapist's unconscious motives. These unconscious motives include aggressive, sexual, and a combination of aggressive and sexual goals.

Those rapists who are motivated by an aggressive aim are actually expressing their angry, hostile feelings by the act of raping a female. In these individuals rape is, "serving to humiliate, dirty, and defile the victim. The degree of violence varies from simple assault to brutal, vicious attacks resulting on occasion in the victim's death." This category of rapist generally chooses a stranger as his victim. He is angry and displaces that anger on his unsuspecting victim. The source of his anger is usually a significant female in his life (mother, wife, or girlfriend), and his victim is the innocent target of misdirected anger.

Cohen asserts that these men usually have a history of difficulty in relating to females. They perceive women as demanding, hostile, and unfaithful. Surprisingly, these are the very types of women they are attracted to, which serves to reinforce their negative feelings about women. They are often "macho types," highly competitive, engaging in exaggerated masculine activities such as aggressive sports, risk-taking activities, or street fighting. Their sense of masculine self is extremely critical to them, and when confronted by a female who threatens their masculinity they become enraged. However, rather than directing their anger at that confronting female, they displace it and victimize an unsuspecting female.

Cohen (1971:313) reports, "These men often have a history of pre-pubertal or post-pubertal sexual trauma with women, frequently, the mother." How does society breed this type of individual? Frequently these men have ambivalent feelings about women and see women as either virgins or whores. They overidealize their own mothers, having an abstract perception of what a real woman is like. They perceive real women as being untrustworthy, depriving, and hostile. The rapist devalues and makes women into objects without identities or feelings. It thus becomes easy to displace anger on them (Cohen et al., 1971).

One case reflects the history of a rapist motivated by aggressive aims. James was referred by his psychiatrist to the authors of this chapter for treatment after he had raped two women. James was a black male in his early twenties and was not prosecuted for either rape because of insufficient evidence. He was an only child. His father died when James was seven, and he was then raised exclusively by his mother. She reportedly, "gave me everything I wanted," but at the same time, was quite controlling of what the patient did, when he did it, and with whom he did it. His usual means of dealing with his mother's control was to remain passive. For example, if he and his mother had been arguing one day, he would sleep late the next day, get up at noon, and leave the house immediately so that he would not be available for further discussion and disagreement. Eventually, the patient joined the armed service to extricate himself from his mother's control. Unfortunately, he received a medical discharge because of a physical disability and had to return home.

Within one month of returning home, his chronic conflicts with his mother began to accelerate. On the one hand, she was the most important person in his life; on the other, his anxiety and discomfort when interacting with her continued to increase because he found it impossible to assert himself with her. One week before his first rape, fights with his mother accelerated even further. This led to his frequently leaving the house and attempting to "cool off" by talking to others. A few hours before his first rape, he had had a hostile argument with his mother. After driving around for two hours, he saw a woman entering her home, followed her, and raped her. A second rape ensued in the next week; the pattern was similar—conflicts with his mother followed shortly by the rape of an unknown woman.

It is interesting that the patient himself reported no direct relationship between his anger towards his mother and his rape of the women. He was quite aware, however, of his inability to cope with his mother's control over his life and his inability to assert himself with her.

Cohen's second category describes rapists motivated by sexual aims. They use aggression only to the extent necessary to complete a rape and gain sexual satisfaction from it. A large percentage of attempted rapes fall into this category. The rapist accompanies the act with the fantasy that the woman actually enjoys being raped, falls in love with him, and wants him to return for further sexual contacts.

This type of rapist frequently participates in sexual deviations, such as voyeurism and exhibitionism. He avoids sexuality by taking a passive approach to sex, being shy and socially withdrawn. This passive approach is reflected in the act of rape. Should the victim offer significant resistance, he usually leaves immediately, rather than accelerating aggressive behaviors as does the rapist in the aggressive-sex category, described below. The "passive-feminine" features of the sexual-aim category of rapist, along with his occasional homosexual urges, tend to frighten this man. As a consequence, masculinity is highly praised, and any behaviors that would be construed as feminine, such as warmth or tenderness, are detested.

The third motivating force for rape is the combination of both sex and aggressive aims, what Cohen calls sex-aggression defusion. This category is characterized by an arousal pattern in which violence is used to sexually arouse the rapist. He brutalizes his victim initially to generate his erection response. After he is sexually excited, he ceases to be physically violent. Cohen defines the type this way:

> He is assertive, overpowering and somewhat hostile in all situations. Warmth and affection are completely absent. The most friendly meeting is punctuated by a bruising one. [p. 322]

His family dynamics involve a father who is psychologically and physically cruel and who demands and reinforces physically aggressive behavior in his children. The mother is usually a warm, compassionate, overly permissive individual.

The following case exemplifies the third category of rapists, whose aim is sex-aggression defusion. In his mid-thirties, Arthur was referred by his lawyer to the authors for psychiatric evaluation following his arrest for two brutal rapes. History revealed him to be one of four children whose parents separated when he was four years old, due to the father's excessive drinking. The patient reported masturbatory fantasies of harming women beginning at age nine and accelerating up to the present. By age 14, he was more anxious than the average child and socially withdrawn.

He married at age 22 and concomitantly began a series of extramarital affairs that continued throughout each of his four marriages. Although he denied sadistically beating his first wife or raping her, he did admit that he was unable to get an erection with her unless fantasizing sadistic thoughts of her. Their marriage terminated after a year and a half, following his severely beating his wife. Within four years, he married a second time and began acting on his sadistic thoughts, sadistically raping his wife on the average of two times per week. As he stated, "I couldn't put my hands on her without hurting her." Following this brief marriage, the patient remarried a third time with marked acceleration of his sadistic behavior with his wife. He would severely spank her with wet towels, striking her breasts and pubic area with his fists.

His fourth marriage, in his early thirties, was yet a further extension of his sadistic impulses. Beatings of his wife occurred three times per week; on one occasion a severe beating involved burning her with cigarettes and sticking pins into her genital organs. He began raping women unknown to him at age 30, completing four savage rapes of women by the time of his referral. At the time of each of the rapes, the patient's inability to obtain an erection prompted him to begin sadistic beatings of the rape victims and, concomitantly, generate an erection.

The psychoanalytic models espoused by Cohen have given us many leads as to means of classifying rapists according to their motivating forces, but these models are limited by the difficulty in confirming or proving the hypothesized forces. Furthermore, it is difficult to translate these findings into specific treatment interventions to assist the rapist in gaining control over his urges to rape. Some argue that it is best not to attempt treatment interventions through psychological means, but rather to rehabilitate rapists through legal avenues such as incarceration or parole.

Legal interventions themselves have several major limitations: (1) fewer than 13.3% of rapists are actually found guilty of charges of rape, and, therefore, incarceration is unlikely; (2) in most states, treatment programs do not exist for those who are incarcerated; and (3) if they are released from incarceration untreated, approximately 35% of rapists repeat the crime within five years (Abel, Blanchard, and Becker, in press). These grim statistics have led Abel and his colleagues to undertake a series of physiologic and behavioral studies to investigate directly the factors that contribute to rapists' sexual arousal as well as other aspects of their behavior repertoires that would appear to be closely linked with the act of rape and, therefore, in need of correction if they are to learn to control their urges to rape.

The physiological measures rely on direct measurement of rapist's erection responses to various sexual stimuli. Using a penile transducer, a small apparatus that encircles the rapist's penis, it is possible to quantify with precision the rapist's erotic preferences (Abel and Blanchard, 1976). In a series of papers (Abel, 1976; Abel, Barlow, Blanchard, and Guild, forthcoming; Abel, Blanchard, and Becker, forthcoming; Abel, Blanchard, Barlow, and Mavissakalian, 1975; and Abel, Barlow, Blanchard, and Mavissakalian, 1974), these authors have reported the isolation of characteristics of rapists that differ from nonrapists. Contrary to popular opinion, in the laboratory, sexual deviates who are not rapists and normal males fail to respond to scenes or descriptions depicting a sexual assualt on a female victim. Rapists, by contrast, clearly respond with large erection responses to such cues.

The key to objective validation of the physiologic differences between rapists and other men relies on (1) exact quantification of male sexual arousal by one of the penile measures and (2) pinpointing various sexual stimuli to which the rapist will respond.

To accomplish the latter, brief, two-minute, detailed audio descriptions depicting three scenes have been devised. The first describes the rapist participating in a scene of mutually consenting intercourse, with a willing, adult partner. In the second one, the rapist is raping that same female in spite of her vigorous, verbal and physical protest. The third describes the rapist physically assaulting the same female with absolutely no references to any sexual goals on his part. Each of these categories of stimuli is presented to rapists and to other men, and their erection responses quantified to each category (Abel, Barlow, Blanchard, and Guild, in press).

Using this method, it is possible to view rapists' responses along a continuum that begins with the nonrapist, extends to the rapist, and ends with the sadistic rapist. The male who is not a rapist, when presented with scenes depicting mutually consenting intercourse, is able to get sexually aroused. Scenes depicting a pure physical assault on a female victim or the rape of the woman fail to generate sexual responses in such normals. Rapists, by contrast, respond to scenes depicting rape and mutually consenting intercourse and somewhat to scenes depicting a physical assault devoid of sexual connotations. The sadistic rapists lack arousal to scenes depicting mutually consenting intercourse (consistent with Cohen's data), respond moderately to scenes depicting rape, and show marked sexual arousal to scenes depicting a physical assault of the female victim, devoid of sexual connotations.

A more refined analysis of the data shows a direct relationship between a rapist's arousal to rape descriptions versus his arousal to scenes depicting mutually consenting intercourse (his "rape index") and the number of times the rapist has raped, the extent of his injury to his victims, and the extent to which he is a sadistic rapist. That is, the greater the relative arousal to rape cues as compared to cues depicting mutually consenting intercourse, the greater the number of rapes the patient has committed, the greater the amount of violence he has used to perpetrate the rape, and the higher the likelihood of his being a sadistic rapist.

These results have provided the first objective means of classifying rapists according to their type of arousal and the extent of their danger to society in terms of their likelihood of having injured their victim. Equally important, however, is that these physiological methods can serve as a means of evaluating therapeutic interventions to treat rapists and prevent their raping again. If rapists are physiologically different from other men, then treatment should involve helping the rapist acquire the physiological responses of those who are not rapists. On a practical level, this first means carrying out the form of treatment that reduces his arousal to rape descriptions so that he is no longer aroused by such stimuli and, thus, on a physiological basis, is similar to normals. Numerous treatments to accomplish this goal are already available (Abel, Blanchard, and Becker, in press).

A second treatment implication of such physiological measurement is that since nonrapists are aroused by mutually consenting intercourse scenes, and some rapists and almost all sadists are not responsive to such scenes, treatment for these individuals would involve methods to help them develop arousal to scenes depicting consenting intercourse. Various treatments are avaliable to accomplish this goal (Abel, Blanchard, and Becker, in press).

In addition to these physiological measures, behavioral assessment of rapists indicates that three areas of potential social skills deficits exist for these aggressive men. These include deficits of heterosocial skills, assertiveness skills, empathy skills (Abel, Blanchard, and Becker, in press).

Heterosocial skills are frequently overlooked as deficits in may sexual aggressives. Some rapists can interrelate with a female with ease, maintain a conversation, eye contact, show interest in the female, and, in general, maintain those behaviors necessary to establish a social relationship between males and females. Other rapists, by contrast, fail miserably in such efforts. When they even think about talking to a female, they become markedly anxious. If able to speak at all, they are quite hesitant in their speech, avoid eye contact with the woman, and allow their speech to taper off in an unintelligible mumble. Individuals this deficient in heterosocial skills may respond to their failures in this area by raping the woman with whom they are unable to communicate.

Recently, checklists have been developed for assessment of such social skills deficits (Abel, 1976, Barlow et al., 1977), and a method of heterosocial skills training has been developed (Abel, Blanchard, and Becker, in press) which explains how rapists with deficits in the heterosocial skills area can be resocialized so as to acquire such skills in a relatively brief training period.

The treatment involves having the patient practice or role-play various social scenes with women of his own age. The rapist's performance is videotaped and played back to him to help him understand what methods or techniques he might use to better maintain social contact with a female. The therapist models for the patient, gives him social reinforcement for successes, points out limitations of his performance, and then the rapist practices the skills again. Such training continues until the rapist has demonstrated his acquisition to social skills consistent with those defined as appropriate for his natural environment.

Heterosocial skills training is based on the premise that the rapist's inability to relate to women heterosocially does not result from basic neurotic conflicts, but is more a product of his lack of socialization and lack of opportunity to practice heterosocial skills with women. This assumption is confirmed by the fact that heterosocial skills deficits can be corrected by a social skills training approach, similar to that described below. In the process of assessment, Ralph, a rapist, was found to be deficient in heterosocial skills. He reported being unable to approach women socially because of his fears of failure.

During Ralph's first session, his therapist asked him to keep track of those situations in his natural environment in which he had the opportunity to relate to an adult female. It is important to recreate these very scenes in the therapeutic interview, so that heterosocial skills training will apply directly to the social situations the rapist meets in the real world. Keeping a diary also places responsibility on the rapist to become directly involved in his therapy so that he sees that it is something he and the therapist are working on together, not something the therapist is requiring him to do.

The usual sequence of skills training is to have the client think about and imagine various methods of opening up a conversation with a woman. He is next asked to select one of these approaches to role-play with the therapist so the therapist and client can closely evaluate his actual performance and help him identify what he does well and how he can improve. A common error is that the therapist attempts to work with too many heterosocial behaviors at once. The therapist may inadvertently try to help the client maintain eye contact with a woman, develop a series of one-line opening comments to say to the woman, and maintain the flow of conversation. When all of these goals are attempted at once, the client becomes overwhelmed and confused, and will probably be unsuccessful. The therapist's goal is to develop successes for the rapist in his heterosocial skills training by concentrating on small components of heterosocial skills, components that can be mastered by the rapist. Once smaller, single components have been learned, several components can be combined into the type of skills needed for complex interactions occurring in his environment.

Rapists with poor heterosocial skills are frequently overcritical of their own heterosocial skills, feeling that nothing they do is right. In actuality, many of their conversations, if they would initiate them, fall very close to normal conversation. Their anxiety about initiating conversations, however, blocks their expression of interest in others; as a consequence they feel greater anxiety in conversing with someone else and never develop these skills. Initially, in heterosocial skills training, the therapist frequently socially reinforces the rapist for even small attempts at heterosocial skills. As therapy progresses however, the therapist gives less social reinforcement, expecting the rapist to perform at a higher effectiveness before social reinforcement is given. Initially, social reinforcement is lavishly given so that the rapist can feel a sense of success and accomplishment and is more likely to continue in therapy.

Social skills training can be done either live in the therapist's office or with the assistance of videotape, if available. When scenes are videotaped, it allows the therapist to go over them in detail with the rapist, stopping the action at various points, and discussing at length alternative ways of saying things or maintaining body posture. Videotaping, however, is not an absolute requirement for heterosocial skills training.

The advantage of actually having the rapist role-play situations involving heterosocial skills is that, although the rapist can talk about his skills (or lack of them), the therapist really doesn't know until he or she sees the rapist attempting to carry out those skills. This allows the therapist to directly observe the rapist's actual behavior and to assess more validly his assets and deficits as he attempts a social situation. The rapist's self-report of his skills is helpful, of course, but role playing a scene is more valid. It gives the therapist access to the rapist's current skills level, and allows the therapist to see how the rapist is proceeding in treatment.

An important conclusion to be drawn from this description of heterosocial skills training is that the process itself is not complicated or cloaked in mystery. Controlled studies have demonstrated that the method is highly effective and transfers outside of the treatment session quite well. Furthermore, our experience with rapists is that they respond to the treatment as others do, improving their heterosocial skills and, equally as important, gaining positive feelings about themselves and their social functioning. Of course, not all rapists need such training, as they already have adequate skills in that area. For those who do need it, however, training must include not only the simple one-line openers of conversation, but other components such as maintaining eye contact with the woman, sustaining an adequate voice volume, and not allowing too many long pauses to occur.

The tragedy of many treatment programs for rapists is that they do not attend to issues such as how to relate to women socially. Furthermore, many of the environments in which rapists are placed (such as prisons) remove them from contact with women. In isolation, their heterosocial skills deteriorate further, and the part that heterosocial skills deficits play in motivating their rape behavior becomes even more exaggerated. The issue that society must face squarely is whether the current, primarily punitive method of dealing with rapists is conducive to their rehabilitation. Unfortunately, the aggressive behaviors are only corrected when concerted effort is made to teach new behaviors.

A second area of potential social skills deficit is assertiveness. The case of James, described earlier, demonstrates the impact of the rapist's inability to communicate appropriately with others, in this case, his mother. For some reason, some rapists (not all) have lacked adequate socialization whereby they learn to communicate their needs, ask for change in another's behavior, or express their feelings and emotions to others. A considerable body of knowledge has been accumulated in this area (Abel, Blanchard, and Becker, in press) that outlines both the means of assessment and treatment of these particular deficits of assertive skills. Our clinical experience indicates that not infrequently rapists without such skills explode with a sexual assault (usually on an unsuspecting or inappropriate victim) when they are unable to assert themselves, as exemplified in James' case. Lack of assertiveness skills appears more commonly in rapists who do lack social skills.

The treatment for deficits of assertive skills falls under the label of assertiveness training. Similar to the heterosocial skills training treatment, such assertiveness training involves the rapist role-playing scenes requiring expression of his feelings, requesting changes in others, and expressing his beliefs. As with heterosocial skills training, role-playing, videotape feedback, social reinforcement, and modeling are all components of assertiveness training.

A final area of deficient social skills includes insufficient empathy or feelings for others, lack of concern for others, and inability to assess the needs and feelings of others. Such skills, long considered essential for a good therapist (Truax and Carkhuff, 1967), are often found lacking in rapists. The majority of rapists view their victims as objects, not real people. This dehumanization of the victim enables the rapist to engage in his aggressive behavior. By teaching a rapist that women have feelings and that his behavior will traumatize as well as stigmatize a woman may serve to inhibit such behavior. Support for this notion comes from a study by Brodsky (1976). Incarcerated rapists were asked to rate a series of videotaped behaviors according to which would be most successful at deterring a rape. A substantial number of rapists rated the establishment of an "interpersonal liaison" as the most effective. One rapist commented,

> Calm talking, asking why are you doing this to me and try to establish in the rapist's mind that she is a real person with real feelings and not just an object . . . in doing so it makes a realization in your mind that you are doing something wrong to a real person. [p. 86]

The authors are attempting to teach rapists to appreciate their feelings about other people and how to express those feelings to others. Although the methodology and means of assessment remain in a rudimentary form at this time, it appears that such empathy training is an important element for retraining some rapists (Abel, Blanchard, and Becker, in press).

CONCLUSIONS

More recent research confirms that definite physiological differences exist between rapists and nonrapists. Measurement of such differences allows the identification of physiological patterns that occur in rapists and not in men who are not rapists. Such studies have identified two treatment needs of rapists: reduction of their arousal to rape stimuli and, in some cases, increased arousal to mutually consenting sexual cues. Fortunately, several treatments exist to implement both these types of needs.

Recent behavioral assessment has similarly identified three potential social skills deficits manifested by some rapists. Treatment methods currently available allow rapists with such deficits to be resocialized through the acquisition of appropriate heterosocial skills, appropriate assertiveness skills, and empathy for others.

The physiological and psychological assessment of rapists and the development of treatment techniques that correct their excesses or deficits cannot be expected to eliminate rape. Rape and other aggressive acts against women are the product of multiple factors impinging upon the perpetrator. The importance of assessment, however, is that such methods are beginning to identify how those who victimize women differ from those who do not. Through qualifying and quantifying such differences, it is becoming possible to trace back, in individual cases, where and how such deficits arose. In this fashion, we should be able to resocialize some rapists, to determine what social interventions would preclude the development of the excesses and deficits that may cause men to become rapists, and, therefore, provide primary prevention of the sexual assault and victimization of women.

The victimization of women by men appears to be directly related to our sexist society in which male supremacy must be upheld at whatever cost. The form that victimization takes varies from subtle and not so subtle discrimination in hiring practices to blatant physical and sexual assaults on females.

The majority of male and female children from a very early age identify with their mothers as a primary model and as the one who meets their needs. Gender role stereotyping taught and reinforced by parents, peers, and society at large programs male children to behave differently from female children. Research indicates that males are more aggressive than females. Furthermore, the amount of aggression shown by children is related to the amount of physical punishment used by the parents. It is not unusual for a child to be exposed to a home environment in which the father physically assaults the mother. In a number of cases, the mother, out of her own frustration and anger, will physically abuse her child. The male child in turn will "grow up" to be an adult who physically abuses women.

The media and literature are replete with sexist stereotypes. Children from an early age are exposed to fairy tales, cartoons, and TV programs and commercials that directly exploit females. Violence is rampant in TV programming. The differential impact of exposure to violence has been demonstrated. Females are learning through observation that they are impotent and passive in the face of any form of threat and that males occupy a dual role, as their protectors and their antagonists.

"Femininity" denotes inferiority, weakness, and passivity to the male subculture. Young males are socialized not to express warm, tender feelings. They are reinforced for the expression of rough, aggressive behaviors. The importance of this is seen in rapists who are truly "macho." As several therapists have noted, sexual aggressives are "frightened" by their passive-feminine characteristics. Many gang and pair rapes illustrate the need for some males to assert and receive peer group reinforcement for their "masculinity."

It will be a difficult task to ameliorate the victimization of women. Progress, however, is being made. Shelters have been established for battered wives and abused children. There are more than one hundred rape counseling centers for women in this country. More programs such as the one described for sexual aggressives need to be established.

More basic goals also need to be set. Gender role stereotyping and lack of equal rights for women are at the core of the victimization of women. Parents need to be educated about the effects of their differential child-rearing practices. The educational system in this country should incorporate teaching modules in which aggression is discussed, and when aggressive behavior is noted in a child, steps should be taken to resocialize the youngster. Human rights should be taught at an early level of the educational system. The criminal justice system, which is male oriented and controlled, needs revision. More women who are sensitive to the basic issues involved in women's rights need to be in positions of power so they may influence policy making. Advances are being made in the area of women's rights, and we look to the future for the needed social policy changes.

REFERENCES

ABEL, G.G. (1976). "The behavior assessment of rapists." Paper presented at Brown University and Butler Hospital, Providence, R.I., October 21.

––– (1976). "Assessment of sexual deviation in the male." In M. Hersen and A.S. Bellack (eds.), Behavioral assessment: A practical handbook. New York: Pergamon.

ABEL, G.G., BARLOW, D.H., BLANCHARD, E.B., and GUILD, D. (forthcoming). "The components of rapists' sexual arousal." Archives of General Psychiatry.

ABEL, G.G., BARLOW, D.H., BLANCHARD, E.B., and MAVISSAKALIAN, M. (1974). "The relationship of aggressive cues to the sexual arousal of rapists." Paper presented at the American Psychological Association, New Orleans, Louisiana.

ABEL,G.G., and BLANCHARD, E.B. (1976). "The measurement and generation of sexual arousal." In M. Herson, R. Eisler, and P.M. Miller (eds.), Progress in behavior modification, Volume II. New York: Academic Press.

ABEL, G.G., BLANCHARD, E.B., BARLOW, D.H., and MAVISSAKALIAN, M. (1975). "Identifying specific erotic cues in sexual deviation by audio-taped descriptions." Journal of Applied Behavior Analysis, 8:247-260.

ABEL, G.G., BLANCHARD, E.B., and BECKER, J.V. (1976). "Psychological treatment for rapists." In S. Brodsky and M. Walker (eds.), Sexual assault. Lexington, Mass.: Lexington Books.

——— (forthcoming). "An integrated treatment program for rapists." In R. Rada (ed.), Clinical aspects of the rapist. New York: Grune and Stratton.

BANDURA, A. (1965). "Influence of model's reinforcement contingencies on the acquisition of imitated responses." Journal of Personality and Social Psychology, 1:589-595.

BANDURA, A., ROSS, D., and ROSS, S. (1963). "Vicarious reinforcement and imitated learning." Journal of Abnormal and Social Psychology, 67:601-607.

BARLOW, D.H., ABEL, G.G., BLANCHARD, E.B., BRISTOW, A., and YOUNG, L. (1977). "A heterosocial skills checklist for males." Behavior Therapy, 1, 8:229-239.

BERKOWITZ, L. (1970). "Experimental investigations of hostility catharsis." Journal of Consulting and Clinical Psychology, 35:1-7.

BINFORD, S. (1972). "Apes and original sin." Human Behavior, 1, 6:64-71.

BORING, E.G., LANGFELD, H.S., and WELD, H.P. (1939). Introduction to Psychology. New York: Wiley.

BRODSKY, S. (1976). "Prevention of rape: Deterrence by the potential victim." In H. Walker and S. Brodsky (eds.), Sexual assault. Lexington, Mass.: Lexington Books.

BROWNMILLER, S. (1975). Against our will: Men, women and rape. New York: Simon and Schuster.

CANTOR, H.G., and ORWANT, J. (1977). "Differential effects of television violence on girls and boys." Paper presented at the Southern Sociological Society, Atlanta, Georgia.

CLEAVER, E. (1968). Soul on ice. New York: Dell-Delta Ramparts.

COHEN, M., GARAFALO, R., BOUSCHER, R., and SEGHORN, T. (1971). "The psychology of rapists." Seminars in Psychiatry, 3:307-327.

DELGADO, J.N. (1969). Physical control of the mind. New York: Harpers.

GOLDSTEIN, J.H. (1975). Aggression and crimes of violence. New York: Oxford University Press.

GREEN R., and PIGG, R. (1970). "Acquisition of an aggressive response and its generalization to verbal behavior." Journal of Personality and Social Psychology, 19:165-170.

HEATH, R.G. (1963). "Electrical self-stimulation of the brain in man." American Journal of Psychiatry, 120:571-577.

KAGAN, J., and MOSS, H.A. (1962). Birth to maturity: A study in psychological development. New York: Wiley.

KANIN, E. (1970). "Sex aggression by college men." Medical Aspects of Human Sexuality, 4:25-40.

LOEW, C. (1967). "Acquisition of a hostile attitude and its relation to an aggressive behavior." Journal of Personality and Social Psychology, 5:552-558.

LoSCIUTO, L. (1972). "A rational inventory of television viewing behavior." In E. Rubinstein, G. Comstock, and J. Murray (eds.), Television and social behavior. Washington, D.C.: U.S. Government Printing Office.

MILLETT, K. (1970). Sexual politics. New York: Avon.

SCACCO, A.M. (1975). Rape in prison. Springfield, Ill.: Charles C Thomas.

SEARS, R., MACCOBY, E., and LEVIN, H. (1957). Patterns of child rearing. Evanston, Ill.: Row, Peterson.

STRAUS, M. (1977). "Sexual inequality, cultural norms, and wife-beating." In J. Chapman and M. Gates (eds.), Women into wives: The legal and economic impact of marriage. Beverly Hills, Calif.: Sage.

TRAUX, C.B., and CARKHUFF, R. (1967). Towards effective counseling and psycho-therapy. Chicago: Aldine.

WATERS, H. (1977). "What TV does to kids." Newsweek (February 21), pp. 63-70.

WOLFGANG, M.E. (1956). "Husband-wife homicides." Corrective Psychiatry and Journal of Social Therapy, 2:263-271.

3

RAPE

DONNA D. SCHRAM

Rape can be the most terrifying event in a woman's life. The sexual act or acts performed are often intended to humiliate and degrade her: bottles, gun barrels, or sticks may be thrust into her vagina or anus; she may be compelled to swallow urine or perform fellatio with such force that she thinks she might strangle or suffocate; her breasts may be bitten or burned with cigarettes. In many instances, her hope is to save her life, not her chastity. Her terror may be so great that she urinates, defecates, or vomits. If she escapes without serious outward signs of injury, she may suffer vaginal tears or infections, contract venereal disease, or be impregnated. For months or years afterward, she may distrust others, change residences frequently, and sleep poorly. Her friends and family may blame or reject her.

If she chooses to report her offense to authorities, she may suffer further trauma. She must relate her account to patrol officers, detectives, medical personnel, counselors, filing prosecutors, and, perhaps, trial prosecutors. She might be *required* to submit to a polygraph or psychiatric examination to determine the veracity of her statement. If a suspect is arrested, she might be subjected to direct and cross-examination at a preliminary hearing and trial. Her testimony may not be protected against inquiries into her previous sexual relationships with other men or with the defendant. Thus, her private life may be exposed in a public and open forum; testimony regarding her prior chastity may be used to discredit her account of the rape.

Given these circumstances, it is not surprising that many women choose not to report rape offenses to the police. Indeed, victimization studies have shown that rape is probably the most under-reported of all major crimes. If victimization estimates are accurate, the *actual* number of rapes is approximately four times the reported number,[1] or one quarter of a million rapes per year.[2] Thus, rape is *not* an infrequent offense; it is simply an infrequently reported offense.

Public interest in the crime of rape has been generated primarily by activists in the women's movement. The act of forcible sexual assault and the subsequent treatment of the victim by criminal justice authorities have come to symbolize the most extreme example of the abuse of a woman's body and her integrity. As these abuses have been exposed to public scrutiny, this previously "unmentionable" act has become the subject of media dramatizations, as well as discussions in public schools, churches, and civic organizations. This attention has created an atmosphere conducive to the reform of antiquated rape legislation,[3] the development of more rigorous procedures for rape enforcement (e.g., Still, 1975; Lichtenstein, 1974; Bard and Ellison, 1974; Cottell, 1974), and an insistence on more sensitive treatment of victims by agents of the criminal justice system and the medical profession (e.g., Putnam and Fox, 1976; Hayman, 1970; Burgess and Holmstrom, 1976). In addition to these more institutionalized changes, rape crisis lines, victim advocacy services, and mental health services have been established to assist victims in communities large and small throughout the United States.[4]

Precisely because of this public interest in the crime of rape, research in this area has proliferated during recent years. The first large national study (Brodyaga et al., 1975) resulted in the publication by the Law Enforcement Assistance Administration of a Prescriptive Package intended to provide guidelines for police, prosecutors, medical personnel, and service groups involved with rape victims. A second national study, and the one from which much of the information for this article was drawn, was conducted by the Battelle Institute Law and Justice Center Study under grants from the National Institute of Law Enforcement and Criminal Justice of the Law Enforcement Assistance Administration.[5] Taken together, these and other studies have helped to identify and understand the dynamics of rape, the circumstances under which such offenses usually occur, the social and psychological implications of victimization, needed legislative change, and improvement in the treatment of victims and the enforcement of rape statutes. Thus, we are beginning to understand this crime and the most appropriate response to it.

THE RAPIST

Despite a rather considerable literature on sex offenders, it is extremely difficult to draw a consistent picture of the rapist, his motives, or his potential for "successful" treatment. For example, rapists have been variously described as antisocial or psychopathic (Henn et al., 1976), autistic and depressive (Takakuwa et al., 1971), less intelligent than other convicted felons (Ruff and Templer, 1976), average or above in intelligence (Cormier and Sickert, 1969; Perdue and Lester, 1972), good treatment prospects (Marshall and McKnight, 1975; Sadoff, 1975), or poor treatment prospects (Pacht, 1976). Still other authors suggest that is a myth to presume that rapists share common characteristics. According to Pacht and Cowden (1974), the obvious lack of homogeneity among assaultive sex offenders suggests that there are more similarities between rapists and ourselves than there are differences. Thus, readers who search the literature on rapists are likely to emerge from the process more confused and perplexed than before they began.

One cause of this confusion is the sampling bias inherent in research on rapists. Of all the rapes actually reported to the police, only a very small number of suspects are ever arrested, charged, and convicted of rape. Recent research conducted at the Battelle Law and Justice Study Center (1977) suggests that suspect attrition is so great at each stage of the criminal process that less than 3% of rape reports are disposed as rape convictions. The remaining 97% of the offenders are never arrested, never charged, never convicted, and never participate in research intended to explore the psychodynamics of sexual assault. The subjects in such research are usually drawn from that tiny fraction of the rapist population which is actually adjudicated and convicted. Whether this small sample of rapists is representative of the entire population of offenders is subject to serious question.

Despite the methodological limitations of research on sex offenders, Cohen et al. (1971) conducted extensive clinical assessments of convicted rapists. These authors describe three basic types of offenders, differentiated on the basis of the underlying motivation for the sexual assault. In the first type, *aggressive aim,* rape serves to humiliate, degrade, and defile the victim. These offenders often describe their own emotional state as anger. The rape itself is often accompanied by sexual multilation or insertion of objects into the vagina or anus of the victim. These rapists are often highly skilled, competitive, and physically attractive. Human relationships, however, are usually shallow, and friendships are rare. Prognosis for treatment is good. In the second type of offender, rape serves a *sexual aim.* Rapes committed by these offenders usually demonstrate a relative absence of violence and lack characteristics of brutality. Victims are almost always strangers. These rapists are shy, socially inept, and isolated from male peers. School records usually show poor performance and, frequently, withdrawal before graduation. Long-term treatment prognosis is good. In the third type of rapist, *sexual aggression diffusion,* the offenders demonstrate a strong component of sadism which appears to be necessary to achieve sexual arousal. These offenders are often impotent until they are able to provoke resistance from their potential victims. In the extreme, lust, murder, or mutilation may occur. These offenders are often assertive, manipulative, and somewhat hostile in all situations. This type of rapist demonstrates the greatest paranoid features and does not appear to benefit from therapy.

This assessment suggests that rapists do not fit any particular stereotype. Furthermore, the sexuality associated with rape may be less important for many offenders than the pain and humiliation they are able to inflict on their victims. Thus, rape might be appropriately viewed as a crime of violence, rather than a crime of passion.

The more recent Battelle study of rape relied on two other methods to examine the characteristics and behaviors of offenders. The first of these methods was an analysis of 1,261 rape victim reports made to the police in Seattle, Detroit, Kansas City (Missouri), New Orleans, and Phoenix. Of particular interest were the age and race of offenders, the circumstances of the initial contact between victims and offenders, the location of the rape offense, and threats or weapons used against the victims. The second research method consisted of interviews with a group of 50 incarcerated offenders who were patients at Atascadero State Hospital in California, a maximum security mental institution for the treatment of sex offenders. Topics explored in the course of the interviews included types of victims selected, the amount and kind of prerape planning undertaken, modus operandi, the effects of victim resistance on offender behavior, and the perceived influence of potentially sexually arousing stimuli, such as victim clothing and pornographic materials.[6] This combination of research methods (police reports and offender interviews) provided the offender information discussed below.

AGE OF OFFENDERS

Victim estimates indicated that the majority of offenders were between the ages of 18 and 25 years old. In much the same way that women over 30 were not likely to be raped, men over 30 were not likely to be rapists. Men 40 years old or older were almost never involved in forcible sexual assaults; they made up less than 4% of the offender population.

RACE OF OFFENDERS

According to victim reports, minority males were consistently overrepresented in the offender population. This overrepresentation was true in all jurisdictions examined, whether the minority population was small or large. In the overwhelming majority (80%) of all cases that involved multiple rapists the offenders were minority males.

NUMBER OF OFFENDERS

There is a substantial literature which suggests that the psychological and sociological dynamics of pair rape (two offenders) or group rape (three or more offenders) differ significantly from those which underlie rapes committed by single individuals. Group rape, in particular, has been variously explained as the manifestation of frustration/aggression, where hostility and inadequacy are coupled with a collective need to dominate (MacDonald, 1974), the eroticized adulation of one boy for another (Blanchard, 1959), or the outcome of social resentment based upon a general pattern of social disorganization (Woods, 1969). Whatever the genesis of paired or group rape, it has been thought to constitute a substantial proportion of all sexual assaults. In Amir's (1971) well-known study of rape in Philadelphia, for example, 43% of the victim reports examined involved more than one offender. From this, one might conclude that multiple offender rapes account for as many as one half of all reported rapes. More recent data, however, do *not* substantiate this conclusion.

Analyses of 1974 and 1975 police reports from Seattle, Detroit, Kansas City, New Orleans, and Phoenix indicate that the overwhelming majority of rapes are committed by a single individual who attacks a lone woman. Paired rapes accounted for 11-17% of the complaints; group rapes accounted for 3-4% of the victimizations. Thus, multiple rapists are rare. When such offenses were observed, they usually involved juvenile males under the age of 18 years.

LOCATION OF FIRST CONTACT PRIOR TO OFFENSE

The traditional view of rape assumes that sex-crazed males lurk in alleys and roam darkened streets in search of unsuspecting prey whom they may assault. Although this type of rape certainly exists, it does not describe the most frequent circumstances under which victims and offenders come into contact. Indeed, in the cases studied, it was not the street that represented the greatest risk of sexual assault to a woman—it was her own home. This location was followed in frequency by street encounters. Of the nine other initial contact locations identified from the police reports, only the automobile of the offender stood out as a consistently high-risk location. Initial contacts established at taverns, social gatherings, and so forth were relatively uncommon.

LOCATION OF OFFENSE

The location of the initial contact between the offender and the victim was not always a good indicator of the actual location of the offense. There was a general tendency to move the actual crime scene to an indoor or more private location. Thus, although the victim's residence remained the most likely location of the assault, the offender's residence or his automobile became the next most frequent locations. Relatively few rapes were actually consummated in public places, such as streets or parks.

THREATS

Approximately 70% of all rape reports included clear indications that the offender threatened force or used force against the victim. In most instances, these consisted of verbal threats of harm or death to the victim or to someone related to the victim. In other cases, the mere presence of a weapon was defined as a threat; no verbalizations were necessary. Occasionally, threats, physical force, and a weapon were all used. The victim statement in one police report illustrates such a case.

> He hit me in the face and knocked me on the floor. He pulled off my robe and nightgown and I screamed and he threatened to kill me. He stuffed the nightgown in my mouth and tied the rest around my throat and the gown strangled me. He tied my hands behind my back and he pressed my neck so hard I passed out. Then he asked me if I needed air and I nodded and he let it loose a bit but still kept it in my mouth. He tied my legs up to the tie on my hands . . . then he got my butcher knife from the kitchen and ran the point all over my body.

WEAPONS

The frequency with which weapons were present or used during sexual assaults varied considerably from one police jurisdiction to another. Nearly 60% of all reported rapes in Detroit involved weapons of some kind; in contrast, only 33% of the rapes reported to Seattle authorities involved weapons.

The weapon of choice was usually a handgun, although knives were used almost as frequently. In addition to guns and knives, an incredible variety of other weapons were also used or threatened. Occasionally these "weapons" were everyday items, such as pencils, metal combs, and rolling pins. In other instances, menacing weapons were formed from broken bottles, fire pokers, burning cigarette butts, and rocks. Some type of weapon was identified in approximately one half of all police reports examined.

TYPE OF VICTIM SELECTED

Rape is not a crime inflicted on random members of the female population. Many victims share similar characteristics which, it is assumed, influence their selection as victim targets. The first and most obvious of these characteristics is age. In general, rape is a crime committed against young women. Based upon analyses of rapes reported in the five police jurisdictions, more than 50% of all rapes were committed against women who were less than 21 years old. Once a woman reached the age of 30, the likelihood of being raped decreased precipitously.

Perhaps no other myth is more prevalent in rape lore than that which asserts that most sexual assaults occur in dating situations in which the victim provoked her own attack. Although such cases may occur, the frequency of such attacks is inconsequential. In one half or more of all rapes, the offender and the victim are completely unknown to one another. Almost without exception, the offenders interviewed at Atascadero committed this type of rape. Even though the victim targets were strangers to these offenders, most of the subjects professed some reasonably firm concept of the type of woman they preferred to rape and the methods necessary to locate such individuals. When offenders were asked to describe their victim preferences in detail, the picture which emerged was that of the "all American woman"—a nice, friendly, young, pretty, white housewife or college student. These same offenders were asked to indicate those characteristics that would make women undesirable victims. Leading the list were females who were crippled, dirty, children, sick, pregnant, retarded, fat, middle-aged, or prostitutes (Chappell and James, 1976:8-9).

PLANNING THE RAPE

Earlier research suggested that a significant proportion of rapes were spontaneous or explosive acts wherein the offender exploited an opportunity to attack a vulnerable target. Thus, a burglar might discover that a dwelling he has entered is occupied by a lone woman. Because of the circumstances, the burglar takes advantage of the situation and woman, and rapes her.

The extent to which a rape of this type is truly spontaneous is a matter of conjecture. A large proportion of the rapists interviewed at Atascadero had prior arrests for both burglary and robbery. While details of these earlier arrests and convictions for offenses other than rape were not obtained during interviews, almost a third of the subjects indicated that their primary objective had been rape in previously committed burglaries and robberies. Further, seemingly spontaneous rapes that resulted in the offenders' present incarceration exhibited a certain degree of premeditation or planning. When questioned generally about the planning engaged in before a rape, 36% of the group said they did none, 52% said some, and 12% said a considerable amount. There was quite a bit of leeway in the definition of planning, as the following three cases illustrate (Chappell and James, 1976:11).

Case 1

It was spur of the moment. I would fantasize it. My sort of planning was that I would just find a piece of ass and take it because I was only concerned for myself. I wanted some sex. Actually there was no planning but there was planning already about the idea. There was no planning like, I would say, a robbery. You know, at 10 o'clock you're going to do this, at 10:05 you're going to be in there. With mine, there was not that kind of tactic planning. I was in the restaurant and I was pretty well bombed and I thought my friend took me home but evidently he didn't. He took me instead to my girlfriend's house. Then she took me home, that was about an hour and a half. Then I blacked out. Somewhere in there I grabbed this woman and had a piece of ass.

Case 2

I found a couple of guy friends I knew. We started a party up—a big party and we went down to a place where a hangout is—where a lot of people hang out—and we picked up three chicks and took them over to the party. All the three chicks were jumping from car to car and were pretty wild and we figured it would be easy to put the make on. So we got over there to the party and we had some weed. We were there about an hour and I asked the girl if she wanted to go out in the car and get some fresh air. Like she had been kind of standoffish at the party towards me and so I imagined the whole thing to take her out in the car and rape her. I didn't know for sure but—anyway, we got out in the car and I tried to kiss her and she pushed me away and that got me mad. I grabbed her neck and told her that if she made a sound or made a struggle, I would kill her.

Case 3

I went to work. There were two girls at work who planned to go to the park—the lake the next day which we did. One girl we dropped off home; the other girl I went to a bar with and she said, "I want to be with you tonight." So I figured I'd have a piece of ass, but I got too drunk and threw up and she went off with somebody else that she picked up at the bar. I went home and woke up angry in the morning and I was determined to get a piece of ass—if I couldn't I would rape. I drove around this area that I knew there were some girls living in these apartments and this one girl that I particularly wanted to rape—I rang her doorbell, this guy answered the door and I made up some excuse about my car being broken down and I wanted some assistance and to use the telephone. I saw this girl walk into her apartment carrying her laundry and I asked her if she had a telephone and she said "yes." And that I could use it and I made a couple of phony phone calls working my courage up and she offered to give me a dime and I grabbed her and pulled her down and I told her I wouldn't hurt her if she cooperated. I was in her apartment and I made sure the door was locked when I went in. I tied her up and took her clothes off and went to the bedroom and raped her. I was feeling angry. Afterwords, I had a cigarette and talked to her about 45 minutes and I split.

The subject in Case 1 denied any specific planning prior to the rape and distinguished the sex offense from robbery in this regard. Case 2 illustrates apparent premeditation, but only after a potential victim had been observed. Indeed, this offender appeared to be attracted by the standoffish behavior of the least provocative woman. Finally, Case 3 portrays an act of pure premeditation. This offender was determined to rape any vulnerable woman while, at the same time, minimizing the risk of interruption or apprehension.

RELEASE OF THE VICTIM

According to the offender interview responses, victims were usually released immediately after the rape event, although a number of offenders subsequently engaged the victim in a conversation or drove her to a less accessible spot before letting her go. Approximately one half of the sample made some effort to convince the woman not to report the offense to police. The most common tactic used to deter such a report was to threaten bodily harm to the victim. Sixteen percent of the offenders also threatened to return again because they knew the identity of the victim and where she lived.

Almost a third of the sample said they would rape the same woman twice. This rather surprising proportion of potentially repeating offenders based their reason for return on the following (in order of importance): victim responded well; they were invited back; a good relationship was established; a desire to further humiliate the woman; the woman agreed not to report the rape to police. The remainder of the offenders expressed no desire to return, usually because of fear of being caught.

In many cases, associated crime was found to be part of the release situation. Approximately three quarters of the offenders indicated that they would commit some additional crime beyond the rape. Robbery was the most common, followed by theft, then assault. After leaving the victim, 18% of the subjects said they would consider committing another rape the same evening (Chappell and James, 1976).

ATTITUDES TOWARD WOMEN

Although many men who rape may suffer serious psychological disturbances, there is no reason to assume that their attitudes toward women, sex, and violence are significantly different from those of other males. Even the offenders interviewed at Atascadero, for example, believed that the prevention or avoidance of rape was the responsibility of the female. When asked specifically how such acts could be prevented, the rapists sounded very much like crime prevention officers. Women were advised not to go out alone (32%), not to hitchhike (36%), to learn self-defense (16%), to buy a dog (8%), to carry weapons (6%), to dress conservatively (6%), and not to drink alone (2%).

These findings and this advice will depress or enrage many women, for they represent an impingement on their basic freedoms. However, the findings and advice should come as no surprise, for they reflect, in part, the male attitudes toward women that have been so thoroughly condemned by feminist writers such as Brownmiller (1975) and Russell (1975).

Offenders at Atascadero not only believed that women were responsible for rape avoidance, they also considered many of their offenses the result of provocative or "lead on" situations created by their victims. The following statements by rapists typify these attitudes:

Case 1

I believe that women who want to be fashionable in some of the styles that are sexually stimulating to men should try to realize some of the consequences of wearing some of these styles before they wear them. Carrying themselves a little better in public when they do wear them—men are going to look, quite naturally, but all men aren't the same. Some of them are going to make more advancements—more aggressive advancements than others in certain situations. If a women just happens to be weak and not realize what it means, then she's in trouble. That's just the way it is.

Case 2

Once again, I would say again, by body language—or unconsciously they flirt—sometimes the way that they dress—their minds say one thing—their bodies say another—or some come on with their seduction-type overall tone—that says one thing but could possibly mean something else. Or they put themselves in the position of being alone.

Case 3

By hitchhiking—being real loose with themselves—maybe not wearing bras or something like this—so you can see through—or where you can tell where they are drooping down or something like that—by wearing short dresses—being alone at night time walking around.

All three statements imply that victim behavior or apparel arouses an overwhelming sexual desire which men are unable to overcome short of ravaging the provocateur. Thus, the responsibility for the rape is shifted from the helpless male to the cunning or careless female. The error of such misplaced responsibility is best expressed by Bromberg and Coyle (1974):

The average rapist . . . rarely admits his aggressive motives, either during or after the offense; he prefers to accept his act as evidence of sexual need which other men will understand. The purely sexual aspect of rape is more congenial to the perpetrator's inner feelings than his basic desire to demean women.

This statement succinctly describes precisely why it is that rape has so often been viewed merely as an unwanted, albeit illegal, act of sexual intercourse. The underlying element of violence and the offender's intent to humiliate and degrade the victim are usually overlooked. Instead, it is the woman's behavior that is judged to determine the extent of her contributory negligence.

THE VICTIM

Most of the information on rape victims comes from those who report offenses to police or to medical personnel. The means by which they report and their reasons for doing so suggest that these victims share much in common. In the course of the Battelle study (1977), for example, victims were asked to specify their main reasons for reporting to police. When victim responses were analyzed, a very interesting pattern of reasons emerged. These victims reported because they wanted the criminal justice system to *do* something to the offender. Anger, revenge, and outrage were common motivations that apparently were so intense that they overcame any concern for personal embarrassment or fear of mistreatment by the criminal justice system. In essence, these women reported because they wanted protection for themselves and for other women.

These same victims were also asked whether, on the basis of their experience, they would advise other women to report a rape to the police. An overwhelming 98% of the victims responded affirmatively; i.e., they would recommend reporting. When victims were asked why women should report, the majority indicated that official complaints might serve to *save* others:

"If a lady lets it go, he might go on to kill another woman."

"Save another woman's life."

"To protect themselves and others from the sickness of people who rape."

or to *punish* others:

"Help get some of these sadists off the street."

"Why let the rapist go fancy free?"

or to assure treatment and emotional support:

"It helps to talk to someone."

"To get medical and counseling help."

Only two victims advised against reporting. In both instances, the victims felt that police treatment was so poor that other women should be discouraged from making official complaints.

In the course of the Battelle research project, 1,261 initial rape complaints were obtained from five large police agencies throughout the United States. On the basis of these reports, it was possible to gather an enormous quantity of data regarding the characteristics of victims, the circumstances prior to and during the sexual assaults, victim resistance, victim injury, and the kinds of forced sexual acts attempted or performed. The information presented below summarizes some of those findings.

AGE OF VICTIMS

Victim ages obtained from police reports clearly demonstrate that rape is a crime committed against young women. More than 50% of the rapes were committed against women under the age of 21. In much the same way that men over the age of 30 were not likely to be rapists, women over the age of 30 were not likely to be victims. Elderly women were almost never raped.

RACE OF VICTIM

In most jurisdictions from which records were obtained, minority women were overrepresented in the victim population. This finding was particularly true in the 61 cases in which there was more than one victim. Fifty-nine percent of all multiple victim cases involved black and Asian-American women.

RELATIONSHIP BETWEEN VICTIM AND OFFENDER

For the purposes of this research, the relationships between the victim and the offender were divided into four categories. The first category consisted of *strangers;* that is, the actors had no acquaintance or knowledge of one another before the sequence of events that terminated in the assault. The second and third categories, *acquainted* or *friends,* were more difficult to distinguish. Victims and offenders were defined as "acquaintances" if they had merely met or were known to one another by reputation prior to the offense. In contrast, the term "friend" was used to define long-standing or previously intimate relationships. The fourth category included all rapes between persons who, either by blood or by marriage, were *related* to one another.

The findings indicated that, among the police jurisdictions studied, approximately one half of all rapes involved strangers. An additional one quarter of all rapes occurred between acquaintances. Rape between friends made up less than 20% of the reported assaults in any jurisdiction. In general, these rapes occurred subsequent to planned dating situations or other social interactions. Finally, rapes involving relatives were extremely rare. When such rapes were reported, they usually involved an offender who was related to the victim by marriage, i.e., stepfather or brother-in-law, for example.

VICTIM RESISTANCE

Police records indicated the majority of women resisted their sexual assault. Initial resistance was usually verbal and fell into one of three categories. The first category included verbal methods whereby the victim attempted to make herself unattractive to the offender or elicit his sympathy; the woman indicated that she was pregnant, sick, diseased, virginal, or menstruating. Examples of this method drawn from case records include the following:

Case 1

He just stood there over the kid with his flashlight in my face and told me to take my nightgown off—QUICK! I didn't move at all. I couldn't see his face because he kept the light in my eyes. He reached down and pulled back the covers. I told him I couldn't have intercourse. I told him I was hemoraging (sic) and had just been to the doctor the day before. He said "Good, you bitch. I can play like you are a virgin."

Case 2

_____ and me had just been listening to music. We had drunk a little wine and he started pulling at my sweater. He told me to take my clothes off and lay on the rug or he would break my arm off. I told _____ that I hadn't ever done it before and I was afraid I would have a baby. ___ said what the hell did I come over there for if I didn't want to screw. Girls just didn't come over and drink his wine and think they could leave when they wanted to.

The second category of verbal resistance consisted of *threats* that, if the offender persisted, the victim would prosecute or seek retaliation from her family or friends. Finally, some victims attempted to feign stipulated consent, that is, they indicated a willingness to engage in sexual activity if they could first use the restroom, change clothes, call a friend, or so forth. Although these latter ruses sometimes allowed an occasional victim to escape the situation, verbal resistance was singularly ineffective in thwarting sexual assaults. Victims were seldom able to deter the rapist with "talk" no matter which of the various verbal tactics were used.

A related method of victim resistance consisted of crying, either from fear or as a means to underscore her lack of consent. Again, as in cases of verbal resistance, rapists were seldom deterred by this behavior.

Approximately 20% of all victims reported that they screamed or used some device (a whistle, for example) in an effort to attract attention. Whether or not the victims' actions actually attracted assistance from others, this was the most effective method of terminating a sexual assault. Unfortunately, it was also likely to cause some offenders to become more violent in attempts to silence the screams.

Many victims attempted to physically resist their assailants. In general, this resistance took the form of struggling, hitting, biting, and kicking the offender. Nearly 20% of the victims attempted to run from the scene. Although struggling or fighting with the assailant seldom terminated the assault, victims who were able to run sometimes escaped their attackers. Examples from police records indicated the futility most victims experienced when they attempted physical resistance.

Case 1

He pulled real hard on my right arm and I fell down on one knee. I bit him hard on the arm but he hit me real hard on my ear with his fist. . . . Then I tried to hit him with my fists but he just laughed. . . .

Case 2

I told ___ I would poke his m—— f—— eyes out if he laid one finger on me. He just sat there for a minute and stared out the windshield. Then he looked back at me and said something like "Ain't six of you could stop me when I get fired up." I tried to hit him but he just grabbed my arms and shoved them over mine [sic] head.

VICTIM INJURY

The rape reports indicated that approximately one third of all victims were injured. In most instances, the physical injuries were relatively minor and consisted of bruises and cuts that did not require extensive medical treatment. More serious injuries usually involved severe bruises or cuts, vaginal tears, internal bleeding or bruising, broken bones, broken teeth, or concussions. (Note: No records of rape-homicide were examined in the course of this research. Thus, injuries that caused the death of victims were not included in this analysis.)

COUNSELING/ADVOCACY SERVICES

During the course of the present research, many different forms of victim counseling and advocacy services were observed. In many cities, for example, rape crisis lines were operated by community volunteers who had undergone some form of specific training in crisis intervention, rape law, and criminal process. These volunteers were usually available around the clock so that they could respond quickly to the immediate emotional needs of rape victims and provide important medical and legal information. In other cities, services were available through mental health professionals who could provide more traditional, long-term counseling and assure proper medical follow-ups.

Although it was impossible to establish the total number of victims who used such services at each of the sites included in this study, the researchers were able to question victim interview respondents about their experiences. Of the 146 victims who answered this set of inquiries, one third had been in contact with a local rape crisis center or rape crisis line. Although most victims learned of the existence of such services from the media (38%) or family/friends (29%), it was not unusual for referrals to be made by police (15%) or by medical personnel (6%). If victims sought assistance from rape crisis centers/lines, they usually did so within one day of the assault.

When victims were asked their *main* reason for contacting the crisis line/center (multiple answers accepted), the most frequently mentioned answer (71%) was that they "needed to talk to someone." Other reasons for contact included the following: "needed criminal justice information" (46%); "needed someone to go with you to the medical facility" (35%); "needed medical information" (25%); and "wanted to make a third-party (anonymous) report to the police" (10%). In general, victims seemed very satisfied with the services rendered. For example, *all* victims believed that the information they obtained from rape crisis workers was accurate, and all victims believed that they were treated either with a great deal of understanding (78%) or with understanding (22%). No victim believed she was treated with indifference or with disrespect.

A total of 114 victim respondents received some form of medical treatment. In most instances, the treatment related specifically to the victim's health, including examinations for injuries and tests for the presence of venereal diseases and pregnancy. The majority of victims also underwent vaginal and/or anal examinations to determine the presence of semen or sperm.

A substantial proportion of all rape victims experience some physical problem as a result of forcible sexual assaults. Among the victims interviewed, for example, 49% reported physical complications whether or not they received immediate medical treatment. The most frequent of these complications were bruises, cuts, or other injury (21%); vaginal infections (15%); urinary tract infections (9%); side effects from "morning after treatment" to prevent pregnancy (5%); venereal disease (4%); and pregnancy (2%). Thus, in addition to the psychological trauma of rape, many victims also experienced significant and lingering physical trauma as well.

Victim assessment of the *quality* of medical treatment afforded them was very mixed. For example, nearly one half of the victims had to wait two or more hours at a facility before they received any medical attention. The examinations themselves often required three or more additional hours. In fact, 34% of the victims spent a total of six or more hours at a medical facility between the time they arrived and the completion of their examinations.

In addition, more than one quarter of the victims were not satisfied with the treatment they received. Examining physicians, in particular, were often believed to have treated victims with indifference (19%) or disrespect (12%). Some victims (20%) complained that they were not given sufficient information about the medical tests performed. Finally, more than one third of all examinations (39%) were performed in general purpose emergency rooms which offered no privacy. Although this lack of privacy did not disturb all victims, many felt embarrassed and humiliated by this procedure.

EMOTIONAL IMPACT OF RAPE

Researchers and medical personnel have interviewed victims of rape immediately after the assault and during the weeks and months that follow. They have observed a common sequential pattern of emotional reactions which has come to be known as the *rape trauma syndrome.* Not all victims follow the identical pattern of response or experience the symptoms with the same intensity. However, virtually all victims experience some of the emotions described; thus the rape trauma syndrome provides a useful way to discuss the general reaction of victims to rape.[7]

The first reaction, or acute phase, can last for several days after the rape and is most commonly characterized as extreme psychological shock. Since the victim may be unable to comprehend her situation or what she should do, she sometimes behaves in ways that appear illogical or irrational. The victim may not, for example, contact the police for several hours after the rape, or she may bathe and wash her clothes repeatedly.

Every victim also experiences some degree of fear or terror. The forcible rape itself is most often perceived as a life-threatening event rather than a sexual intrusion. In all likelihood, threats were made on her life. This fear, once aroused, does not always diminish immediately upon termination of the sexual assault. It is this continued sense of apprehension and danger that may determine and explain many victim actions during the hours and days immediately after the rape.

In addition to fear, the victim is likely to experience a variety of other emotions. These can include anger, shame, guilt, anxiety, revenge, powerlessness, and humiliation. It is common for a victim to experience severe and abrupt mood swings immediately after the rape. A counselor or police officer may be talking with a victim when suddenly she demonstrates a surge of anger followed by expressions of guilt and self-blame. Such mood swings can be as surprising and unexpected to the victim as they are to the interviewer. Victims experience these feelings at different times and in different ways depending on the manner in which they normally cope with crisis.

A common style of victim response to an interview situation during this time is a calm, composed "I'm okay" demeanor which is sometimes known as the controlled reaction. Unfortunately, this type of response occasionally causes others to doubt the victim's account because she appears too "flat" and unemotional. Furthermore, this reaction of external calm allows others to form the mistaken belief that the victim will have no emotional consequences from the sexual assault.

During this time of crisis, a victim can revert to a state of dependence or helplessness. Because the sexual assault has disrupted her normal coping abilities, decision-making can become an ordeal. For some victims, it is easier and safer to seek direction and protection from friends, family members, or a person in a position of authority. This factor can be important if, for example, a relative or a friend has a strong opinion that the victim should or should not prosecute the rapist. The victim is also very sensitive to the attitudes and behavior of patrol officers, detectives, and prosecutors involved with her case. Lack of support from criminal justice personnel is likely to render the victim confused and uncooperative.

Victims often report significant disruptions in their daily routines. Some women, for example, are unable to sleep at night and are easily awakened by noises that would not have bothered them previously. Eating habits can also be affected by the stress of the rape. Frequently, women report loss of appetite or inability to eat. Others find that eating causes nausea and vomiting, especially if they were forced to perform oral sex. The victim's ability to concentrate may be greatly diminished and her attention span temporarily shortened. In sum, the victim's normal methods of coping with daily stress work so ineffectively that almost all of her life functions are temporarily disrupted.

Following the victim's intense emotional reaction to the rape, she often gives every appearance that she has learned to cope with the experience. Very often she does this by blocking out all thoughts of the rape and rearranging her daily life so that she is not reminded of the crisis. Although denial is usually only a temporary stage, it can interfere with criminal justice proceedings because the victim may wish to withdraw her complaint or become uncooperative with detectives or prosecutors who want her to relive the incident.

The final stage of dealing with rape trauma occurs over a long period of time and requires the victim to fully integrate the experience into her life as a whole. Because rape so dramatically upsets a woman's normal routines, the crisis can be a time for self-evaluation and new decisions. Many facets of the victim's life may be different after the rape. Some women find it necessary to change residences to feel safer and more secure. This is a particularly common behavior for women who are raped in their own homes or apartments. Other women spend a great deal of time, energy, and money to secure their living quarters with new locks, bolts, and alarm systems.

Victims may perceive themselves as changed by the rape either because they feel differently about themselves or because they believe that others see them as changed. Family support can be crucial at this time. Unfortunately, family members sometimes respond in ways that are not helpful to the woman. Victims describe husbands who doubt their account of what happened and are suspicious and accusatory. Parents sometimes find it difficult to talk about the sexual assault and try to dissuade the victim from thinking or talking about the incident. While they may wish to save the victim from recalling disturbing emotions surrounding the rape, it is not uncommon for the victim to conclude that what has happened to her has brought shame and embarrassment to her family.

Dreams, especially nightmares, are a common experience for women who have been raped. The dreams often consist of vivid pictures in which the victim relives the terror of the rape situation. The paralyzing feeling of doom is recreated with such reality that the victim awakens to the frightening powerlessness, loss of autonomy, and life-threatening fear of the rape itself.

In summary, the emotional impact of rape is often intense and may persist for months or even years. It is clear, however, that these symptoms can be alleviated if victims receive support from friends, family, criminal justice personnel, and the community. Certainly, rapes occur with sufficient frequency and destructiveness that the victims deserve special consideration.

RAPE LAW

The last half decade has seen unprecedented activity in the area of rape law reform. During the years 1973-1976, for example, new rape legislation was enacted in 36 states and proposed in an additional 13 states.[8] The majority of these legislative changes have taken two forms: adoption of new and wider definitions of rape, and/or relaxation of the proof requirements for the crime. Rape has sometimes been redefined in terms of sex-neutral assault or battery, with several degrees based on the dangerousness of the circumstances of the assault or the kind of assault. One state, Michigan, has entirely abandoned the traditional law of rape and has created a new legal terminology to define a variety of sexual crimes.

Changes in proof requirements have taken a variety of forms. In many states, corroboration requirements have been eliminated or minimized. In addition, many legislatures have moved to restrict the admission of evidence of the victim's prior sexual conduct, and to eliminate both the cautionary instruction to the jury that the testimony of the victim is suspect and the chastity instruction that permits the jury to infer that a woman who has once consented to sexual intercourse is more likely to consent again than one who has not.

Other legal modifications include legislative mandates to provide special training for police and special medical procedures for the examination of rape victims. Some states have begun to provide high school instruction in self-defense. Finally, an earlier trend toward protecting the victim from public exposure (particularly exposure through the media) has been noted, although this movement has largely disappeared as a result of several Supreme Court cases which expanded freedom of the press with respect to criminal proceedings (Battelle Report, 1977:7).

TRADITIONAL RAPE LAW

Traditional rape law evolved through case-by-case judicial determination of what acts constituted the crime. This process of lawmaking, known as the common law system, defined rape as *unlawful carnal knowledge of a woman by force and against her will.* The slightest sexual penetration by the male penis of the female vagina was sufficient to complete the crime if the other elements were present. The common law instituted a resistance standard for the victim as a means to distinguish forcible carnal knowledge (rape) from consensual carnal knowledge (fornication or adultery). Both forms of carnal knowledge were crimes, but if the act were forcible, the victim escaped punishment for fornication or adultery (Battelle Report, 1977:11).

Legal theory has long held that

a crime exists only when there is concurrence of an unacceptable act and a criminal intent with respect to that act. The unacceptable act is called the *actus reus;* the criminal intent is called the *mens rea.* In traditional definition of rape, the *actus reus* is the unconsented-to sexual intercourse and the *mens rea* is the intention or knowledge of having the intercourse without the consent of the victim. Lack of consent of the victim is ultimately the characteristic that distinguishes rape. The concurrence of the act and the intent requires both that the victim in fact not consent and that the perpetrator know at the time that the victim did not consent. [Battelle Report, 1977:34]

Thus, according to theory and common law tradition, the definition of rape depends upon both the perception of the victim that the intercourse was not consensual, and the perception of the defendant of that lack of consent. This two-pronged legal requirement raises obvious problems of interpretation since there will be no criminal intent in many instances where there is an unacceptable act. The victim may well perceive an intercourse as rape when the perpetrator does not.

REDEFINITION

As a result of this legal dilemma, several states have redefined rape in terms of the conduct of the rapist (force), rather than the behavior of the victim (resistance) or her state of mind (lack of consent). To date, eight states have eliminated the word "rape" from their statutes and developed a new vocabulary, using terms such as "criminal sexual assault" or "sexual battery," to connote a crime defined by the behavior of the offender. In addition, many states have made the crime of rape sex-neutral, thereby eliminating the presumption of female victims and male offenders (Battelle Report, 1977:17).

PROOF REQUIREMENTS

Although statutes differ from one state to another, there are generally three elements that must be proven in cases of rape: (1) the occurrence of sexual penetration or other forms of sexual contact; (2) the identification of the perpetrator; and (3) the establishment of force or lack of victim consent. Evidentiary rules to establish these elements are generally the same as those that apply to all criminal cases. However, a special set of rules that applies only to cases of rape has been devised.

Traditional common law did *not* require corroborative evidence of each element of the crime to support a criminal conviction for rape. Courts simply relied upon juries to weigh the evidence, which might consist of nothing more than the victim's testimony, and render a verdict. It was assumed that a false complaint would be exposed in the adversary process, with the presumption of innocence serving to protect the defendant. Some courts departed from this tradition and established special corroboration requirements to confirm the victim's testimony (Battelle Report, 1977:69).

Where all three elements of the crime have required corroboration, very low conviction rates have been obtained. This result was most graphically shown under the strict corroboration requirements of the New York rape statute prior to 1972. In 1969 in New York City, for example, there were 1,085 arrests for rape and only 18 convictions. However, relaxation of the corroboration requirement does not necessarily lead to high rates of conviction.

> Even in states where there is no corroboration requirement, few cases are taken to trial without corroborating evidence. Furthermore, some states without corroboration requirements have erected other barriers to conviction, such as cautionary instructions or psychiatric examination of the victim. Thus, regardless of the formal corroboration requirements, an informal corroboration requirement and other screening devices may operate to exclude uncorroborated charges from the criminal justice system. It is only where corroboration requirements are extensive and narrowly interpreted that there appears to be a significant negative impact on the conviction rate. [Battelle Report, 1977:71]

In lieu of corroboration, some states have utilized an instruction to the jury that warns them to consider the testimony of the victim with caution. In its most common form, the instruction reads as follows:

> A charge such as that made against the defendant in this case, is one which is easily made and, once made, difficult to defend against, even if the person accused is innocent. Therefore, the law requires that you examine the testimony of the female person named in the information with caution.

The cautionary instruction, which arose from the 18th century writings of Sir Mathew Hale, has been eliminated in all but 13 states. The instruction has been attacked by feminists because it symbolizes a contemptous attitude toward rape victims by the criminal justice system. Prosecutors have also objected to the instruction on the grounds that it creates unjustified doubt in the minds of jurors.

Some states have adopted a provision for the psychiatric examination of victims as an alternative to corroboration requirements. According to Wigmore (1970) and other legal scholars, all rape complainants should be psychiatrically examined as a means to eliminate false rape complaints. This belief is premised on the assumptions that many complaints are false, that false complaints arise from mental disorders, and that psychiatric examinations are able to discriminate between the truthful and the false complaints (Battelle Report, 1977:80).

Both victims and prosecutors have strongly opposed these examinations. The examination may constitute an affront to the victim that her account is inherently untrustworthy and her integrity questionable. She may choose to withdraw her complaint rather than accept this insult (Battelle Report, 1977:82).

Corroboration requirements, cautionary instructions, and psychiatric examinations of victims have all served to limit successful rape prosecutions. Although all of these special exceptions have been introduced to protect innocent defendants, they have done so by assuming that victims are lying. In addition, the attitudes that created these special requirements in rape cases have so infiltrated the criminal justice system that, even without common law or statutory exceptions, prosecution of rape cases often appears extremely timid. It is hoped that the recent legislative activity to remove these exceptions may make the proof for rape similar to the proof for other major crimes and, at the same time, alter attitudes to increase the successful prosecution of this offense.

CONCLUSION

Interest in rape victimization and its aftermath is not likely to dissipate in the near future. Although this interest may change its focus or form, rape will never again be an "unmentionable" topic to be kept from the ears and eyes of children and teenagers. Rape is a terrible crime that often imparts devastating consequences on the lives of victims and their families. Fortunately, society and its institutions seem to be responding in ways which suggest that rape victims will someday be treated with the respect they deserve.

NOTES

1. An approximate ratio of one reported rape for every four actual rapes has been observed in several studies. In 1965, for example, the National Opinion Research Center of the University of Chicago conducted a victimization survey and found that the actual rate of forcible rape in their sample was 3.66 times greater than the reported rate. See the President's Commission on Law Enforcement and Administration of Justice, 1967:21. Also, see State of California, 1950, which estimated that the ratio of reported rapes to actual rapes was 1 : 5; and the Minnesota Department of Corrections, 1964, which estimated this ratio to be 1 : 4.

2. In 1975, the Federal Bureau of Investigation indicated that 56,090 rapes were reported to law enforcement authorities in this country. When this number is multiplied by four (unreported estimate), as many as 225,000 rapes might have been committed. See the Federal Bureau of Investigation, 1976:22.

3. For a summary of these legislative issues, see Battelle Law and Justice Study Center Report, 1977. Also, see Luginbill, 1975; Johnson, 1975; Cobb and Schauer, 1974.

4. For an excellent discussion of the developmental history of victim services, see Brodyaga et al., 1975.

5. Most of the material for this article was excerpted from Schram, 1977. This report was prepared under Discretionary Grant Number 76-NI-99-0056 and is available from the National Institute of Law Enforcement and Criminal Justice, Law Enforcement Assistance Administration, U.S. Department of Justice, Washington, D.C. 20530.

6. For an extensive discussion of the offender interview data, see Chappell and James, 1976:1-37.

7. For more extensive discussions of the emotional impact of rape on the victim, see Burgess and Holmstrom, 1974. Also, see Burgess and Holmstrom, 1976; McCombie, 1976; Notman and Nadelson, 1976; Sutherland and Schere, 1970.

8. For a state-by-state summary of rape legislation, see the Battelle Law and Justice Study Center Report, 1977.

REFERENCES

AMIR, M. (1971). Patterns in forcible rape. Chicago: University of Chicago Press.

BARD, M., and ELLISON, K. (1974). "Crisis intervention and investigation of forcible rape." Police Chief, (May):68.

Battelle Law and Justice Study Center Report (1977). Forcible rape: An analysis of legal issues. (Published by the National Institute of Law Enforcement and Criminal Justice.) Washington, D.C.: U.S. Government Printing Office.

BLANCHARD, W. (1959). "The group process in gang rape." Journal of Social Psychology, 49:259-266.

BRODYAGA, L., GATES, M., SINGER, S., TUCKER, M., and WHITE, R. (1975). Rape and its victims: A report for citizens, health facilities, and criminal justice agencies. Washington, D.C.: U.S. Government Printing Office.

BROMBERG, W., and COYLE, E. (1974). "Rape. A compulsion to destroy." Medical Insight, 22:21-25.

BROWNMILLER, S. (1975). Against our will: Men, women and rape. New York: Simon and Schuster.

BURGESS, A., and HOLMSTROM, L. (1974). "Rape trauma syndrome." American Journal of Psychiatry, 131(September):9.

——— (1976). "Copying behavior of the rape victim." American Journal of Psychiatry, 133(4):413-418.

CHAPPELL, D., and JAMES, J. (1976). "Victim selection and apprehension from the rapist perspective: A preliminary investigation." Paper presented at the Second International Symposium on Victimology, Boston, September.

COBB, K., and SCHAUER, N. (1974). "Legislative note: Michigan's criminal sexual assault law." Journal of Law Reforms, 81(1):221.

COHEN, M., GAROFALO, R., BOUCHER, R., and SEGHORN, T. (1971). "The psychology of rapists." Seminars in Psychiatry, 3(3):307-327.

CORMIER, B., and SICKERT, S. (1969). "Forensic psychiatry: The problem of the dangerous sexual offender." Canadian Psychiatric Association Journal, 14(4):329-335.

COTTELL, L. (1974). "Rape: The ultimate invasion of privacy." FBI Law Enforcement Bulletin, (May):2-6.

Federal Bureau of Investigation (1976). Uniform crime reports. Washington, D.C.: U.S. Government Printing Office.

HAYMAN, C. (1970). "Sexual assaults on women and girls." Annals of Internal Medicine, 72(2):447-452.

HENN, F., HERJANIC, M., and VANDERPEALL, R. (1976). "Forensic psychiatry: Profiles of two types of sex offenders." American Journal of Psychiatry, 133(6):894-896.

JOHNSON, E.G. (1975). "Evidence—rape—trials—victims' prior sexual history." Baylor Law Review, 27(2):222-237.

LICHTENSTEIN, G. (1974). "Rape squad." New York Times Magazine, March 3, p. 10.

LUGINBILL, D. (1975). "Repeal of the corroboration requirement: Will it tip the scales of justice?" Drake Law Review, 24(3):669-683.

MacDONALD, J. (1974). "Group rape." Medical Aspects of Human Sexuality, 8(2):58-88.

MARSHALL, W., and McKNIGHT, R. (1975). "An integrated treatment program for sexual offenders." Canadian Psychiatric Association Journal, 20(2):133-138.

McCOMBIE, S. (1976). "Characteristics of rape victims seen in crisis intervention." Smith College Studies in Social Work, 46:137-158.

Minnesota Department of Corrections (1964). The sex offender. St. Paul: State of Minnesota.

NOTMAN, M., and NADELSON, C. (1976). "The rape victim: Psychodynamic considerations." American Journal of Psychiatry, 133:408-413.

PACHT, A. (1976). "The rapist in treatment: Professional myths and psychological realities." In M. Walker and S. Brodsky (eds.), Sexual assault. Lexington, Mass.: D.C. Heath.

PACHT, A., and COWDEN, J. (1974). "An exploratory study of five hundred sex offenders." Criminal Justice and Behavior, 1:13-20.

PERDUE, W., and LESTER, D. (1972). "Personality characteristics of rapists." Perceptual and Motor Skills, 35(2):514.

President's Commission on Law Enforcement and Administration of Justice (1967). The challenge of crime in a free society. Washington, D.C.: U.S. Government Printing Office.

PUTNAM, J., and FOX, D. (1976). "A program to help the victims of crime." Police Chief, 36(March).

RUFF, C., and TEMPLER, D. (1976). "The intelligence of rapists." Archives of Sexual Behavior, 5(4):327-329.

RUSSELL, D. (1975). The politics of rape: The victim's perspective. New York: Stein and Day.

SADOFF, R. (1975). "Treatment and violent sex offenders." International Journal of Offender Therapy and Comparative Criminology, 19(1):75-80.

SCHRAM, D. (1977). Final report: Techniques for improving the effectiveness of the criminal justice response to forcible rape. Washington, D.C.: National Institute of Law Enforcement and Criminal Justice.

State of California, Subcommittee on Sex Crimes of the Assembly Interim Committee on Judicial System and Judicial Process (1950). Preliminary report 26. Sacramento: Author.

STILL, A. (1975). "Police enquiries in sexual offenses." Journal of Forensic Social Sciences, 15:183-187.

SUTHERLAND, S., and SCHERE, D. (1970). "Patterns of response among victims of rape." American Journal of Orthopsychiatry, 40:503-511.

TAKAKUWA, M., MATSUMATO, Y., and SATO, T. (1971). "A psychological study of rape." Bulletin of the Criminological Department, Ministry of Justice, Japan.

WIGMORE J. (1970). Evidence.

WOODS, G. (1969). "Some aspects of group rape in Sydney." Australian and New Zealand Journal of Criminology, 2(2):105-119.

4

SEXUAL ABUSE OF CHILDREN

KEE MacFARLANE

Growing interest and social action on behalf of battered children over the past 10 years have highlighted an even more distasteful form of child victimization. Long believed to be extremely rare, or a problem occurring only in primitive cultures or lower classes, sexual abuse of children is now recognized as far more prevalent than once imagined. Hard data on the subject are scarce, but many signs, including increased public awareness and reporting, indicate that it is a problem which is more widespread, more serious, and more difficult to discuss than many other similarly sensitive social issues. While many social problems are as complex as child sexual abuse, few are as distressing.

Disturbing as the actual experience of sexual victimization may be for a child, the long-term effects of that victimization may hold the greatest significance for the child and for society as a whole. It is an experience that, even by the most conservative estimates, probably shapes the lives of thousands of women each year. For the victims of child sexual abuse, like those of rape, spouse battering, commercial sexual exploitation, and a number of other forms of victimization, are overwhelmingly female. The feminine pronoun is used throughout this chapter because child sexual abuse is primarily the victimization of young girls.

Child sexual abuse can also be recognized as a fundamental betrayal of childhood trust and an affirmation of the powerlessness of being young and female in a society where victimization is often not recognized and protection is not guaranteed. Most child victims of sexual abuse are not attacked by sick strangers who appear from

AUTHOR'S NOTE: The opinions expressed herein are the author's and do not necessarily reflect the position or policy of the Department of Health, Education and Welfare.

the shadows when a child is out alone. They are abused, for the most part, by men whom they know and trust. Their exploitation is usually at the hands of their own fathers, family members, or other familiar adults. Moreover, they are generally not physically harmed because their fear, their trust, and their deference to male authority preclude the need for violence. Most children are unprepared and unable to protect themselves against what is perceived as an adult prerogative. As a result, many of them internalize their roles as victims—within the sexual relationship and in the broader context of their own worlds.

It is the instilling of this "victim mentality" in the mind and the developing personality of a young girl that is, perhaps, the most insidious aspect of her sexual exploitation. It is not only pervasive in the many areas of her life in which it may be reenacted, it is an extremely difficult self-concept to change and can be a devastating source of continued self-depreciation.

Almost every society contains cultural taboos against incest and sexual abuse of its children, yet, the problem of child sexual abuse has always existed. It is a problem with "a long past but a short history"—one surrounded by myth and misconception, by ideas we must dispel in favor of a more disturbing reality if we are to move toward protection of the thousands of children who are its victims.

The universal revulsion felt toward acts of child sexual assault and the strong emotional reaction of most people toward the adult who sexually abuses a child are rarely coupled with an understanding of the problem, its causes, or its effects. This lack of knowledge, shared by professionals and lay persons alike, appears to result from at least three major factors: the scarcity of published research, clinical data, or case material on the subject; the accepted sanctity of matters that happen within or directly affect the family; and the aura of secrecy that has traditionally surrounded this subject and sexuality in general. In addition, traditionally held beliefs and cultural taboos have fostered fears and reactions toward child sexual abuse that are largely unfounded and misdirected, and that contribute to the inappropriate responses often accompanying its discovery.

The existing research and literature dealing with the subject of child sexual abuse is so limited, and the number of cases studied so small, that they must be regarded as presenting a largely nonrepresentative picture of the problem. Therefore, although this chapter has drawn on material from existing literature, the reader is cautioned against the temptation to generalize from it to all situations of sexual abuse.

The first step in confronting any social problem involves developing an understanding of the situation, those involved, and the dynamics that support it. Needed is knowledge of all the forces that influence those involved—the ones that motivate people as well as those that keep them from acting.

Sexual abuse reaches deeply into the lives of women—as child victims, as mothers who see their daughters victimized, as adolescents whose development is shaped by the experience, and as adults whose sense of identity may be irrevocably marred by their inability to shed the memory of their early exploitation. The victims of childhood sexual abuse represent a population whose long-term vulnerability should not be minimized. They have experienced a betrayal of the most fundamental tenet of an adult-child relationship and, while many have successfully overcome the experience, for others the costs are immeasurable. Those who seek to help such children and their families must consider well the impact of their own actions. They must arm themselves against overreaction and insure that remedial action is always in the best interest of the child.

CHILD SEXUAL ABUSE—DEFINITIONS

One of the difficulties encountered in any discussion of child sexual abuse involves the definition of terms. The term "sexual assault" brings to the minds of many people an image of sexual violence and physical attack. While such incidents do occur and periodically capture our attention in sensational newspaper headlines, they actually represent only a small proportion of the reported incidence of child sexual abuse. The fact is that sexual abuse of children takes many forms, involves varying degrees of violence and emotional traumatization, and is defined in a variety of ways, depending upon the source, context, and purpose of the definition.

Our laws provide little insight into the definitional issues of sexual abuse since there is little uniformity in states' legal definitions. State laws prohibiting incest vary considerably in definition and detail. The penalties for incest range in severity from simple fines to fifty years in prison. Some laws developed out of an initial concern for the production of biologically defective offspring; such laws recognize incest only as sexual intercourse among consanguineous, or blood, relations. Other states, however, reflect the current sociological and psychological thinking which recognizes that sexual relations between children and close family members create an atmosphere deleterious to the healthy personality development of the child and interfere with normal family functioning (Tormes, 1967). In these states, incest is recognized as occurring between a variety of family members related by blood and/or law, including adoptive or stepparents, siblings, stepsiblings (in certain cases), and grandparents.

Statutes relating to the sexual assault of children are found in both the criminal codes and the civil codes of most states. The former generally represent a judicial focus on the behavior, conviction, and punishment of the perpetrator, while the latter usually reflect an orientation toward child protection and therapeutic intervention. Whether a sexual abuse case is brought before the criminal or juvenile court is highly dependent upon who is making that decision, and is the object of considerable debate. The decision often depends as much upon such questions as the extent of evidence available or the immaturity of the witness as upon the nature or degree of what was actually done to the child.

Since the passage of the Federal Child Abuse Prevention and Treatment Act of 1974, more and more states are specifically requiring the reporting of sexual abuse, and a degree of uniformity is being established with regard to who is legally responsible for reporting the different types of child abuse. Yet the definition of what constitutes the physical, emotional, and sexual abuse of children still remains largely a matter of jurisdictional and individual interpretation. Furthermore, since most reporting laws address themselves to child abuse by parents or persons legally responsible for a child's welfare, an act of sexual abuse committed by a person outside the family may be defined and handled quite differently from the same act committed by someone legally responsible for the child.

As an example of the different terminology used, in the state of California, the definition of sexual abuse includes: compelling illicit relations by menace, abduction to force defilement, incest, sodomy, sexual contact, assignation or procuring female by force or false inducement, oral sex perversion, seduction, exciting the lust of a child, and so on. To complicate matters even further, the sexual abuse of children is often defined not only in terms of what is done to the child, but the victim's age and the relationship of the abuser of the child are also taken into account. New York state law defines degrees in the crime of sexual abuse with different penalties for each crime. For example, an act of sexual abuse is treated differently if: the victim is less than 11 years old, if the victim is under 14 years old, if sexual contact is without the subject's consent, or if the offender is less than five years older than the subject. In other states, sexual abuse has been imprecisely defined as: "A person is guilty of sexual abuse when he subjects another person to sexual contact." Many state laws provide little guidance as to the meaning of the words "sexual abuse," preferring to leave the matter of interpretation to the courts (McKerrow, 1973:40).

While practitioners and law enforcement officers may bemoan the lack of a specific definition for child sexual abuse, the problem is obviously too complex to lend itself to a simple operational definition. This chapter, therefore, will take a rather generic approach to the issue of child sexual assault. For purposes of this discussion, the terms "sexual abuse" and "child sexual assault" will be used to mean those sexual contacts or interactions between a child and an adult when the child is being used as the object of gratification for adult sexual needs or desires.

SCOPE OF THE PROBLEM

The sexual abuse of children is not a new problem; references to its occurrence date back to Old Testament times. Moreover, it is not as rare a phenomenon as many people would like to believe. But child sexual abuse, like rape, is one of the most underreported crimes in our society. Although estimates of its frequency vary, those cases of sexual abuse that are officially reported to appropriate authorities clearly represent only a fraction of the cases that actually occur.

Statistics from the American Humane Association's study of official reports indicate that, in 1975, approximately 12% of all reported cases of child abuse involved some form of sexual abuse. While there are no reliable figures on the true incidence of sexual abuse, it is believed by some to be more widespread than the physical abuse of children, which is currently estimated to affect over 200,000 children a year in the United States. Statistics maintained over a 10-year period in Hennepen County, Minnesota (Jaffee et al., 1975), revealed 660 reports of physical abuse, and

2,400 reports of child sexual abuse. Assuming that Hennepen County is not atypical of other parts of the country, a picture of the possible proportions of the problem emerges. The American Humane Association has estimated that in every major U.S. city as many as 4,000 cases of sexual abuse may occur each year (DeFrancis, 1965). Other studies indicate that some form of childhood sexual abuse may be experienced by as much as one third of the population. (Landis, 1956).

The reported incidence of sexual abuse is appropriately referred to as "the tip of the iceberg" in an area characterized by fear, denial, and reluctance on the part of family members and professionals alike to bring the problem out in the open. In recent years, the public has become increasingly aware of the plight of women victims of rape and sexual assault; it is not as well known that a large number of recipients of sexual assault are children. As is the case with physical abuse and neglect of children, it is not known whether the higher reporting rate among some segments of the population reflects their greater visibility to the public social service and law enforcement systems, or whether the true incidence is actually higher among some groups. Reported incidences do show that child sexual abuse is not limited by racial, ethnic, or economic boundaries.

The most prevalent myth about child sexual abuse is the commonly held belief that its perpetrators are shadowy, raincoated strangers who haunt our parks and playgrounds in search of young victims. While it is certainly wise to warn children not to take candy or accept rides from strangers, in doing so we are alerting them to what appears to be only a small percentage of the population that actually poses a sexual threat to children. The familiar images of "perverts," "molesters," and "dirty old men" are not accurate portraits of the majority of persons responsible for the sexual abuse of children. Warnings to children might take on quite a different tone if it were more widely known that the great majority of sexual offenses against children are committed by their friends, acquaintances, and relatives. Major studies have shown that in as many as 80% of all cases, children are sexually abused by people they know and trust; parents, relatives, and parent figures are found to be either directly or indirectly responsible for up to 50% of reported cases (DeFrancis, 1969; Sgroi, 1975). These figures are especially alarming in light of the fact that intrafamily sexual abuse is even less likely to be reported than sexual assault by a stranger (Schulz, 1972).

TYPES OF SEXUAL ABUSE

Because the circumstances, reactions, and dynamics of child sexual abuse appear to differ depending on whether the perpetrator is a stranger or someone with whom the child is closely acquainted, it is useful to examine the two situations separately. In cases of assault by a stranger, the behavior of the perpetrator is more likely to be an expression of deviant or abnormal sexual preference than is that found within the family constellation, where normal or appropriate sexual preference may have become thwarted, disoriented, or inappropriately directed toward a child. Even so, most persons who sexually abuse children, whether they are strangers or known to the child, do not fit the usual nightmarish stereotype of the "child molester." Many have extremely poor self-concepts and dysfunctional personal relationships, but the majority are not considered to be "sick" as society has traditionally held (Peters, 1976; Weiner, 1964).

While aggressive sexual offenses, such as rape and sadism, do occur, they are the exception rather than the rule. The majority of cases do not involve penetration, contraction of venereal disease, or infliction of serious injury. Exhibitionism and fondling by strangers, often compulsive and habitual forms of behavior, are rarely violent and may have minimal impact on their victims, depending upon how the situation is subsequently handled. Pedophiles, those who receive their primary sexual gratification from minor children, are only a small percentage of sexual abusers. Although some pedophiles are homosexuals, the correlation in many people's minds between homosexuality and child molesters is a fallacious one that is unsubstantiated by fact. The vast majority of known child sexual abusers are heterosexual in their sexual orientation.

Sexual abuse by strangers is usually a single episode, occurs most frequently during the warm weather months, and usually takes place out of doors, in an automobile, or in a public building. In contrast, sexual abuse by family members or acquaintances is more likely to occur in the home of the victim or the perpetrator, to be accompanied by a host of other interpersonal and family problems, and occur repeatedly over a period of time (DeFrancis, 1969; Peters, 1976).

While there are cases of sexual abuse by adult women, the overwhelming majority of perpetrators are men. Girls are victimized or at least reported at a much higher rate than boys (the estimated ratio is 10:1), and although victims have been found to be as young as four months old, the average age is 11 years old (DeFrancis, 1969). Thus, in speaking of sexual abuse, we are primarily talking about sexual encounters between young girls and adult men with whom, more often than not, they are personally acquainted.

Since the offender is usually known and trusted by the child, incidents of sexual abuse are seldom accompanied by physical violence or extreme force. Children are accessible targets for a number of reasons. They have been conditioned to comply with authority; they are in subordinate positions and are fearful of threats; they are intensely curious; they are susceptible to bribes and the promise of reward. In addition, children are often naive with regard to social norms and values, and they are sensual beings who may respond willingly to intimate and gentle contact which they may associate with feelings of being loved, cherished, and cared for. Thus, the use of physical violence is rare because it isn't necessary: children by their very nature make ideal victims of sexual exploitation.

DYNAMICS OF THE PROBLEM

The sanctity of the home is such an established aspect of our society, traditionally and legally, that it is not difficult for a family to isolate itself from public view and public censure. Moreover, despite increased public awareness of the issue of children's rights and protection, children are still largely regarded as the property of their parents, whose right and privilege is to raise their children as they see fit. It is, therefore, extremely difficult for agents of society outside the family structure to act to deter or prevent the occurrence of intrafamily sexual abuse.

Incestuous behavior, the definition of which includes, for purposes of discussion, a wide range of child-focused sexual behavior by parent figures as well as parents and other close relatives, rarely exists as a single event. A sexual relationship between father or father figure and child may begin innocently enough and progress from touching and caressing to fondling and overt sexual stimulation. Although most children recognize at a very early age that what is happening is "wrong," it does not always begin as an unpleasant experience for children. For some, it represents the first time they experience what they perceive to be recognition or special attention from the parent or parent figure. As is the case with some battered children, even negative, painful, or distasteful attention is better than none at all.

Despite the facade of contentment that might be maintained outside the home, incestuous families are often characterized by a high degree of family disruption and poor personal relationships. In cases of father-daughter incest it is often the relationship between the adults in the home, not the parent-child relationship, that is the key factor. The sexual relationship between the adults is often strained or nonexistent, and a great deal of underlying hostility may be present on both sides (Giarretto, 1976a). In some cases, the mother has essentially abdicated her role as wife and mother, while the daughter, in a classic role reversal situation, has increasingly taken on the adult role and responsibilities in the family. The mother, who may have experienced a cold and rejecting relationship with her own mother, may be unable to avoid recapitulating this role with her daughter. There are indications that a number of these mothers were themselves sexually abused as children (Raphling et al., 1967). Thus, intrafamily sexual abuse, like the physical abuse and neglect of children, is likely to become part of a troubling cycle of dysfunctional family interactions that play themselves out in each successive generation.

The notion that incestuous fathers or stepfathers are highly sexed and aggressive men is generally false. Many are weak, resentful, and ineffectual individuals both within and outside the family; their negative self-concepts and low personal esteem make them prime targets for the adoption of behavior that is destructive to themselves and to others (Giarretto, 1976b).

Motivations for intrafamily sexual abuse and incest are often as diverse and complex as the families themselves. Although sexual gratification for the participating adults seems an obvious motive, the factors contributing to the breaking of such a stong cultural taboo as incest are rarely that simple. As previously mentioned, an unhealthy marital relationship is a prime factor in the development of resentment between husband and wife and the channeling of attention in other directions. Likewise, a daughter who sees her mother as rejecting, unjust, or dependent, may consciously or unconsciously use her father as a means of revenge. The justifications used by some men include the notion of furthering their daughter's sex education, protecting the child's physical health by preventing the contraction of venereal disease from other men, or the explanation that this is the way love and affection are expressed in their family. Incestuous fathers are often extremely conservative in their sexual beliefs and practices, and generally do not engage in a variety of sexual practices or extramarital relationships. As one outraged father indignantly exclaimed as he was being brought to the police station, "I am a decent man. I provide for my family, I don't run around on my wife, and I've never slept with anyone except my wife and my daughters."

Family isolation, both physical and emotional, overcrowding, and alcoholism, which tends to lower impulse control, are frequently cited as antecedents to sexual abuse. Contrary to some commonly held assumptions and unlike the usual battered child syndrome, it is not uncommon for more than one child in a family to be sexually abused. The sexual relationship may begin with the oldest child and eventually include younger siblings as well. It is not uncommon for a girl finally to report an incestuous family situation having discovered after silently enduring the relationship for years to protect her siblings, that her father had been engaging the other children in the same behavior all along. Her request for protection of younger sisters often comes only after she herself has run away or grown old enough to leave home. Some girls report that their greatest sense of disillusionment came, not from their father's physical behavior toward them, but from the betrayal of this type of "silent pact" to protect their siblings.

In cases of intrafamily sexual abuse, it is important to understand the role of the mother, though her role may vary greatly depending upon the individual situation. Although many women are caught in a drama that they neither see nor understand until it is publicly brought to light, this is not always the case. In some family situations, the mother's knowledge and subsequent denial of the incestuous behavior is often a key to its continuation. Sexual relationships of any kind that occur over a period of time have visible and emotional antecedents, and, in many cases, it is unlikely that a spouse could remain totally unaware of the changed personal dynamics that occur when sexual abuse or incest is present. Full sexual contact between an adult and a child within a family is invariably preceded by a long series of verbal and nonverbal expressions of growing sexual interest. The mother, in such situations, has been described as "an active nonparticipant" (Weich, 1968); her conscious attempt not to see what is happening is often motivated by her own feelings of powerlessness and horror. Whether her collusion in the incestuous relationship is conscious or unconscious, the mother's strong denial of the situation may act to provide tacit permission for the relationship to continue.

Poznanski and Bloz (1975), in their study of incest, have explained that in some families, the nonparticipating members go to great lengths to avoid acknowledgement of the presence of sexual behavior between an adult and a child. It is not uncommon, for example, to learn that a child has gone to her mother or other family member to report what is actually transpiring between her and her father, stepfather, uncle or grandfather, only to find that she is either not believed, accused of being nasty or wicked, or has caused the mother such emotional upset and anxiety that the child ends up regretting the revelation even more than the behavior itself. Many mothers in families where incest is discovered, initially express outrage and denial of what has occurred, but may later admit to having known of the incest and experience a great deal of shame.

To understand the role of the mother who is aware that some form of sexual abuse is occurring in her family, it is important to recognize that her behavior is rarely motivated by the conscious desire to hurt her daughter or intentionally subject her to the sexual advances of the father or father figure. More often than not, the mother herself is a victim of her circumstances and her own poor self-image, so immobilized by a situation in which she feels powerless and ineffectual that she can take no action to protect her child. Public recognition of the sexual abuse in her family may serve to expose her inadequacies as a wife and mother. She fears the disintegration of her family and marriage, perhaps the loss of her only sources of economic and emotional support. A number of these mothers are themselves the objects of physical violence and battering at the hands of the men with whom they live. Trapped within the boundaries of their own violent relationships and often aware of the precarious and temporary nature of the protection that society is able to offer them, they are afraid to intervene actively on behalf of their children. In the dejected words of a battered mother of a sexually abused 15-year-old runaway, "I tried to give her the only things I had to offer: some money and the strength to get the hell out of here."

Fear of exposure, humiliation, or personal harm all act to increase the mother's already strong dependency on the family member who may be both the source of her subjugation and her protection from the outside world. Too often, in such situations, the protection of the child is sacrificed in the process of the mother's victimization.

Mothers who have been truly unaware of the sexual involvement within their families endure their own private victimization once the incest is discovered. Their initial shock may soon turn to feelings of extreme guilt over what has happened to their children. Many are plagued by self-recrimination over their inability to protect their daughters, and demean themselves for not suspecting what was going on. The realization that the victimization of a child is at least partially possible as a result of her mother's trust in the abuser is a painful one. The aftermath of such a discovery for many women involves not only their feelings of guilt, but a fundamental sense of betrayal.

In the case of child sexual assault by a stranger or person outside the family, the responsibility of the parents for the child's protection and supervision is sometimes in question. Similarly, in intrafamily abuse, the role of the mother and degree of active participation by the child may vary greatly depending upon the individual situation. Nonetheless, the discussion of these various dynamics should not be interpreted to mean that it is difficult to assign ultimate responsibility when sexual intimacy occurs between an adult and a child. Although an accurate and inclusive psychological profile of the child sexual offender does not exist, the matter of accountability is not at issue. Regardless of a child's specific behavior or apparent needs, and despite any of the interpersonal dynamics which may be operating in the home, it is the adult who must exercise control (DeVine, 1977). The assignment of blame is generally not a productive approach to the problem, but the acceptance of full responsibility for his actions is usually an important aspect in the treatment of the offender. Understanding the roles of other involved persons, including the victim, is important to our efforts to prevent and treat the problem, but when the violation of an adult-child relationship takes the form of sexual exploitation, the responsibility clearly rests with the adult perpetrator.

EFFECTS ON THE VICTIM

It is impossible to make a general statement about the effects of sexual abuse on children. Aside from the fact that there has been little research on the effects of sexual abuse, children react differently to different situations depending on a number of variables that may be operating at the time of the occurrence. While it is not possible to generalize across the population of abused children, this section attempts to describe some of the most serious repercussions that have been observed, and to identify a number of important variables that operate in determining a child's reaction to a sexual abuse situation.

Children who are sexually abused are not special children with special characteristics; they are not of one age, one sex, one race, or one social class. They are not victims of one particular offense, nor do they sustain identical injuries. Their role in the abusive situation, their disclosure of the incident, their relationship to the perpetrators, and their reactions, both long- and short-term, all differ (DeVine, 1977). Nonetheless, a number of key factors are commonly believed to be of critical importance in determining the ways in which a child reacts to the experience. These factors include the child's age and developmental status, the relationship of the abuser to the child, the amount of force or violence used by the abuser, the degree of shame or guilt evoked in the child for her participation, and, perhaps most importantly, the reactions of the child's parents and those professionals who become involved in the case.

It is not difficult to understand why some incidents of sexual abuse by a stranger may be far less traumatic to a child than those committed by someone close to her. In most such instances, the parents will rally to the aid of the child, and, while they may overreact to the situation, their anger and feelings of retribution are generally directed toward the perpetrator. There is less likely to be any question about possible provocation on the part of the child, who is usually the recipient of expressions of concern, protection, and support from family and friends. The degree of violence or physical coercion used by the offender, is, of course, another important factor in cases of sexual assault. If a child has been raped or otherwise physically hurt by an outsider, both the short- and long-term effects can be expected to be far more serious than if, as is usually the case, the assault has been nonviolent. Many, if not most, cases of nonviolent sexual assault by a stranger can be treated with short-term crisis intervention techniques that emphasize putting the incident in perspective and returning the family to its former state of equilibrium.

Intrafamily sexual abuse, including that initiated by persons whom the child or other family members hold in high esteem, usually has far more complicated temporary and long-term repercussions. It is believed that the closer the emotional ties between the child and the perpetrator, the more emotionally traumatic the situation is likely to be for the child (Sgroi, 1975); nonetheless, the degree of emotional impact will vary greatly depending on the nature of the individual relationship.

The child's role—or the manner in which she perceives her role—in the sexual relationship can have a strong influence on the way she reacts to the situation once it has been disclosed. Very young children often have difficulty separating fact from fantasy and may have a very different and less distressing image of what occurred than others in the family have. Their view of the world may provide a layer of unconscious self-protection that enables them to react only to what it is they imagine has happened to them. However, this type of initial reaction may be quickly colored by the more violent reactions of the adults around them.

If the sexual behavior between adult and child has occurred over a long period of time, if it has involved a series of progressively intimate incidents, or if the child is old enough to understand the meaning and cultural taboo of what has occurred, then the effects may be more profound. Extreme feelings of guilt are a common consequence of intrafamily sexual abuse and cause many victims a great deal of anguish. Guilt feelings may be intensified by a number of factors, including the degree to which the child actively participated in or encouraged the sexual contact, and whether she herself experienced pleasure when it happened. Regardless of whether her pleasure stemmed from the accompanying feelings of acceptance and adult approval or from a normal physical reaction to sexual stimulation, the acknowledgement of some level of enjoyment is a painful source of shame for many children. With children for whom the experience was totally repugnant and upsetting, guilt may stem from the fact that they allowed the situation to continue because they felt too fearful and powerless to take any action to stop it. Such guilt is particularly poignant if a child believes that her passive acceptance of the situation resulted in the subsequent abuse of her siblings.

The reactions of a child's family can do much to either lessen or enhance her guilt feelings following disclosure of the abuse. DeFrancis (1969) has described initial parental reactions as either child-oriented, self-oriented, or offender-oriented. The object of a family's blame or support in such situations is dependent upon a number of variables. The degree of public humiliation experienced by family members and their concern for what other people will think may undermine any support for the child's position. As with many personally traumatic experiences, the need to blame somebody for what has happened is sometimes a strong one. The mother may put complete blame on the offender, or she may blame herself for failing to protect the child adequately. While both reactions may be normal ones under the circumstances, unless they are accompanied by a focus and concern for what the child is undergoing, they may not be constructive reactions.

As mentioned earlier, the benefits of supporting the child may be outweighed by the very concrete losses that the family might experience if the father or family provider is put in jail or ordered to keep away from the home. In such cases, the family's anger and frustration may be focused on the victim who may find herself being blamed for initiating and perpetrating the sexual relationship or for breaking up the family by revealing the situation, or both. This form of "blaming the victim" can have a devastating impact on a child who is usually already guilt-ridden from the blame she has imposed on herself.

Even if a child has not experienced extreme guilt or confusion as a result of the sexual contact itself, she is often likely to discover it once she comes into contact with the so-called "helping system." Due to the seriousness of the crime of sexual assault, such accusations are often viewed with a great deal of suspicion. Again, as has been the experience of many rape victims, the child victim may find that it is her own credibility which is in doubt, and her strongest emotional reactions may occur as a result of this recrimination. Even when a very young child has incurred physical damage as a result of sexual assault, her reliability may be questioned, as in a case cited by Walters (1975) of a four-year-old girl who was hospitalized with massive internal injuries, and was asked by an emergency room nurse, "Were you 'playing with yourself'?"

In cases where the sexual contact itself was not immediately traumatizing to a child, the ensuing separation of a child from her family may be the event that carries the most severe or lasting emotional impact of all. Feelings of grief mixed with guilt over the loss of a special person or relationship, regardless of the pathology involved, may be the effect felt most strongly by the victim.

Behavioral indicators of the effects of either the abuse or its disclosure can take many different forms. Some children manifest their reactions by regressing to earlier types of behavior such as thumb sucking, bed wetting, or becoming afraid of the dark or certain locations which have negative associations for them. Others develop a variety of behavioral disorders such as sleepwalking or difficulty in eating and sleeping. Such physical symptoms may constitute the child's way of acting out those disturbing feelings and reactions that she is unable to verbalize.

Even less is known about the long-term effects of sexual abuse than about the short-term reactions. Sexual abuse has been referred to as a "psychological time bomb" because of the dormant nature of some of its aftereffects—many of which may not be realized until the child is old enough to establish adult sexual relationships of her own. It is then that she may discover her inability to disassociate the sexual aspects of that relationship from her negative experiences as a child. It is believed by some that the low self-esteem and self-interest of many victims leads them to engage in a variety of self-destructive behaviors. Girls who react by turning their self-hate inward may be likely to become involved in drug or alcohol abuse. In studies of female drug abusers, as many as 44% of them had been sexually abused as children (Benward and Densen-Gerber, 1976). Similarly, some girls display their internalized feelings through such outward displays of self-abuse as adolescent promiscuity or prostitution. James (1971), in her study of prostitutes, found that approximately 30% of them had been sexually exploited during childhood. For some, the exploitation of their own sexuality may become the only way they know to relate to others.

A number of girls appear to jump into early marriages as a means of escaping their family situations, or dealing with their feelings of aloneness. Many experience a sense of isolation when they realize that they do not have any peers who could understand what they are going through. Depression and confusion about their own identities are not uncommon reactions of many victims. Some report feeling "marked" or stigmatized for life and may have suicidal tendencies. Others, with support and understanding, may be able to comprehend their roles as child victims within the perspective of adult responsibility for what occurred, and thus may not suffer lasting consequences of the abuse.

No two children or families will react in exactly the same way to the presence of child sexual abuse. Also, because they are under a great deal of stress, their reactions and behavioral signs—whether conscious or unconscious—are subject to misinterpretation. Generalizations about the effects of any kind of interpersonal crisis often do a disservice to all the individuals involved. Children, no less than adults, need interpreters in society who can hear the unique story that each has to tell.

VICTIMS OF THE SYSTEM

Although society reacts with predictable horror at what is done to children by sex offenders, it apparently does not share a similar concern for what subsequently may happen to them at the hands of our law enforcement and child protection systems. Whether a child has been sexually assaulted by a stranger, an acquaintance, or a member of her own family, when the incident is brought to light the family is usually found to be undergoing a state of crisis as it works through feelings of anger, fear, shock, and confusion. In the midst of such vulnerability, the criminal justice, health, and social service systems may descend upon a child and family with such a devastating impact that its recipients are left with the feeling that the "cure" is far worse than the symptoms. Many authorities agree that the emotional damage resulting from the intervention of "helping agents" in our society may equal or far exceed the harm caused by the abusive incident itself (DeFrancis, 1969; Giarretto, 1976b; Miner, 1966; McKerrow, 1973; Sgroi, forthcoming).

More parents and professionals might be willing to report suspected cases of sexual abuse if they could be confident that the effect of their actions would not be to appreciably add to the trauma the children already were experiencing. It is an assurance that few communities are able to make. Once a case of known or suspected sexual abuse is reported, a series of investigative, protective, or prosecutorial procedures spring into action. Although the specific steps vary, depending upon state law and procedures, whether the report is made to the police or to the department of social services, and whether the case is handled under civil or criminal statutes, it can be a complicated and overwhelming process for those involved.

The child, who is usually under a great deal of emotional stress already, may be required to recount the details of the case over and over at various stages in the legal process. If the situation is reported to the police, as is required by law in several states, she may have to tell her story first to a patrol officer during the preliminary investigation, and later to a police detective—neither of whom may have had any specialized training in dealing with a child witness. When child protective services are involved, a separate investigation may be initiated, which involves an interview with at least one social worker.

During the process of investigation, the child may be taken to a hospital or private physician for a medical examination. Here, again, the child is usually expected to recount the incident or incidents leading to the report. Concerned physicians, such as Sgroi, have pointed out that a thorough and gentle examination can serve to calm and reassure a child that she is physically all right (Sgroi, forthcoming). However, as many women and most rape victims attest, a gynecological exam, even when performed under the best of circumstances, can be an upsetting experience. This may be true especially if the girl is very young, if it is the first time she has undergone such an examination, if the physician is a male and a stranger to her, or if physical restraints or strong words of admonition are used to calm her. The situation can be exacerbated if the medical personnel are not trained or sensitive or willing to spend the time and patience required to handle these disturbing cases.

If the case is to be handled under criminal statutes, it will most likely be referred to the Prosecuting or District Attorney's office, where the girl will again be interviewed, sometimes more than once, in order to evaluate the force of the evidence, the victim's credibility as a witness, and the strength of the case in general. Even if there is a decision not to press criminal charges, the case may go to civil or juvenile court to determine such matters as child custody and supervision. In this case, the child may be interviewed still another time by the court attorney, city solicitor, or guardian ad litem appointed by the court to represent the best interests of the child. In the end, it is not unusual for a child to have to repeat her story six or seven time or more, even if the case never goes to court.

Although many children are spared the agonizing ordeal of a full trial since such cases are often resolved by plea bargaining and dropped charges, a criminal case may quickly develop into an adversary proceeding between child and adult. In cases where preliminary hearings are held to determine whether the accused should be bound over for trial in superior court, the child must confront her assailant (possibly for the first time since the assualt or since the report was made—even if the assailant is her father) in a courtroom situation. Once again, she must recount the exact details of the abusive situation, and her testimony is subject to cross-examination.

The differential and complex way in which our society treats children who come into the criminal justice system is a subject of considerable relevance for the victims of sexual abuse. Although the United States was the first society in the world to establish a separate justice system for its juveniles, that system was not designed to protect *all* children who must undergo criminal proceedings, only those accused of committing criminal offenses. Our juvenile courts were established on the belief that the special needs, vulnerabilities, and limited experience of children make them significantly different from adults; thus they warrant a court system that is sensitive to those differences. Presumably, a young child who is either a victim or a witness to a crime committed by an adult is in need of at least as much special consideration as a juvenile offender. Unfortunately, in the criminal court there may be little allowance made for the child victim's limited ability to comprehend and compete with her adult counterparts (Stevens and Berliner, 1976).

Testifying at an open trial is a stressful experience for even the most secure adult, and is often the most difficult encounter of all for the child victim of sexual abuse. The child may have to sit alone on the witness stand answering a series of complex questions and pointing out the accused in a courtroom filled with spectators. This author will never forget the look on the face of a 9-year-old incest victim when her father was brought into the courtroom with chains and handcuffs around his hands and waist. With support and reassurance from concerned professionals and family members, she had, up until that point, coped remarkably well with the rigors of the judicial process. Her only comment before she withdrew into a spasmodic, twitching episode (which recessed the trial for the day) was, "I did *that* to my Daddy?"

Regardless of a child's age, she is usually not protected from the Defense Attorney's attempts to attack her credibility on the witness stand. As have many adult rape victims, children who have been sexually abused—some of them as young as 7 or 8 years old—may quickly find that their own personal lives and behavior appear to be on trial. Often judges and prosecutors are reluctant to intervene for fear of appearing too protective or of swaying the jury. The child is often expected to provide information on dates, times, and sequences, plus a detailed description of the abusive situation and events that preceded and followed it. Her story is often regarded with a great deal of suspicion, and a number of concrete external proofs of abuse, such as witnesses, physical injury to the child, presence of semen or penetration, must usually be present. It often seems that society's primary interest in the child is in the testimony she can give for the conviction of her abuser. The entire process has the effect of abandoning the child to a set of abstract principles of justice (Stevens and Berliner, 1976).

Even when a child is not directly involved in a criminal court proceeding, the only methods available in most communities for dealing with intrafamily sexual abuse involve the forcible, or sometimes voluntary, separation of perpetrator and victim. Giarretto (1976a) has pointed out that, with rare exceptions, the repertoire of law enforcement, judicial, and social service personnel handling child sexual abuse cases is limited to two devices—separation and punishment. In cases where the burden of reporting or testifying lies primarily with the mother, she may be put in the position of having to decide who will go, her husband or her child. Either way, there are often serious repercussions for the child. If charges are pressed, and the father or father figure goes to jail, the girl will often see herself as responsible for breaking up the family. If she is taken out of the home to be placed in a foster home, she may internalize her removal as evidence of her own innate badness and guilt. This perceived assignment of legal guilt not only serves to allow other family members to maintain a destructive denial of their own responsibility, but, as is so often the case, the girl may, in her foster home, act out her feelings of shame, guilt, and confusion to the point where she has to be placed in another home. This drama may be re-enacted in a series of foster homes and institutional placements until the child has convinced herself, if not those around her as well, that she is a thoroughly unlovable and destructive individual.

Although society has traditionally looked to the machinery of the criminal justice and protective service systems to provide the best available assistance to victims of sexual abuse and their families, the process has often meant additional traumatization for *all* persons concerned. There are pitifully few treatment programs available to the perpetrators of sexual abuse, prison sentences are usually not of long duration, and offenders, if they do go to jail, receive few if any rehabilitative services. Convicted sexual offenders find when they reach prison that, even in a society of criminals, they occupy a pariah status and are in physical and sexual danger from the other inmates (McCaghy, 1971). They quickly become the victims of another kind of system, where they find themselves holding the most despised status on the reordered social scale.

In situations where there is already a high degree of family disruption, the threat of forced family dismemberment may take on much greater significance to family members than anything that has previously happened to the child. The legal process may act to entangle the entire family in a web of retribution. There are few sights more disturbing than watching a mother transfer her support and allegiance from her young daughter to her husband or lover as they progress through the justice system. The child may be left with no functioning adult ally in the household once her sacrifice is seen as a way of salvaging the adult relationship; she is left alone in the role of accuser. Caution should be exercised with regard to criminal prosecution in such cases. There are indications that, in the absence of any continued protection from the mother or other adult family members, a child who is put on the witness stand to publicly accuse her father of incestuous behavior may be in real physical danger if he is subsequently aquitted and allowed to return home.

Perhaps the most telling indictment of our present system of child protection is contained in an interesting theory regarding one way to determine the difference between a report of actual intrafamily sexual abuse from one fantasized by the child. It is believed by some that, in the case of true sexual involvement between a child and another family member, the child will often be back in a week or two to deny all of her charges and retract the report. This happens, it is hypothesized, because the societal intervention that has occurred during the ensuing days or weeks has proven to be even less tolerable and more upsetting to the girl than the previously existing situation. The abused child came seeking protection and an end to the abuse, not an end to her family. The girl who falsely accuses a family member, on the other hand, may be more likely to stick by her story because society has given her exactly what she wanted: retaliation and total family disruption.

Although more and more communities are developing specialized child-centered services for the victims of sexual abuse, we have a long way to go. It is not surprising that perhaps the most frequently chosen solution is for the child, as soon as she is old enough, to rebel and leave home. It is, unfortunately, the case that, for many children and their families, society, no matter how well intentioned, is the cruelest assailant of all.

PRESCRIPTIONS FOR CHANGE

Perhaps the most important thing to keep in mind, for those who seek to help children and families who are the victims of sexual abuse, is contained in an ancient expression familiar to the medical profession: primum non nocere—first, do no harm. We are often helpless to prevent or undo the negative interactions that occur between adults and children; we *can* do something about what happens to a child following disclosure of the incident. It is important to remember that sexual abuse in its various forms does not *automatically* leave permanent emotional scars on its victims. This is said with no intent to minimize the negative effects of sexual exploitation, but with the belief that children need the adult world to respond appropriately to their individual needs and circumstances. By reacting out of our own needs for retribution or immediate resolution of a repugnant situation, we can, and repeatedly do, make life worse for the children involved.

The first step toward insuring that we don't compound an already stressful situation is to consider the effects on the children involved of every ameliorative action contemplated. While any major disruption in a child's life is bound to cause anxiety and fear, especially if it threatens his or her basic family structure, constant maintenance of a child-centered orientation at each step of the process can go a long way toward reducing the stress. A child's world revolves around the family, and no matter how dysfunctional that family may be, it is usually the only one she has ever known. Most maltreated children want the abuse, not their families, to end. It is difficult for most children to accept the fact that it could be their parents, not they, who are wrong or who have behaved badly. Understandably enough, this is especially true if the child is taken out of the family. In their young minds, parents are parents, and it is children who are bad and get punished. The author once worked in an institution largely populated by children who had experienced the most extreme forms of physical, sexual, and emotional abuse at the hands of their parents. These children had very diverse backgrounds and had coped with their experiences with varying levels of emotional adjustment; but they all had one thing in common—they all wanted to go back home to their families. They would insistently promise that, if allowed to return home, they would be careful not to provoke their parents to hurt them, abandon them, or sexually misuse them again.

It is important to keep the perceptions of children constantly in front of us, not because it is always possible to keep from compounding their private pain, but so that we always strive to provide "the least detrimental alternative to the child" (Goldstein, Freud and Solnit, 1973). We cannot always avoid splitting up families or placing a child in a foster home when there is no other way to protect her from further abuse, but such action should be a resource of last resort, not an attempt to appease our initial feelings of horror. Although society is not, for a variety of reasons, presently able to tolerate the possibility of recurrence of intrafamily sexual abuse, the time has come to question whether the immediate removal of a child from her own home, or her participation in the arduous process of a court trial, is ultimately in her best interests. There have been cases of long-standing sexual involvement in the home where children have been forcibly removed by the police within an hour following disclosure of the situation. A child may find that, in the space of one afternoon, she is living with strangers, prohibited from seeing her parents, and in a new school district away from friends as well.

It should also be remembered that many children have a distorted sense of time; a few days can seem an eternity to a young child. When we speak of temporary foster care, we would do well to bear that in mind. Many "temporary" foster and institutional placements of children stretch on into years of separation, until the child has virtually no family as she knew it to return to. Children have the right to a home in which they can be assured of permanence; if we judge their own to be inadequate and are unsuccessful in an intensive attempt to rehabilitate it, then we at least owe them permanence in another setting.

In most cases of sexual abuse, as with many other family problems that threaten the well-being of children, if we really want to help the child we will first do our best to help save the family. Again, it is not always possible, but far more could be done than is presently being attempted. There are few sexual abuse treatment programs associated with the prisons in this country. There are also few programs that attempt to involve the whole family in treatment. The Santa Clara County Child Sexual Abuse Treatment Program in San Jose, California, is one of the only programs in the country specifically developed to treat incestuous families.[1]

Treatment programs are obviously only one aspect of our system for dealing with child sexual abuse which needs improvement. Attention must be focused on the needs of children and families from the time that a situation is discovered. Special units or teams of professionals in hospitals, police departments, and social service agencies should be trained to deal with sexual abuse and to become sensitive in their interactions with children. Whenever possible, cases should be handled by social workers or at least plainclothes policewomen, since children are often frightened by police officers in uniform.

In our desire to protect children from distressing situations, we cannot ignore the reality of many existing legal and medical procedures. Criminal laws that involve the child witness will not be disposed of simply because they make therapeutic intervention difficult. They must be changed where they are destructive or insensitive to their effects on children, and, where families are involved, they must be humanistically refocused on rebuilding rather than destroying family units. Children should undergo a minimum of interviews about what happened; if ten professionals must hear the story, let it be recorded on tape the first time around. Medical examinations of young girls should be conducted only when necessary and by female physicians or by a doctor known to the child. They should be performed with the utmost sensitivity and care. Every attempt should be made to handle court cases in pretrial conferences, judges' chambers, or special settings adapted to use by children and not open to the public. Child victims should, at a minimum, be entitled to the same considerations and special provisions as child offenders. In addition, they require careful treatment and follow-up to determine what long-term effects the abuse may have. It is not enough to remove a child or other family member to another setting and call it treatment, though our present system often functions as if it were. Whether children are abused by strangers or by someone they know well, they need to be treated with compassion and understanding; we must stop treating them merely as evidence. The procedures and requirements of our judicial and protective systems make it difficult not to add to the trauma child victims experience. But we should at least be able to promise that the "help" we provide will not leave them preferring the previous sexual abuse to the abuse imposed by an insensitive system.

CONCLUSION

Our knowledge about the sexual abuse of children appears to be evolving in a pattern similar to that of knowledge about the problems of battered women, battered children, and rape victims. This pattern begins with the disturbing discovery that the prevalence of the problem and the number of extreme situations are much greater than previously imagined. Then a concerted effort to gather more information typically reveals an insidious, secondary level of abuse; i.e., the way victims are treated by society and its institutions following disclosure of the abuse. It is not until the scope and ramifications of the problem are fully realized that we see improvement in the lot of victims and the restructuring of social institutions.

Another important aspect of child sexual abuse has to do with prevention and how we raise our children. Little girls learn at a very early age how to be provocative and coy. They are surreptitiously encouraged by the myriad of material things that surround them— their toys, the television, and what they read. Parents and friends knowingly and unknowingly encourage them to grow up fast, to use their wiles to their advantage. Their sexiness may be reinforced before they are old enough to understand what it means. When sexuality in young children is encouraged, they become confused as to its appropriate purpose and function. The very behavior and dress they use to get adult attention and approval may make them vulnerable to kinds of sexual exploitation they are emotionally or developmentally able to manage.

Similarly, young boys are often raised with inappropriate expectations about sexuality and women in general. The notion that sexual pleasure may be taken, either by physical force or coercion, or that women and children "ask for" sexual exploitation by their behavior or vulnerable status, is one which is all too often subtly reinforced in our society. As long as prevailing societal attitudes reflect a view of women as sexual objects, and as long as the rights of children receive such casual regard, female children will remain an especially vulnerable target for sexual abuse. True confrontation of a problem as insidious yet as pervasive as child sexual abuse ultimately requires the type of primary prevention which seeks to change the contributing attitudes and behaviors found in our society. Thus, one aspect of preventing child sexual abuse involves the projection of images and values onto children. Children must not grow up with the kind of expectations and attitudes which will allow them to objectify others to the point of exploitation; at the same time, they must have help in insuring that they do not covertly or overtly elicit sexual behavior with which they cannot cope.

Another aspect of prevention is to adequately prepare and protect children from inadvertently becoming trapped in the role of victim. One way to do that is to provide them with more education about the nature and indicators of sexual abuse and what to do if they experience it. The fear, of course, is that in so doing we will make our children paranoid or unduly distrustful of the people they know and of any intimate or affectionate behavior. The fear is a legitimate one, but it is most likely outweighed by the potential benefit of such an educative process. If sensitively handled, it can provide a child with the kind of psychological armor he or she might need to successfully prevent exploitation. We may tell our children not to talk to strangers, but we often neglect to tell them why, so that if and when they are subjected to sexual abuse they are unsure of what is happening and what to do about it. If they can be taught the differences between appropriate and inappropriate adult-child physical interaction (regardless of who the adult may be), they are in a better position to prevent or at least seek help for their own victimization. As one former sexually abused child so pointedly put it, "They told me never to accept rides or candy from strangers, so I never did. They never told me to watch out for my own father or why."

Our challenge is to prepare children for any eventuality of sexual exploitation without scaring them to death. We must counterbalance their natural passivity and deference to authority by providing them with a strong sense of what other people should and should not be permitted to do to them under any circumstances. They must know that they will be supported in their efforts to act and speak out against being victimized. If, for whatever reason, they are not being protected within their own homes, they need to know that there are other supportive avenues of help available. In that regard, school personnel and other adults who have contact with children must be alert to the visual signs and halting messages of children in trouble. Child victims of sexual abuse can only be as strong and effective in acting on their own behalf as the protective system and the adults who are standing behind them.

Sexual abuse of children has existed for centuries, though it has only recently come into the light of public attention. Even when the problem is recognized, it is often compounded by our clumsy and ineffectual attempts at immediate solutions. Except in a minority of cases, the problem cannot be effectively dealt with simply by invoking the retribution of our criminal justice system. Our desire for retaliation may provide a consoling outlet for our initial feelings of outrage, but it rarely solves the underlying issues. Children need education about sexual abuse and sexuality in general. They need a sense of themselves that will help to insulate and protect them against victimization and victim mentality. Parents need to be helped to handle their own sexual feelings appropriately, and protect their children from the exploitation of others. Professionals need training to help them recognize the symptoms of sexual abuse, and the criminal and protective service systems need to be changed so that they deal fairly and humanely with the problem.

A cause for optimism lies in the fact that the process of identification, assessment, and resource development has begun in other problem areas similar to that of child sexual abuse. In rape cases, the past five years have seen the incidence of reporting rise, judicial impediments modified, and public attitudes slowly change. Certainly much remains to be done for the victims who learn daily that what society offers is insufficient to meet the need. All victims of our society's cult of violence and self-gratification deserve our compassion, our energies, and our voices for change, but none more than our children, who have no voices of their own.

NOTE

1. Hank Giarretto, Director, Child Sexual Abuse Treatment Program, Santa Clara County Juvenile Probation Department, San Jose, California 95110.

REFERENCES

BENWARD, J., and DENSEN-GERBER, J. (1976). "Incest as a causative factor in anti-social behavior: An exploratory study." Paper read at the American Academy of Forensic Sciences, 27th annual meeting (February), Chicago, Illinois.

BESHAROV, D.J. (1975). "Building a community response to child abuse and maltreatment." Children Today, 4 (September-October):2-4.

BURGESS, A.W., and HOLMSTROM, L.L. (1975). "Pressure, sex, and secrecy." Nursing Clinics of North America 10 (3):551-563.

CAVALLIN, H. (1966). "Incestuous fathers: A clinical report." American Journal of Psychiatry, 122:1132-1138.

CORMIER, B.M., KENNEDY, M., and SANGOWICZ, J. (1962). "Psychodynamics of father-daughter incest." Canadian Psychiatric Journal, 7(5):203-217.

DeFRANCIS, V. (1965). Protecting the child victim of sex crimes. Denver: American Humane Association, Children's Division.

––– (1969). Protecting the child victim of sex crimes committed by adults, final report. Denver: American Humane Association, Children's Division.

DeVINE, R. (1977). "Sexual abuse of children: An overview of the problem."

GIARRETTO, H. (1976a). "Humanistic treatment of father-daughter incest." Pp. 143-158 in R.E. Helfer and C.H. Kempe (eds.), Child abuse and neglect–The family and the community. Cambridge, Mass.: Ballinger.

––– (1976b). "The treatment of father-daughter incest: A psychosocial approach." Children Today, (July-August):2-5, 34-35.

GOLDSTEIN, J., FREUD, A., and SLONIT, A.J. (1973). Beyond the best interests of the child. New York: Macmillan.

GREENE, N.B. (1977). "A view of family pathology involving child molest–from a juvenile probation perspective." Juvenile Justice, (February):29-34.

HEIDER, K.G. (1969). "Anthropological models of incest laws in the United States." American Anthropologist, 71:693-701.

HENDERSON, J.H. (1972). "Incest: A synthesis of data." Canadian Psychiatric Association Journal, 17(4):299-313.

JAFFEE, A.C., DYNNESON, L., and TEN BENSEL, R.W. (1975). "Sexual abuse of children; An epidemiologic study." American Journal of Diseases of Children, 129(6):689-692.

JAMES, J. (1971). "Formal analysis of prostitution." Final report to the Division of Research, State of Washington Department of Social and Health Services, Olympia.

LANDIS, J.T. (1956). "Experiences of 500 children with adult sexual deviation." Psychiatric Quarterly, 30:91-109.

MACHOTKA, P., PITTMAN, F.S., and FLEMENHAFT, K. (1967). "Incest as a family affair." Family Process, 6:98-116.

McCAGHY, C.H. (1971). "Child Molesting." Sexual behavior, 1(5):16-24.

McGEORGE, J. (1964). "Sexual assaults on children." Medicine, Science and the Law, 4(October):245-253.

McKERROW, W.D. (1973). "Protecting the sexually abused child." Pp. 38-44 in Second national symposium on child abuse. Denver: American Humane Association.

MINER, L. (1966). "Sexual molestation of children, a medicolegal problem." Acta Medinale Legalis et Socialis, 19 (April-June):203-205.

PETERS, J.J. (1973). "Child rape: Defusing a psychological time bomb." Hospital Physician, 9 (46):46-49.

––– (1976). "Children who are victims of sexual assault and the psychology of offenders." American Journal of Psychotherapy, (July):398-421.

POZNANSKI, E., and BLOS, P. (1975). "Incest." Medical Aspects of Human Sexuality, (October):46-77.

RAPHLING, D.L., CARPENTER, B.L., and DAVIS, A. (1967). "Incest, a genealogical study." Archives of General Psychiatry, 16:505-511.

SARLES, R.M. (1975). "Incest." Pediatric Clinics of North America, 22 (3):633-642.

SCHULTZ, L.G. (1972). "Psychotherapeutic and legal approaches to the sexually victimized child." International Journal of Child Psychotherapy, 4:115-127.

––– (1973). "The child sex victim: Social, psychological and legal perspectives." Child Welfare, 52 (3):147-157.

SGROI, S.M. (1975). "Sexual molestation of children." Children Today 4(3):18-21.

––– (forthcoming). "Child sexual assault: Guidelines for investigation and assessment." In A.W. Burgess, A.N. Groth, L.L. Holmstrom, and S.M. Sgroi, Sexual assault of children and adolescents. Lexington, Mass.: D.C. Heath.

STEVENS, D., and BERLINER, L. (1976). "Harborview social workers advocate special techniques for child witness." Response, 1(2) (December):1.

SUMMIT, R. (1975). "Sexual abuse: A frustration of love." Frontiers, Parents Anonymous Newsletter, (Midsummer):2-3.

TORMES, Y. (1967). Child victims of incest. Denver: The American Humane Association, Children's Division.

WALTERS, D.R., (1975). Physical and sexual abuse of children: Causes and treatment. Bloomington, Ind.: Indiana University Press.

WEICH, M.J. (1968). "The terms 'mother' and 'father' as a defense against incest." Journal of the American Psychoanalytical Association, 16(4):783.

WEINER, I.B. (1964). "On incest: A survey." Excerpta Criminologica, 4:137-155.

5

BATTERED WOMEN: SOCIETY'S PROBLEM

DEL MARTIN

Wife beating is a complex problem that involves much more than the act itself or the personal interaction between a husband and his wife, despite what many prefer to believe. It is a social problem of vast proportions with its roots in historical attitudes toward women and the institution of marriage. The socialization of women and men in our society and the assignment of women to inferior roles that keep them economically dependent make women vulnerable to abuse by the men with whom they live. This victimization of women, who are married to or who live in quasilegal relationships with men, is reinforced by law enforcement, social service agencies, mental health professions, educational insitutions, and the economy. Protections, legal or otherwise, to which a wife may resort when she has been brutalized or her life threatened, are more theoretical than practical. In application they are virtually nonexistent because they are geared to protect the marriage, not its victims. Any solution to family violence must address the values and the structure of the society that permits and thus perpetuates crimes against women. Clinical approaches cannot be effective unless pervasive social attitudes and the institutions that now give tacit approval to the practice of wife beating are drastically changed.

Wife abuse is not just slapping or shoving—it is described (Gayford, 1975; Gelles, 1972; Eisenberg and Micklow, 1974) as punching with fists, choking, kicking, knifing, slamming the victim against the wall, throwing her to the floor, or shoving her down the stairs. Beatings can last anywhere from a few minutes to over an hour. Threats of violence—punching holes in the wall, breaking down doors, and wielding a gun—can be as frightening and intimidating as actual physical attack.

The reluctance of society to recognize the prevalence of violence in marriage and to interfere with the privacy of the family is best illustrated by the inability to obtain data on the incidence of marital violence. Obvious sources like the police, attendants in hospital emergency rooms, the district attorney, private physicians, the courts, social workers, family service counselors, and other mental health professionals do not keep such records.

The FBI believes that marital violence is the most unreported crime, probably ten times more unreported than the crime of rape (Durbin, 1974:64). From the pockets of evidence available and the educated guesses of experts who have conducted limited research or have come in direct contact with complaints from victims, we can say that the number of battered women nationwide reaches into the millions.

While wife beating has only recently surfaced as a major social problem, it is highly doubtful that its incidence is increasing. Admittedly, some men who feel threatened by the concept of women's liberation may beat their wives to keep them in their place and to reassert their "manhood." But the truth is that men have beaten their wives with impunity for centuries.

HISTORICAL ATTITUDES TOWARD WOMEN

The historical roots of wife beating are ancient and deep. Frederick Engels (1948:53-58) placed its beginnings with the emergence of the first monogamous pairing relationships, which replaced group marriage and the extended family of early promiscuous primitive societies. This new arrangement came about because women sought protection from what Susan Brownmiller (1975:16) called "open season on rape" and because men wanted to authenticate and guarantee their identity and rights as fathers. Prior to the pairing marriage, women, as mothers, were the only discernible parents and were held in high esteem. But with the new "father right," the strictest fidelity was demanded of women. Polygamy and infidelity remained men's privileges, however. The cost to women for the "protection" of one man from the sexual ravages of other men came high. Monogamy brought about the complete subjugation of one sex by the other.

With the advent of the pairing marriage, the man seized the reins in the home and began viewing the woman as his property. The sole purpose of woman was seen as that of satisfying her husband's lust, bearing his children, and tending to his household. Women were relegated to certain parts of the home, isolated, guarded, and their public activities restricted. If a woman showed any signs of having a will or a mind of her own, she was beaten in the same way that a strong-willed horse might be whipped and finally subdued.

The church sanctioned the subjection of women to their husbands "in everything" (Ephesians 6:22-24). Abused wives were advised by priests that a husband's displeasure was best dispelled by the woman's increased devotion and meek submissiveness. Physical cruelty, even murder, of the wife or a serf were allowed in medieval times (Davis, 1971:255) if it was inflicted for "disciplinary purposes." Women were burned at the stake for many reasons, including scolding and nagging, talking back, refusing to have intercourse, *miscarrying* (even though the miscarriage was caused by a kick or blow from the husband), and permitting sodomy (even though the husband who committed it was forgiven). These inhumane practices and attitudes toward women were incorporated into the dominant culture by law, allowing men to avoid responsibility for their own behavior.

In the 1880s, the British Parliament, through a series of legal reforms (Davis, 1971:311), began to deal with the sorry plight of the married woman. The law was changed to allow a wife who had been habitually beaten by her husband to the point of "endangering her life" to separate from him, though not to divorce him. Another law prohibited a husband from selling his wife or daughter into prostitution—but only if she were under 16 years of age. Special legislation was enacted to prevent a husband from keeping his wife under lock and key.

In our own country, a husband was permitted by law (Calvert, 1975:89) to beat his wife as long as he didn't use a switch any bigger around than his thumb. It was not until the end of the 19th century that such laws were repealed. An old town ordinance, still on the books in Pennsylvania in the 1970s (Fleming, 1975), prohibited a husband from beating his wife after 10 o'clock at night or on Sundays.

THE MARRIAGE CONTRACT

Despite recent gains of the women's movement in correcting some of the inequalities between the sexes, the legal and social authority of the husband in marriage still persists. Time-honored traditions and laws are not easily or quickly changed. According to early English common law, which is the basis for American jurisprudence, "The very being or legal existence of the woman is suspended during the marriage, or at least is incorporated and consolidated into that of the husband, under whose wing, protection, and cover she performs everything" (Blackstone, 1765). In other words, the husband and wife were regarded as one person in law, and the rights and property of the marriage were vested in one person—the husband. With few modifications, this is still true today.

The married woman's loss of identity begins with the loss of her name. She takes her husband's domicile; she becomes his legal dependent. Traditional marriage vows still exhort her to "love, honor, and *obey*" her husband. He is designated by both church and state as the head of household. This authority of the husband over his wife is reinforced by the courts, the Internal Revenue Service, the Census Bureau, economic dependence, and the socialization of the sexes. The marriage contract and the restrictions it imposes have been justified by the state's overriding interest in keeping the traditional family structure intact, for marriage is the mechanism by which the patriarchy is maintained.

The law says the husband is responsible for the support of the family, and the wife is responsible for the household and the children. With the notable exception of five states (Arizona, California, Idaho, New York, and Washington) where women recently won rights to joint management of community property, the husband has sole financial authority in marriage. The wife who does not have an outside income is thus dependent upon her husband's generosity and good will for her economic and physical well-being. If a husband decides to give her no money or clothing and provides her with only a roof over her head and groceries on the table, she has no legal recourse. In 1953, a Nebraska judge ruled (DeCrow, 1974:164-165) that the living standards of a family are not the concern of the court. That the home is maintained and the parties are living as husband and wife is all that is required by law, he said. A 1962 court decision in Connecticut (Weitzman, 1974:1187) was more specific about the obligation of the wife to perform her household and domestic duties *without compensation.* "A husband is entitled to benefit of his wife's industry and economy," the court ruled.

The economic disadvantage of the wife makes her vulnerable to the whim of a supposedly benevolent despot. In return for the promise of the protection and security of her husband, she is required to reshape her personality to conform to his expectations. Should she fail to accommodate herself and accede to his standards, he may abuse her economically, emotionally, and physically. When this happens and she seeks help, she is likely to find support systems of society are geared to keeping the marriage intact, no matter the danger to her well-being or that of the children.

THE FAILURE OF THE LEGAL SYSTEM

Today, wife beating is a crime just as any other crime that constitutes bodily harm: assault and/or battery, aggravated assault, intent to assault or to commit murder. But the law becomes ambiguous in its application when the parties involved are husband and wife. The sanctity of the family home and the adage that a man's home is his castle, which pervade the whole fabric of society, are reflected in the legal system. Police admit that a large percentage of the calls they receive are DD's (domestic disturbances), but they do not differentiate between family "squabbles" and incidents of violence. They seldom make arrests in either case.

A study conducted by the Kansas City (Missouri) Police Department in 1971-1972 revealed that 46,137 DD calls were received during one year. Of the city's homicides, 40% were found to be cases of spouse killing spouse. In more than 85% of these homicides, police had been summoned at least once before the murder occurred, and in almost 50% of the cases, the police had been called to the scene five or more times within the two-year period prior to the homicide. Escalation of marital violence was also noted in figures for aggravated assault (domestic disturbance accounting for one third of these crimes) and the equally high percentage of repeated calls for help prior to the incident.

FBI statistics (Murphy et al.:n.d.) show that one out of every five officers killed in the line of duty in 1974 died trying to break up a family fight, and that the majority of injuries sustained by patrol officers are due to domestic disturbances. The danger to police may explain their reluctance to respond to DD calls and why many departments have instituted family crisis intervention training—training that places a high priority on teaching officers how to protect themselves in volatile home situations. But it does not explain why the police ironically persist in viewing these cases as mere family "spats." If these situations are perilous to trained police officers, they are certainly even more dangerous to the defenseless woman and her children.

The police are probably the worst possible choice for a woman to call to her rescue, according to Deputy Chief James D. Bannon who has been with the Detroit Police Department since 1949. Policemen, like most males, are imbued with perceptions of masculine-feminine roles which translate into dominance-submission terms. They perceive the husband as the boss and the wife as his subordinate. These attitudes develop naturally into a laissez-faire policy. "In Detroit, as in many other cities, the treatment of female victims of assault of the domestic variety could charitably be termed cavalier. Not so charitable, but perhaps more accurate, would be an allegation of misfeasance." Bannon declared in a speech before the American Bar Association in Montreal in 1975.

Police officers are usually directed by their superiors to avoid making arrests in domestic disputes except in cases of severe injury. In a training bulletin on "Techniques of Dispute Intervention," the nonarrest policy of the City of Oakland (California) Police Services (1975:2-3) is stated explicitly: "The police role in a dispute situation is more often that of a mediator and peacemaker than enforcer of the law." The officer is told that an arrest may only aggravate the dispute or create a serious danger for the arresting officers because a husband is likely to exert desperate resistance to prevent loss of face in front of his family. The manual goes on to say that when no "serious" crime has been committed but one of the parties demands arrest, the officer should attempt to explain the ramifications (loss of wages, bail procedures, court appearances, and other hardships) and "encourage the parties to reason with each other."

Implicit in these guidelines is the refusal of police to take wife beating seriously, even though it has been shown in their own experience and that of researchers that these beatings, when unchecked, are repeated and become more and more severe as time goes on. It is hard to imagine any other situation in which police would be officially advised to encourage a victim to "reason" with an attacker. Furthermore, encouraging victims to refrain from exercising their rights is in effect denying them their rights. Wife/victims are entitled to be apprised of the law and its procedures without prejudice. It is not the function of the police to give legal advice or to base decisions on what might happen. Nor is it the function of police to help the violent offender "save face" at the expense of the victim. The safety and protection of the victim should take priority over all other considerations.

While it is true that police in most jurisdictions cannot make an arrest unless they actually witness a misdemeanor, the victim still has the option of making a citizen's arrest. Usually she is not aware of that right, and the officer should be required to so inform her and to take the offender into custody if she chooses to make an arrest. Instead, police are prone to point out to the woman that if her husband is taken to the station he will be out in a few hours on bail or on his own recognizance and will probably return to give her an even more severe beating for turning him in. Additionally, she is reminded of her dependence upon her husband's paycheck, which he could lose if he were found guilty of the charges and jailed. Some women, fearing for their lives and faced with the realization that the system offers them no physical or economic protections, renege and drop the charges. By so doing they give law enforcers the excuse, "They won't follow through," for placing a low priority on cases of marital violence.

Two class action suits have recently been filed by wife/victims: one in federal court against the Oakland Police Department and the other in the state court against the New York City police and the Family Court clerks and probation officers because of their failure to provide protection to battered wives. The 102-page New York complaint charges that the police unlawfully refuse to make arrests and employees of the Family Court unlawfully refuse to allow victims to see judges to ask for orders of protection. In one of the complaints, a neighbor called the police, and when they arrived the beating was still going on. Even though the two officers had to pry the husband's hands from around the wife's neck, and several neighbors present cried, "Arrest him; he will kill her!" the police refused to do so. They merely shrugged, said, "There is nothing we can do. We can't do anything in marriage fights," and left.

If the husband is arrested or the wife files a complaint with the district attorney, the victim faces still another test. District attorneys, who are understaffed and overburdened with caseloads, tend to count stitches and rely on the availability of witnesses in deciding which cases they will prosecute. Rarely are there witnesses to violence in the home other than the children, who are routinely protected from making court appearances. Justice and protection of the victim are sacrificed for the "We'll only go with the cases we know we can win" philosophy. According to Sgt. Barry Whalley, who conducts family crisis intervention training for the Oakland Police Department, only one out of a hundred complaints filed ever reaches the courtroom. Bannon said that of 4,900 formal complaints filed in Detroit one year only 300 were tried in court.

When the police and district attorney do follow through and prosecute a wife-beating case, there is no assurance that the judge will take the case seriously. Judges also have a tendency to dismiss marital violence as family quarrels. If they find the husband guilty, more than likely they will let him off with a suspended sentence, probation, or a small fine. A classic case in New York City (Hart, 1975) was that of "Loretta," who brought charges in criminal court against her former common-law husband on five occasions for five different incidents within a year and a half. Each time she pressed charges, followed through, and testified in court, and each time the judge released "Thomas" on his worthless promise the he wouldn't do it again. The fact that Loretta had been hospitalized on at least two occasions and had lost an eye and part of an ear because of the savage beatings she had suffered obviously had no effect on the judges who heard her complaints.

The civil remedy—issuance of temporary restraining orders or orders of protection—is equally farcical. As many attorneys point out, they aren't worth the paper they are written on. When a man is of a mind to beat his wife, he'll do it. Violations of court orders are considered contempt of court offenses and are subject to the same restrictions as other misdemeanor arrests. The victim is generally referred back to her attorney to obtain another court order, which must again be served on the husband, to appear at another show cause hearing. The procedure, which requires costly and time-consuming paper work and court appearances, offers the woman no practical protection and, again, no guarantee that the offender will be incarcerated and the beatings stopped. For this reason, many attorneys who handle divorce and domestic relations cases refuse to obtain these orders of "protection" for their clients. Others continue to go through the motions on the outside chance that such an order will have a restraining effect on the husband.

A proposal for a three-year study to test the effectiveness of legal remedies for wife abuse has been submitted to the Ford Foundation by Nadine Traub, associate professor of Rutgers Law School, and Ann Marie Boylan, attorney-at-law. They contend that comparatively little attention has been given to the question of whether available legal remedies would be effective in reducing marital violence if, indeed, they were actually used and enforced to a greater extent. In addition to the usual legal avenues a wife may pursue (criminal charges, divorce, orders of protection, suing for damages, or using child abuse laws), the attorneys suggest it may be appropriate in some instances to ask the court to use the remedies of prosecution for obstruction of justice or pretrial detention. These remedies, which would protect the victim/plaintiff from threats or harmful assaults to "persuade" her to drop the charges or perjure her testimony, are seldom invoked. The legal system routinely has placed its emphasis upon the protection of the defendant's civil rights, among them the "rule of disclosure" requiring the complainant to disclose her current address to the defense. The plaintiff's right to physical protection and the prevention of intimidation of witnesses are rarely considered in marital violence cases.

This demonstration project would be most helpful in determining the facts about wife abuse laws and their effectiveness. While the grant application applies only to a test of New Jersey law, and laws differ somewhat from state to state, still the data from such a study could have an impact nationally by suggesting legislative reforms necessary to make state laws workable.

THE INADEQUACIES OF SOCIAL SERVICES

Many women are trapped in violent homes because they have no place to go and no means of supporting themselves and their children if they were to leave. Attempts to seek help from other sources can be as discouraging as calling the police to intervene. In the first place, most beatings take place at night or on weekends, when social agencies are closed. A woman, fleeing in the middle of the night and fearing for her life, often finds herself wandering the streets aimlessly not knowing where to turn or what to do.

The most pressing need is for emergency shelter. Although there are about 70 refuges for battered women and their children in England and a network of shelters across Scotland and Holland, few exist in the United States. Task forces across the country are grappling with this desperately urgent problem. Unfortunately, efforts to establish shelters are coming at a time when money is scarce, government budgets are being pared to the bone, and private foundations are cutting back on the number and size of grants. Also, past funding patterns show that federal monies are available for research but not for services, and less than one fifth of one percent of the billions of dollars granted annually by private foundations goes to women's projects (Tully, 1975:26).

In many localities, surveys of existing emergency housing reveal that a disproportionate number of beds are available to men rather than to women and that stays are generally for a maximum of three nights. Admissions in many instances are limited to alcoholics, former mental patients, or exprisoners. Few places are prepared to take in women with children, and those that do sometimes have rules that exclude sons over four years old. A traditional shelter may meet a victim's immediate need for refuge. But, because of the limitation on the number of nights she can stay, it protects her from immediate danger at best and allows for a "cooling off" period at least. It does not allow a battered woman enough time ro reevaluate her situation, consider her options, and perhaps seek a more permanent solution to her predicament. More than likely she has no money and only the clothes on her back. She may have no work experience or job skills. She needs more time and the opportunity to acquire vocational counseling, training, and placement. The experience of the shelters set up specifically for battered women and their children shows that when they are allowed to stay for at least three weeks to a month, they are more likely to become independent. To give them time to get on their feet and make their own way, they need public assistance.

Runaway wives who apply for funds through the Aid for Dependent Children program (AFDC) are often turned away because the husband's income makes the family ineligible for welfare. The social services system doesn't bend for the wife who is trying to make a break from an unbearable situation and has no money of her own. Technically, she is neither homeless nor destitute. She has a husband who is obligated to support her and a home to which she can return. A woman cannot qualify for financial assistance unless she has filed for divorce and is established in a separate domicile of her own. But to establish that domicile, she needs money. Consequently, many victims are forced to return to their violent husbands.

Should a woman be lucky enough to have the money to rent a place, she may still need food, clothing, and other necessities. Welfare is not obtained instantaneously. In crowded urban areas where there is high unemployment, applicants sometimes have to wait as long as 10 days to two weeks for the first interview to determine eligibility and, if they qualify, another two weeks or more for their first check.

Government services are no more prepared to meet emergencies than is the legal system. Rules and regulations are rigid and do not permit social workers the flexibility needed to respond adequately to crisis situations. Contingency funds to meet unusual emergencies are virtually nonexistent. Thus, victims are frequently referred to privately funded agencies which may then refer them to others. Victims who tenaciously follow every lead often report that they wind up full circle—back to the agency where they originally sought help, and, more likely than not, back to the home where they are in jeopardy of further physical abuse.

When it comes to mental health services, battered women are far more likely to be recipients than their irrationally violent husbands. Women are told to be more compliant and to be cautious about their own behavior, especially when their husbands are in a bad mood. They are given tranquilizers along with the "grin-and-bear-it" advice. Unable to change her situation, the wife often falls into depression and despair. The majority of women who sought refuge at Chiswick Women's Aid in England (Gayford, 1975) had spent time in mental institutions for depression or suicide attempts. In fact, some women have committed themselves as one means of getting away from their abusive husbands.

Few batterers, even those who may be genuinely remorseful when they see the damage they have wrought, seek treatment on their own. According to the League of Women Voters (1975), California law allows involuntary custody for up to 72 hours "if a person is a danger to himself, to others, or gravely disabled." After the 72-hour detention period for evaluation and treatment, if the person is still considered dangerous and will not accept voluntary treatment, a certification for intensive treatment for another 14 days can be obtained. When diagnosed as "imminently dangerous," a person can be held for a period not exceeding 90 days. If a woman's husband is dangerously violent, and she wants him hospitalized, she must go to court and show reasonable cause. The man, naturally, has the right to hire an attorney and request a jury trial contesting the decision to hospitalize.

Considering how battered women are treated when criminal charges are at issue, there is little reason to believe the victim would fare any better in taking this approach. Getting mental health professionals and judges to agree that the man is "dangerous," let alone "imminently dangerous," when wife beating is the only "symptom," is a bit far-fetched. It is far easier for a husband to get his wife committed when she is so depressed and tranquilized that she no longer has the will to resist. Besides, everyone she has turned to for help has told her that she is really to blame for her husband's violence.

THE "BLAME" BIAS

Mental health professionals and researchers generally view wife beating in terms of personal relationship and individual background. Concerned chiefly with the psychological interaction between the offender and the victim, they tend to adhere to theories of victimology, in which the victim is perceived as having provoked or instigated the offense. This translates into the old saw, "a wife has masochistic needs that are gratified by her husband's assaultive behavior." The husband is thus vindicated for his act of violence by the shifting of responsibility from the assailant to his victim. Mother, who is traditionally blamed for all family ills—particularly the antisocial behavior of the males in her family—is blamed once again. Her punishment is the beating she "brought on herself."

One battered wife stated emphatically (Martin, 1976:3): "No one has to 'provoke' a wife-beater. He will strike out when he's ready and for whatever reason he has at the moment. I may be his excuse, but I have never been the reason." Indeed, reports from victims as to what triggered their beatings (she broke the egg yolk when she was cooking his breakfast, she raised her voice, she wore her hair in a ponytail, she prepared a casserole dish instead of fresh meat for dinner) indicate that the incidents are trivial in the extreme. Other women said their husbands came home late at night, and without any warning, started beating them as they lay fast asleep in bed. They had no idea what prompted their husbands' violence.

In *Practical Psychology for Physicians,* Ray Fowler (1975), the executive director of the American Association of Marriage and Family Counselors, describes the wife abuser as "generally an obsessional person who has learned how to trigger himself emotionally." A man may perceive a reasonable comment by his wife as a nagging remark or a whining complaint, mull it over and exaggerate it until, in his own mind, he provides himself with a justification for his behavior.

"There is no warrant for jumping to the conclusion that since suffering exists, there is therefore a tendency to incur it or enjoy it," according to Karen Horney (1973:261). Elizabeth Truninger (1971:260) agrees that the pattern and frequency of wife beating merely demonstrates that some women *tolerate* violence, not that they invite it. Reasons for a woman continuing to tolerate the beatings are myriad: she is afraid to leave, she feels ashamed or guilty and doesn't want anyone else to know; to admit the failure of her marriage is to admit her own personal failure as a woman; she is dependent upon her assailant. She has no place to go and no way to support the children on her own; she is unaware that she has any option but to stay. Underlying these reasons are the ways in which women are socialized to be emotionally and economically dependent upon men and the ways in which all of our institutions are geared to keep the family together, no matter what the consequences.

Batterers, for the most part, do not seek counseling or therapy. They usually feel their actions are justified, and they have no need of help. For this reason, and because they are seldom apprehended or detained by either the criminal justice or the mental health systems, little is known about batterers. What we do know we have learned primarily from the victims. At one time the court in Framingham, Massachusetts, referred husband/offenders to the psychatric clinic for evaluation and treatment. The psychiatrists (Snell et al., 1964) found the husbands uncooperative and unwilling to admit there were any problems in their marriages that warranted outside intervention.

On the other hand, the wives, who wished to put a stop to the beatings, welcomed the opportunity for marital counseling. The doctors therefore interviewed the wives and wound up writing a paper called "The Wife-Beater's Wife" (Snell et al., 1964), the gist of which is the everpresent sexist line that "a husband's behavior may serve to fill a wife's needs even though she protests it." The doctors concluded, "We have come to feel that the offender cannot be adequately understood, and treatment and correctional measures appropriate to him devised, until one knows whom he has offended, how and why. One cannot understand the offender and his offense without having some understanding of the people with whom he has to deal."

That may be true to a certain extent, but, unfortunately, that is where these good doctors stopped. They took the easy way out because the wives were willing subjects. Psychiatrists, like all others in our society, are socialized to believe in sex-typed roles in marriage. In this study they saw role reversal as a causal factor in marital violence. They depicted the wives as efficient, masculine, frigid, and masochistic. The husbands they viewed as shy, passive, indecisive, and sexually inadequate. The beatings were the means by which husbands reasserted their masculinity and took revenge upon their castrating wives. "The devised treatment and correctional measures appropriate to the *offender*" were never determined, of course. Getting the victim to change *her* behavior became the modus operandi. The psychiatrists cited a measure of success in one instance where the husband continued to drink, "but in a more controlled manner, and with less violence in the home."

They also noted, "In none of the cases we studied did the husband express any intent to kill his wife, although some of the beatings were severe." As therapists, they seemed to be satisfied that their work had *lessened* the violence, admitting that it did not stop completely. The implication is that the men meant no real harm and that they should be encouraged to develop less explicit, physically injurious expressions of their male power over their wives.

The problem with psychiatry as a discipline is, Naomi Weisstein (1970:210) says, that findings which are based upon "insight, sensitivity and intuition" rather than upon empirical evidence can confirm for all time the biases that one started out with. She also finds fault with the personality theory (1970:209) which "has looked for inner traits when it should have been looking at social context." If a psychiatrist accepts the traditionally defined sex roles as gospel, believes (as Freud did) that women are innately masochistic, and is convinced that somehow a battered wife precipitates the crimes committed against her, the woman doesn't have a chance. If the wife accepts her "feminine" role, she is set up for a slave-master marital relationship which in and of itself invites abuse. But the tradition-bound psychiatrist would see her "inner need" for abuse, not the social imperatives that made her vulnerable.

Those who operate refuges for battered women report that wife/victims who take advantage of their services are generally submissive and have a very low self-esteem. Most of them need assertiveness training because they have spent their lives being passive (feminine) and have made every effort to please their husbands in order to avoid beatings. The point is that these wives are in a no-win situation. If they are passive, they are doormats that invite abuse. If they are aggressive, they invite the beatings to put them in their place.

Nathan Caplan and Stephen D. Nelson (1974:101-102) complain that a "person-blame" bias arises from too much concentration on the victim and not enough on the offender. Person-centered research and clinical therapy may have validity, they say, but the danger is that the situation can be vastly oversimplified and the labeling of groups (in this case, women, who are already socially, politically, and economically vulnerable) reinforced. The alternative is a "situation-centered" examination of the problem, which takes into account the social variables involved. When studying wife beating, the insitutional history of marriage, the lack of effective sanctions by relevant social agencies, and the general status of women must be taken into account.

More often, studies to determine factors that contribute to the practice of wife abuse concentrate on alcohol use, unemployment, jealousy, stress, "innate" male aggression, and victim provocation. While they may have a certain amount of value, in the long run their chief function is to provide the husband with an excuse for beating his wife. He can say, "I was drunk and didn't know what I was doing"; "She was pregnant, and I panicked because I couldn't face the added financial responsibility"; "I was distraught because I lost my job."

All the trails that are followed in an effort to determine the etiology of wife beating lead to some kind of excuse for or vindication of the assailant/husband. Researchers, therapists, and law enforcers often miss two very salient points: (1) There can be no justification for even a "little" violence. No matter what she may have said or done, no woman deserves to be beaten; (2) The underlying factor that breeds and perpetuates hostility between the sexes is the male-supremacist, patriarchal system which depends upon the sexist structure of the family unit and other social institutions.

As already discussed, violence, if allowed to continue, escalates in intensity. What begins as a slap can lead to a broken jaw the second time around and to murder the third. This chronology of events actually happened to one San Francisco woman (Martin, 1976:20). There is no way to "control" the severity of the beatings even if that were an appropriate goal, which it is not.

Wife beating is, without question, an example of power abuse. Therapists who support the oppressive status quo—the man-over-woman power relationship in marriage—only validate the man's right to exert power over his wife. Expecting the husband to be a benevolent despot is no guarantee that physical force will not be used. The prevalence of wife beating belies such expectations.

WHAT ABOUT THE CHILDREN?

Any solution to the problem of marital violence has to begin by making the public keenly aware of its prevalence and of how it affects the children in the home. An increasing number of people are becoming alarmed about the violence in our society. They berate the police for not protecting them on the streets. They protest the inordinate amount of violence in television programming, which they feel must relate to the increased incidence of muggings and rapes. They express their outrage against child abuse, but fail to see the correlation between child abuse and wife beating or any connection between wife beating and violence in the streets.

The seeds of violence begin in the home where much of the socialization of children takes place. Children who witness their mother's beatings or hear her cries in the middle of the night react with shock, fear, and guilt. They cringe in the corner not knowing what to do. They are afraid to interfere and feel guilty when they don't. Some children, who have been taught that the police are there to protect people from harm, will run to a neighbor to call the police. How the police officer handles the situation will have a strong effect on the children.

In Morton Bard's study (1971:161) of family violence in New York City's 30th Precinct, children were present in 41% of the cases in which police were called to intervene. "If this is typical, one can only speculate on the modeling effects of parental aggression on such children—not to speak of the effects of a variety of police behaviors on the perception of children in such situations," he says. If the police officers (usually male) identify with the husband and treat the incident lightly, they will be reinforcing the role models of violent imperious male and powerless female victim. But if police efficiently calm down the parents, and, whether or not an arrest is made, effectively communicate the attitude that violent behavior is not to be excused or tolerated, the children will receive healthier signals.

Richard Gelles's research (1972:173) shows that people who as children observed violence between their parents or who were themselves victims are more likely to become batterers and victims than people who never saw their parents fight or were not subject to corporal punishment as children. From his investigations, Gelles (1972:171) concluded, "Not only does the family expose individuals to violence and techniques of violence, the family teaches approval for the use of violence."

Violence in the home takes many forms. The wife very often acts as the buffer between father and child. She takes the husband's abuse, and he leaves the children alone. In many instances, however, the husband beats the wife *and* children. Sometimes the battered wife, in her desperation, will strike out against the children. Violence then follows the "pecking order" pattern: the husband beats the wife, the wife beats the child, and the child beats the dog.

In a study of 100 battered wives in England, Gayford (1975) found that 37% of the women admitted taking their frustrations out on their children, and 54% claimed their husbands committed acts of violence against the children. The breaking point for many of these women came when the children became victims of abuse, too. At that point these women resolved, or tried, to leave.

But leaving then may be too late if, as Gelles indicates, "merely" witnessing violence in the home as a child has a deleterious effect on adult marital behavior. Instead of reacting with abhorrence to the violence they saw, as one might hope or expect, the children tend to see violence in another way—as a way of life and a means of problem solving. If children are imbued with this concept, is it any wonder that violence extends beyond the home? The reluctance of the criminal justice system to enforce the law, the failure of social services to provide emergency support systems for victims and their families, the blaming of the victim and related social factors that tend to vindicate the perpetrator—all of these serve to condone the father's violence. It is not surprising then that many sons believe that violent behavior is an assertion of one's masculinity, not only excusable but expected of them.

Robert Whitehurst (1971:41) reminds us that "men are not programmed to be other than aggressive" and that "much of the aggressive hostility vented on wives must be seen as a product of our sexually schizoid culture." He concludes, "Our culture teaches men to be tough and ready to fight if necessary. To expect men to also become tender lovers and responsive husbands seems to be asking more than logic can allow."

Change will not come about by itself. To break through the cycle of violence that has our society in its grip is an enormous task, involving nothing less than a cultural revolution of attitudes and values. If we are to reduce aggression and violence in our society, we must begin with the children. They must be trained to relate to one another as individuals, as human beings rather than as stereotypes.

Seymour and Norma Feshbach (1973:95) believe that parents and school administrators need to find alternatives to physical punishment for discipline and behavior control. They also see a need to develop procedures that will enhance empathy in children as an inhibitory mechanism by which to check the use of violence. When the individual perceives another as similar to oneself, it is more difficult to injure that person. Through role-playing techniques, the child could learn to perceive situations from someone else's perspective and to experience the other person's feelings. Emphasis should be placed on the broad dimensions of similarity that unite us in our humanness rather than on the narrow ones that divide us into antagonism-inducing categories.

James W. Prescott (1975) alludes to pleasure and violence as having a reciprocal relationship in that the presence of one inhibits the other. He sees deprivation of touching, body contact, and movement as a basic cause for a number of emotional disturbances, including violence. Prescott backs his theory by citing studies on child abuse showing that parent abusers were invariably deprived of physical affection during childhood and studies of other cultures demonstrating that societies giving infants the greatest amount of physical affection had low crime and violence rates. Murray Straus (1977) points out, however, that the warmth and affection ideology of child rearing is already espoused in America. He claims additional research is needed to determine the social and psychological conditions that prevent some parents from exhibiting such behavior toward their children and then to translate the results into programs that will assist these parents.

Prescott also sees the double standard—the rigid values of monogamy, chastity, and virginity for women—as helping to produce physical violence. "The denial of female sexuality must give way to an acceptance and respect for it," Prescott (1975:18) says, "and men must share with women the responsibility for giving affection and care to infants and children." He recognizes, too, that to replace materialistic values with human values would mean drastic change in the socioeconomic system and men's concepts of work and home.

Recognition of the problems inherent in sex role stereotyping is not enough to change attitudes and behavior. Men, though they may accept the need for change intellectually, naturally resist giving up their power and privileges. Parents who are locked into inflexible masculine and feminine roles teach their children these same roles from birth. Teachers, too, are apt to treat boy and girl children differently. Researchers Lisa A. Servin and K. Daniel O'Leary (1975) have found that nursery schoolteachers are much more likely to react to a boy's behavior, bad or good, than to a girl's. By thus rewarding boys for aggression and girls for passivity, however unconsciously, teachers mold behavior that will cause both sexes pain later.

Psychologist Marcia Guttentag and a research team (Tavris, 1975) designed a six-week curriculum to be offered in three large, ethnically diverse school districts in Boston. The course, aimed at counteracting stereotypical conditioning and raising the children's consciousness, was given to three age groups: kindergarten (age 5), fifth grade (10), and ninth grade (14). The methodology included reading stories, viewing films, acting out scenes from plays, and working on special projects. The children learned that it is possible for both sexes to share desirable personality traits—that is, men can be sensitive and warm, and women can be assertive and competent.

From tests administered before giving the course, the researchers found that most five-year-olds are already ripe old sexists. Children, no matter what their social class or economic background, had by then been thoroughly indoctrinated to "masculine" and "feminine" sex roles. Whether their mothers worked outside the home made no difference in their belief that boys are strong and can do all sorts of interesting things, and girls are weak and silly and are best kept at home.

Efforts to broaden the children's view of sex roles did not work as well as the researchers had hoped. The girls were consistently more ready to accept the new ideas, and some turned into feminist fledglings, aware of new vistas open to women and eager to experience new roles. Most of the fifth and ninth grade boys, however, persistently held to traditional concepts, and some became even more outspoken about a "woman's place."

The degree to which the students were positively influenced by learning about changing role concepts depended, in large part, upon the teacher's enthusiasm and the extensive use of class materials. But another influencing factor is the child's observation of adult behavior outside of the classroom. Children pick up far more from the ways in which adults act than from what they say. Boys can't help but observe that men have the power and that they, too, can have things their own way if they take the power their maleness commands in our society. Their observations, unfortunately, still reflect the reality.

CHANGING POLICE ATTITUDES

First, we need to deal with the immediacy and the danger involved in marital fights. We must find ways to stop the violence when it occurs and to prevent it from reoccurring. Still the most obvious thing to do, in spite of what has been said, is to call the police for protection. Neighbors, who hear a fight going on and have reason to believe it has become violent and therefore dangerous, should call the police immediately. Neighbors, friends, and relatives must be made to realize that once violence erupts, what transpires between husband and wife can no longer be shielded by concerns for privacy. When a husband abuses his wife physically, he automatically forfeits that right. Prompt action is required to protect the wife, and possibly the children, from severe injury. A quick phone call may even prevent a murder.

When the police receive domestic disturbance calls in which violence or the threat of violence is reported they must give them top priority. Those who receive and dispatch calls should be specially trained in distinguishing wife-beating calls from nonviolent family hassles. They should be made particularly aware of the danger involved so that they get sufficient information from the caller to forewarn the responding officers. Police departments also need to develop some method of separating wife-beating incidents from the usual categories of domestic disturbance or violent crime. When arrests are made for the specific crime (assault, battery, murder), the marital relationship between victim and offender should be noted and tabbed under the heading of spouse abuse. Quasilegal relationships should, of course, be included in this category. Such a system of recording and tabulating incidents would enable us to derive the statistics that are now nearly impossible to obtain. Cross-referenced filing of incidents by name and address is also necessary so that the dispatcher can run a check for any previous reports involving the same parties and determine the probable danger.

On arrival, police should treat these cases routinely, as they would any other investigation of violent crimes. Once a determination has been made that a crime has been committed, officers should be careful to gather evidence, determine the means of force used, and be aware of all possible corroborating witnesses, including the children. Fact finding is the job of the investigating officer. Under no cricumstances should the police assume that the case won't go anywhere or that the victim will drop the charges. Therefore, a detailed report of the facts should be filed in every instance, whether or not an on-the-scene arrest is made.

The wife who claims to have been struck or physically abused by her husband should be treated as a victim, even though her injuries are not visible to the officer. Police should be sensitive to the trauma the woman has just experienced and the emotional as well as physical stress she may still be suffering. She may not be in a state where she can make necessary decisions about the case. If strong circumstantial and physical evidence exists in a felony case, the officer can proceed on his own and make an arrest for probable cause without the wife's cooperation. In a misdemeanor case, the officer is obliged to state why police cannot make an arrest, and advise the woman of her right to make a citizen's arrest. Should she choose not to exercise that right at the moment, the officer should nonetheless proceed with the investigation, which may serve to validate or disprove a complaint filed later with the district attorney. If the wife needs medical attention, the officer should see that she gets it. Police should have the information needed to refer the victim to appropriate agencies where she can find financial aid, emergency shelter, legal assistance, and counseling.

The husband should be viewed as a possible criminal suspect. As part of the fact-finding process, the officer needs to determine whether the incident was an accident, a matter of self-defense, or a criminal offense. If the officer determines during questioning that a crime has indeed been committed, then the husband must be apprised of his constitutional rights before he is interrogated. Regardless of personal feelings about a domestic situation, the officer should take the matter seriously at all times.

When possible, man-woman police teams should be sent out on marital violence calls. Experience shows that women officers have a high success rate in defusing volatile situations. With both sexes responding to these calls, and with each officer serving as a check on the other, there would be less chance for sex-biased reporting of incidents.

How police officers handle themselves in marital violence situations is crucial to their own safety, to the safety of others involved, to the perceptions of the assailant as to the seriousness of the act he has committed, to the trust and commitment of the victim to pursue the case, to the perceptions of the children about violence as accepted behavior, and to the confidence of witnesses in the criminal justice system.

A policy of arrest promotes the well-being of the victim. Many battered wives who have tolerated their husbands' violence in the past have felt alone in coping with the problem. The officer who takes the situation seriously and initiates legal action may give the wife the courage to proceed with her case and change her life situation. Documenting these cases, regardless of expected outcome, builds a record of the husband's actions and intent, which may prove useful for future prosecution. Additionally, the policy of arrest may place pressure on the prosecutor and the courts—pressure that may force them to join in the struggle to find adequate legal remedies and to institute programs that will prevent repeated offenses.

To strengthen the effectiveness of the temporary restraining order as an inhibitory measure to prevent further violence, arrangements were made recently in San Francisco, at the behest of an ad hoc committee of women, to computerize such orders. In this way, the officer can call in to communications, check whether there has been a previous restraining order, and take appropriate action. With this system the officer can no longer beg off from responsibility by referring the woman back to her attorney.

DIVERSIONARY MEASURES

Many people prefer some alternative to arrest and possible jail sentences for the violent husband. One reason given is that he is the "breadwinner," but few would think of using this excuse as a saving grace for an assailant whose victim was other than his wife. In an effort to bypass criminal procedures, and perhaps hold the marriage intact, various diversionary programs have been developed.

In Hayward, California, the police department have established Project Outreach. Mental health specialists, hired by the police, go out on marital violence calls with the responding officers on weekends, when most family fights occur. When the police feel relatively sure that they have successfully quelled the violence, they are free to leave, and the therapists stay on to counsel the couple. Additionally, up to ten counseling sessions are made available free of charge to couples who wish to receive such help. After working with the project for three years, Sue Gershenson, who is a psychiatric social worker, said at a California Senate Subcommittee hearing (1975:112) that she is "convinced that the combination of trained mental health professionals and police who are sensitive and trained in crisis intervention can not only help prevent marital violence, but can also provide assistance in the resolution of family disputes." An evaluation of the project revealed that the number of repeat DD calls to police has decreased.

Project Outreach can be helpful, indeed, if the psychiatric social workers who go out on police calls can persuade the husbands to take advantage of the counseling they offer. Danger lies, however, in viewing marital violence solely as a mental health problem and in measuring the success of the project by the reduction of calls to police. If a batterer rejects counseling, as so many of them do, the wife may decide that calling the police is useless.

Some counties have started Night Prosecutor Programs to mediate disputes in ongoing personal relationships. Hearings are held in various communities in Clackamas County, Oregon, as frequently as volume demands. Volunteer mediators are screened and trained by professionals. The emphasis is on resolution of problems rather than judging right and wrong. The Night Prosecutor Program in Columbus, Ohio, is coordinated by prosecutors and conducted by law students (Martin, 1976:112). If the situation is particularly volatile, the prosecutor or hearing officer may warn of possible legal consequences if the conflict continues. Officials who started this "Citizens Dispute Settlement" concept were motivated to find a way of handling "minor" cases such as "simple assaults" and family disputes in a supervised setting outside of the traditional judicial system, to alleviate caseload pressure on the court, thereby permitting a higher degree of attention to "serious" crimes. Such informal hearings also save money, they claim, by avoiding costly court proceedings. During the first year of this program, only 2% of 3,626 direct complaints resulted in criminal charges.

Here again, wife beating is seen as a minor offense, and the husband is let off with a warning. To make the woman believe that such hearings do something for her is a cruel hoax. What about her future safety? Warnings and threats are useless unless the district attorney is prepared to follow through if the husband calls the system's bluff.

A unique judicial process that seems far more helpful has been developed in Pima County, Arizona. Under the Pre-Trial Release Program, every criminal defendant eligible for release is interviewed by a trained investigator. If, during the initial interview at the county jail, the investigator finds that the alleged offender resides with the victim, a call is made to the Victim Witness Advocate (VWA) Program. A counselor there contacts the complainant to verify the information and asks what conditions of release she would like to recommend. The counselor then relays the wishes of the complainant to the Pre-Trial Release investigator, who so advises the judge.

"Battered women have been very practical about the conditions of release they would like," states David A. Lowenberg (1976), program coordinator of the VWA Program. Consequently, judges have been receptive to their wishes and have usually complied with the suggested conditions of release. Usually the defendant is released on his own recognizance to a relative's or friend's residence with the proviso that he not contact the victim by telephone or in person during the course of the judicial proceedings. A substantial number of wife/victims ask that the defendant be given treatment for severe alcohol or emotional problems.

"From the time a criminal complaint has been issued until the final case disposition, the VWA staff keeps the battered woman apprised of the status of her case and informs her of the date, time, and place of the trial," Lowenberg says. In addition, a member of the VWA staff will escort her to court and arrange day care for her children, if she needs these support services.

The alternative to treatment of wife beating as a crime is to treat it as a mental health problem. As previously discussed, getting a batterer to seek help is extremely difficult. Because he believes not only that he has the right to beat his wife but that other husbands are doing it, too, he considers his behavior to be "normal." Therefore, he believes he has no problem and no need for outside help. The only way to get him into therapy or counseling would be for a judge to order it as a condition of release. Lt. George Rosko of the San Francisco Police Department (Martin, 1976:118) suggests that a first-time offender be remanded to a counseling center in the same way that traffic violators are sent to traffic school. The batterer would be warned explicitly that if he "ever lays a hand on his wife again" he will be sent to jail. If judges would take such a hard-nosed position and make it stick, Rosko believes there would be a marked reduction in the incidents of wife abuse.

An assistant district attorney in Spokane proposes a quicker method of obtaining results: peer pressure. If men would stop making jokes about wife beating, if they would declare wife abuse off limits and bring pressure to bear upon offenders and let them know in no uncertain terms that such behavior is not acceptable, if men would work with batterers in much the same way as women are working with victims, we might well be on our way to solving the problem.

REFUGES FOR BATTERED WOMEN

Under present conditions, however, the need for emergency shelter for battered women and their children is paramount. Women have been trapped in violent homes out of fear and economic dependency or, as one victim put it (Martin, 1976:3), "because the social structure of my world says I cannot do anything about a man who wants to beat me."

Since feminist groups have made the plight of the battered woman a national issue and because the media have been so responsive in giving the subject public exposure, help is now on the way. Consortia, coalitions, or task forces are being formed across the country to provide emergency services and shelter for battered wives and their families. These groups usually start with women banding together to help women. Initiative may come from feminist groups, such as the National Organization for Women, the local women's center or switchboard, or the rape crisis hotline. In other instances, more established groups like the Commission on the Status of Women or the Y.W.C.A. may take it upon themselves to pull together a representative group of women, among whom are attorneys, social workers, mental health specialists, or members of Junior League and Soroptimists. Experts in fund raising and proposal writing are essential to such women's support coalitions.

Gradually these groups expand to form a second more community-oriented coalition which includes both men and women from the social service agencies that relate in any way to the various problems battered wives face. Among these agencies are the police, district attorney, court, legal aid, mental health association, family service agencies, welfare, government social service and mental health departments, emergency hospital physicians, child protective services, AFL-CIO community services, and alcohol and drug abuse programs. University schools of social work, sociology, psychology, medicine, nursing, and law may provide students to conduct research or field work that can be helpful in designing a workable program to provide for the varied needs of battered women.

Invariably the groups see the value in working together to coordinate available services and identify those that are lacking. Most notable is the lack of adequate emergency housing, which usually becomes a top priority of both the women's support coalition and the secondary community resource coalition.

In forming a shelter for battered women, it is essential that the second coalition see its function as supportive of the first. Experience shows the importance of women supporting women as *women* rather than as professionals "helping" clients find solutions to their problems. According to Sharon Vaughn (Martin, 1976:203), the professional "treatment" model automatically creates a barrier that serves to further isolate and dehumanize the woman who is already the victim not only of her violent husband or lover, but of society itself. Vaughn was instrumental in the founding of Women's House in St. Paul in 1974 and the Harriet Tubman Emergency Shelter for Women in Minneapolis in 1977. She contends that peer counseling is the crucial factor. Having the opportunity to talk with other women who have shared her own experience and seeing their strength growing as they cope with emotional and economic problems, the battered woman takes on a new sense of self. She no longer feels isolated and begins to see her own strengths. Even if she decides to return home, the bond between herself and the other women remains.

As soon as a refuge opens its doors, it is filled to capacity almost immediately and has a long waiting list. That this has been the experience of existing shelters throughout the world belies the popular assumption that the wife remains with her battering husband because she has a compelling need for such abusive treatment. The *need* is for an escape hatch—for a place to go. When help is really available, battered women take advantage of it in such numbers that shelters need to tap other resources, like private homes or traditional short-term accommodations, until a vacancy arises in the refuge.

Insofar as possible, under such crowded conditions, the shelter should maintain a homelike atmosphere, particularly for the children's sake. They have already been uprooted from their homes and their friends, and they, too, suffer from the traumatic effects of the violence they have seen or felt. Children often form the majority of the residents in the refuge. Services must be provided for them while the mother is trying to pull herself together and make plans for their future. Funding agencies often lop off from their budgets funds necessary for child care services under the premise that mothers should take responsibility for their own children. They fail to see that the children may have emotional problems requiring special professional attention and that the mother, in a state of recovery herself, needs peace and time in which to work through her personal problems. She may require medical treatment, therapy, assertiveness training, job rehabilitation and placement, legal counseling, or other services provided by the shelter and its support and resource coalitions. The wife/victim needs help in caring for her children while she is reevaluating her situation and pursuing new options—perhaps creating a whole new life for herself and her family.

The biggest problem shelter task forces face is funding. Somehow when women's projects come along the vast well of funding sources suddenly runs dry. Government pleads that there isn't enough money to cover the budgetary needs of already existing programs. Officials continue to pour large sums of money into research on violence rather than reorder priorities to provide vital services for victims. Private foundations, usually traditional and conservative in outlook, are more apt to put funds into programs that are less threatening to the ongoing family relationship. Because of the tremendous need for shelters—there should be, at the very least, one in each county—it is really incumbent upon communities to find local sources to assume responsibility and produce the necessary funding. This can probably be done best by not relying upon only a single source for funding. The combination of some government funds, private donations, small grants from local foundations, and community fund-raising events— while not all that sure or secure—keeps La Casa de las Madres going in San Francisco. Those shelters lucky enough to tie into government or foundation programs must face the fact that these grants are only for a specified period; they are not ongoing. The shelter must find other sources for future needs. One means of raising funds is to set up a business (telephone answering service, mail order, catering service) in the shelter itself. The women could receive training and experience so that they can later qualify for jobs and get out on their own.

REMEDIAL LEGISLATION

Because of conditions in the criminal justice system that allow for discretion and inequities, and because of the need to reorder government spending policies, remedial legislation is being introduced at both the state and federal levels. Legislation introduced in Congress would establish a national clearinghouse for information, research, training workers, funding shelters, and a national hot line. The bill is modeled after legislation that created the national centers for the prevention and treatment of rape and child abuse. Pennsylvania, which previously had no legal provisions for evicting an abusive husband from the home or for issuing protection orders, enacted such a law to provide relief for battered women. What is unique about the statute is that it covers anyone residing in the household; it therefore extends protection to women in "common law" marriages who are not usually covered under existing law in other states. The new law also eliminates the traditional proviso that the woman must file for divorce before she can obtain a restraining order.

Revisions to New York law are being offered by State Senator Carol Bellamy so that a woman who flees her home in fear for her life cannot be divorced later by her husband on grounds of "desertion." This quirk in the law had previously placed the wife/victim "at fault," and therefore at a disadvantage, in custody and financial settlement considerations in divorce proceedings. Legislation to fund, at least partially, four to six emergency shelters for battered women has passed in California. Bills introduced in Florida, Maryland, and California would require all social agencies (police, doctors, social workers, and others who come in direct contact with marital violence cases) to report them to a central state registry. In this way, data could be gathered which might prove helpful in suggesting other solutions. These bills have been rejected by state legislatures because this information gathering would be too costly. Yet these same legislators require statistics that are otherwise unobtainable to prove the need for other "battered wives" legislation, such as funding for shelters.

Women's legislative advocates should work with attorneys who specialize in family law, directors of emergency shelters for battered women, and women's organizations to assess the inadequacies in the law and to initiate changes.

CONCLUSION

Recent developments to alleviate the plight of the battered wife by beefing up the law and law enforcement or by establishing shelters for family victims are, admittedly, only stop-gap, band-aid measures. Such intervention only serves to stop immediate violence in a particular home and to prevent imminent injury or loss of life. There is no guarantee that it won't happen again with this couple, nor that violence will not erupt in other families. Intervention is not synonymous with prevention.

Hopefully, however, these emergency measures will serve as a catalyst for dramatic and widespread change in social attitudes. When we refuse to accept marital violence as a given in some homes, when we publicly deny the husband's misconceived notion that he has a right to beat his wife, when we recognize that children are being trained to violence—then we have already begun that process of change.

For too long we have placed value upon the institution of marriage in and of itself. For the most part, we have neglected or impeded the *quality* of the marital relationship. Marriage counseling comes after the fact—after the damage is done. So long as women are relegated to subservient positions in society and in the home, they can only be victims.

Sex roles, in and out of marriage, need to be re-examined and redefined. The concept that the man is head of household and sole breadwinner for the family must be eliminated. Laws that reinforce man-over-woman power relationships in marriage must be repealed. Family life classes should be instituted in early childhood—at preschool nurseries and in kindergarten—rather than in high school, when it is too late to counteract the effects of sex-role stereotyping. Teachers and parents alike need to be trained to overcome their own sexism so as not to infect the children.

Prevention of marital violence means a whole restructuring of our society so that equality between the sexes is guaranteed in marriage and the family, in the schools, in the work force, and in government. Only when marriage is seen as an egalitarian relationship or partnership will we be able to eliminate the "battered wife syndrome."

REFERENCES

BARD, M. (1971). "The study and modification of intra-familial violence." Pp. 149-164 in The control of aggression and violence: Cognitive and psychological. New York: Academic Press.

BLACKSTONE, W. (1765). Commentaries.

BROWNMILLER, S. (1975). Against our will. New York: Simon and Schuster.

California Senate Subcommittee on Nutrition and Human Needs (1975). Hearings on Marital Violence and Family Violence transcript, July 21.

CALVERT, R. (1975). "Criminal and civil liability in husband-wife assaults." Pp. 88-91 in S.K. Steinmetz and M. Straus (eds.), Violence in the family. New York: Dodd, Mead.

CAPLAN, N., and NELSON, S.D. (1974). "Who's to blame?" Psychology Today, (November):99-104.

City of Oakland Police Services (1975). "Techniques of dispute intervention." Training Bulletin III-J, (June 19).

DAVIS, E.G. (1971). The first sex. New York: Putnam.

DeCROW, K. (1974). Sexist justice. New York: Random House.

DURBIN, K. (1974). "Wife-beating." Ladies Home Journal, (June).

EISENBERG, S., and MICKLOW, P. (1974). "The assaulted wife: 'catch 22' revisited." Unpublished manuscript. A version of this study will be published in Women's Rights Law Reporter.

ENGELS, F. (1948). The origin of family, private property and the state. Moscow: Progress.

FESHBACH, S., and FESHBACH, N. (1973). "The young aggressors." Psychology Today, (April):90-96.

FLEMING, J. (1975). Wife abuse. Unpublished manuscript.

GAYFORD, J.J. (1975). "Wife battering: A preliminary survey of 100 cases." British Medical Journal, (January 25):194-197.

GELLES, R. (1972). The violent home. Beverly Hills: Sage.

HART, A.W. (1975). "Thomas promised that he would." The New York Times, (June 10).

HORNEY, K. (1973). The neurotic personality of our time. New York: Norton.

Kansas City Police Department (1971-1972). Northeast Patrol Division Task Force. "Conflict management: Analysis/resolution." Unpublished manuscript.

League of Women Voters (1975). Challenge of the 70's.

LOWENBERG, D.A. (1976). "Pima county services for battered women." Response, (December):3-4.

MARTIN, D. (1976). Battered wives. San Francisco: Glide.

MURPHY, R.B., McKAY, E., SCHWARTZ, J.A., and LIEBMAN, D.A. (n.d.). "Training patrolmen as crisis intervention instructors." Unpublished mansucript.

Practical Psychology for Physicians (1975). Summer:75.

PRESCOTT, J.W. (1975). "Body pleasure and the origins of violence." Bulletin of the Atomic Scientists, (November):10-20.

SERVIN, L.A., and O'LEARY, K.D. (1975). "How nursery schools teach girls to shut up." Psychology Today, (December):57-58, 102-103.

SNELL, J.E., ROSENWALD, R.J., and ROBEY, A. (1964). "The wifebeater's wife." Archives of General Psychiatry, Volume II, (August):107-112.

STRAUS, M. (1977). "A social structural perspective on the prevention and treatment of wife-beating." In Maria Roy (ed.) Battered women. New York: Van Nostrand-Reinhold.

TAVRIS, C. (1975). "It's tough to nip sexism in the bud." Psychology Today, (December):58, 102.

TRUNINGER, E. (1971). "Marital violence: The legal solutions." Hastings Law Journal, 23(1) (November):260.

TULLY, M.J. (1975). "Funding the feminists." Foundation News, (March/April):24-33.

WEISSTEIN, N. (1970). " 'Kinder, kuche, kirche' as scientific law: Psychology constructs the female." Pp. 205-220 in R. Morgan (ed.), Sisterhood is powerful. New York: Random House.

WEITZMAN, L. (1974). "Legal regulations of marriage: Tradition and change." California Law Review, 62(4) (July-September):1169-1288.

WHITEHURST, R. (1971). "Violently jealous husbands." Sexual Behavior, (July).

6

TREATMENT ALTERNATIVES FOR
BATTERED WOMEN

LENORE E. WALKER

The battered woman is usually pictured as a small, fragile, haggard woman who might once have been pretty. Bruises, broken bones, a painful look of fear are evidence of her batterings. Because of her reluctance to change her situation, it is assumed she enjoys being hurt. It is believed that she provokes her own injuries. Friends and professionals become angry with her for not allowing them to help her. They label her masochistic, mentally sick, a martyr, or just plain stupid. Before long they begin to believe her lament that there are no alternatives for battered women and withdraw their support.

Two years of research have demonstrated that these images and assumptions about battered women are not true (Walker, 1976a, 1976b, 1977). Nonetheless, battering behavior has been concealed for so long that many other images and assumptions must be destroyed before researchers can learn who battered women really are and establish effective alternatives. Until recently, talking about such assault, reporting it to the police, and conducting research on abused women have been taboo, despite the fact that the history of wife abuse is ancient. Brownmiller (1975) provides a description of the trade off women historically have made to obtain economic and physical security. To protect themselves against the threat of violence from many men, women gave up their freedom and mated with one man. Martin (1976) traces the effect of this compromise upon society's institutions, which have allowed violence to exist between the bonded couple. Today, women are no longer willing to be treated as man's property. They are insisting that the previously concealed crime of battering be brought out from the privacy of the home for study and action.

As the high incidence of battering is publicized, more and more women are admitting to being battered. Estimates of battered women soar upwards to one woman out of two. The Federal Bureau of Investigation estimates that over 50% of all murders of women are committed by men with whom they have intimate relationships. Informal reports indicate that a high proportion of women who kill their men previously suffered from battering. The Denver women who participated in this author's research (Walker, 1976a, 1976b, in preparation) indicated that fewer than 10% ever reported serious violence to the police. These women reported being too ashamed or scared to call for help directly. If they did seek assistance, it was usually under some pretense that typically went unrecognized as an indirect call for help. This lack of response reinforced the women's belief that alternatives were not available to them, and they retreated further into isolation. Most of these women said that they were on the verge of asking for direct help and would have admitted to being battered if the helper had asked them. In fact, in one hospital emergency room where the nurses were trained to ask about battering in suspicious cases, the women did admit to being battered. The exact number of battered women is thus not known, but indications are that the number is considerable.

The definitions of battering also have caused confusion in identifying battered women. Many researchers have used physical violence resulting in bodily injury as a primary definition. Straus (1976) supports the use of this admittedly narrow definition because of the ease with which such abuse can be documented. Physical violence also has been the accepted standard for research in the area of child abuse. Gelles (1974) added the criterion of police contact when he selected 80 families for his in-depth study of family violence. Early reports of women who sought safety in the refuges for battered women in England gave futher credence to the assumption that battering meant physical abuse (Gayford, 1975; Select Committee of Parliament, 1975). As more refuges were established in England, however, it became obvious that large numbers of women were seeking safety from psychological abuse, which was at least as detrimental to their lives as the physical abuse. In this author's pilot research (Walker, 1976a, 1976b), both physical and psychological coerciveness were examined. It was found that both forms of violence exist in assaultive couples, and they cannot be separated, despite the difficulty in documentation. Further data have confirmed this finding and underscored the need to develop measurement techniques. It is relatively easy to count black eyes and broken bones and assign a severity rating according to medical standards. To measure psychological abusiveness, the severity must be estimated from both the frequency and the subjective impact on the woman. For example, one woman described life-threatening physical assaults, one of which resulted in broken vertebrae in her neck. She was in physical pain for months following this beating. However, when she was asked to describe the most painful battering incident, she said that it was when her husband commanded her to get on her hands and knees and make sounds like an animal. This psychological degradation was far more humiliating and painful than the physical abuse she suffered. Battered women repeatedly cite psychological humiliation and isolation as their worst battering experiences, whether or not they have ever been physically abused. Furthermore, the threat of physical violence was always present for these women. They all stated they believed their batterer was capable of killing them.

Using this expanded definition of battering behavior as both physical and psychological, the heretofore invisible battered woman becomes more identifiable. The stereotypic physically abused woman living in a poverty environment probably accounts for only about 20% of all battered women. These battered women have been the most visible, as they must depend upon society's institutions to help meet their basic survival needs. The overt and frequent violence in their environments usually brings them to the attention of the police and criminal justice system. Only now are we beginning to realize that battering behavior in perhaps 80% of the cases has gone unrecognized, because the violence occurs in more privileged environments. Battered women come from all walks of life. Social class, family income, level of education, occupation, and ethnic or racial background make no difference. Professional men batter their women as do unemployed and unskilled laborers. Highly successful business and professional women are battered as well as those with no job skills. The common trait among battered women is their low self-esteem, a common result of any kind of repeated victimization. For some, their sense of powerlessness exists only in their relationships with men; for others, it permeates their entire existence.

The man who batters is typically described as having a dual personality. He is seen either as very charming or as exceptionally cruel. He is both selfish and generous depending upon his whimsical moods. Although he sometimes uses alcohol or drugs to excess, his battering behavior is described as independent of whether or not he is drunk. He is described as extraordinarily possessive and extremely jealous. Probably his greatest fear is that his woman will leave him. Despite these characteristics, most men who batter would not be recognized as batterers unless they actually were observed physically abusing women. The small bits of psychological coercion that can be predictors of further violence occur so frequently in interpersonal relationships that they usually are discounted until a major event erupts.

CYCLE THEORY OF BATTERING INCIDENTS

Preliminary data obtained on battered women indicate the existence of a cycle of battering behavior. Rather than constant or random occurrences of battering, there is a definite cycle that is repeated over a period of time. This cycle appears to have three distinct phases that vary in time and intensity both in the same couple and between different couples. The three phases are: the tension building phase, the explosion or acute battering incident, and the calm, loving respite. So far it has proven difficult to discern how long a couple will remain in any one phase. Predicting the length of one complete cycle also is not yet possible. There is evidence that situational events can influence the timing. Relationships that have lasted 20 or more years indicate several different cycle patterns corresponding to different stages of life. There is also evidence that some interventions are more successful if they occur at one phase rather than another. The available data are still too limited to make any conclusions, but trends suggest the desirability of further investigation.

PHASE ONE

The first phase of the cycle is the tension building phase. During this time, minor battering incidents occur. The incidents may be handled in a variety of ways. The woman usually attempts to calm the batterer, using techniques that have had previous success. She may become nurturing, compliant, and anticipate his every whim, or she may stay out of his way. She lets the batterer know she accepts his abusiveness as legitimately directed toward her. She believes that what she does will prevent his anger from escalating. If she does her job well, then the incident will be over; if he explodes, she assumes the guilt. In order for her to maintain this role, the battered woman must not permit herself to get angry with the batterer. She denies her anger at unjustly being psychologically or physically hurt. She reasons that perhaps she did deserve the abuse and often identifies with her aggressor's faulty reasoning. When he throws the dinner she prepared for him across the kitchen floor, she reasons that maybe she did overcook it, accidentally. As she cleans up his mess, she may think that he was a bit extreme in his reaction, but she is usually so grateful that it was a relatively minor incident that she resolves not to be angry with him. She also may blame a particular situation for the man's outburst. Perhaps he had trouble at work or was drinking too much and did not know what he was doing. If she waits it out, she reasons, the situation will change and bring an improvement in his behavior towards her. This reasoning unfortunately does not bring an improvement, only a postponement of the second phase of the cycle, which is the acute battering incident.

Women who have been battered over a period of time know that these minor battering incidents will get worse. However, to help themselves cope, they deny this knowledge. They also deny their terror of the inevitable second phase by believing they have some control over the batterer's behavior. During the initial stages of this first phase, they indeed do have some limited control. As the tension builds, they rapidly lose this control. Each time a minor battering incident occurs, there are residual effects. The battered woman's anger steadily increases, even though she may not recognize it. The batterer, spurred on by the apparently passive acceptance of his abusive behavior, does not bother to control himself. Society's laissez-faire attitude reinforces his belief in his right to discipline his woman. He is aware that his behavior is inappropriate, even if he does not acknowledge it. This creates further fear that she may become so disgusted with him that she will leave him. He thus becomes more oppressive in the hopes that his brutality and threats will keep her captive.

This behavior historically has been successful. Battered women have been trapped in dangerous relationships by man's physical and economic superiority and society's unwillingness to make its institutions responsive to her needs.

The battered woman's attempts to cope with the minor battering incidents that occur during this tension building phase are the best she can do. Most women in a sexist society probably experience similar minor battering incidents. The difference between most women and battered women is that the battered woman has learned that she is powerless to prevent the rest of the cycle from occurring. Many couples are adept at keeping this phase at a constant level for long periods of time. An external situation often will upset the delicate balance. One woman reported that this phase lasted for longer periods of time as her children grew older. Once they were out of the house, the phase could last for several years before an acute battering incident would occur. Ten years had passed without an acute battering incident when one child was killed in an accident. The woman's husband expressed his grief by beating her so severely she spent several months in the hospital recuperating. Five years have past since that acute battering incident.

As the batterer and battered woman sense the escalating tension, it becomes more difficult for their coping techniques to continue to work. Each becomes more frantic. The man increases his possessive smothering and brutality. Psychological humiliation becomes more barbed. Battering incidents become more frequent and last longer. The battered woman is unable to restore the equilibrium. She is less able to defend against the pain and hurt. The psychological torture is reportedly the most difficult for her to handle. She usually withdraws more from him, which causes him to move more oppressively toward her. He begins to look for expressions of her anger, sensing it even though she still denies it or thinks she is successfully hidng it.

PHASE TWO

There is a point toward the end of the tension building phase where the process ceases to respond to any controls. Once the point of inevitability is reached, the next phase, the acute battering incident, will occur. The release of tension must occur, and it is almost always destructive. Thus phase two is characterized by the uncontrollable discharge of the tensions built up in phase one. The lack of control and its major destructiveness distinguish the acute battering incident from the relatively minor ones in phase one. This is not to say that those incidents that occur during phase one are not serious and do not constitute unlawful assault. It is the seriousness with which phase two's incidents are viewed by the couple that makes the distinction between the phases.

During phase two, the batterer fully accepts the fact that his rage is out of his control. The battering behavior in phase one is usually measured as he metes it out. The battering incident in phase two may start out with the man justifying his behavior to himself; however, it ends with him not understanding what happened. The batterer's rage is so great that it blinds him to his behavior. He usually starts out wanting to teach the woman a lesson, not wanting to inflict any particular injury on her. He stops when he feels she has learned her lesson. By this time, however, she generally has been physically abused. When batterers describe acute battering incidents they concentrate on justifying their behavior. Often they recite lots of petty annoyances that occurred during phase one. Sometimes, if they are alcoholics, they blame their drinking. The trigger for moving into phase two is rarely the battered woman's behavior; rather, it is usually an external event or the internal state of the man.

The battered woman occasionally does provoke a phase two incident. When this occurs, the couple usually has been involved in battering behavior over a period of time. The woman often senses the period of inevitability is very close and cannot tolerate her terror or anxiety. She knows the third phase of calm will follow the acute battering incident. She would prefer to get the second phase over with than to continue to dread its certain occurrence, so she provokes the batterer into an explosion. She then has control over when and why the incident occurs, rather than being totally at his mercy. The battered woman often does not realize she is provoking the incident, although some women do. An example of the latter is a woman who wanted to go to a family party with her husband in a pleasant mood. She knew an acute battering incident was about to occur, so she deliberately provoked an explosion during the week so that by the weekend her husband would be pleasant for the party. She was not being masochistic in inviting this beating. The pain of her bashing was simply less noxious than her reward, which was a loving husband to present to her family. Many women report the same kind of relief once phase two is completed.

This second phase is briefer than the first and third phases. It usually lasts from 2 to 24 hours, although some women have reported steady abuse for a week or more. From the battered women's reports of past events leading up to a battering, it has been virtually impossible to predict the extent of the violence or discover incidents that might lead to violence in the future.

The high incidence of police fatalities when intervening during an acute battering incident (Straus, 1976) attests to the difficulty of interrupting phase two. It is important to acknowledge the self-propelling nature of this phase when helpers attempt to intervene. Those advocating police training programs on how to deal with battered women often fail to understand the tenacity of the batterer's behavior during an acute incident. Police are taught to counsel the victim and the batterer and then leave the couple alone. The counseling techniques might be useful during other phases of the battering cycle but not during phase two violence. Most battered women report that acute battering increases after the police leave. A recent study in Kansas City found that over 80% of all non-stranger homicides had had unsuccessful police intervention several times prior to the murder. Further research specifically dealing with wife abuse is under way.[1]

Police usually are called during phase two, if they are called at all. The battered women interviewed in the Denver sample (Walker, 1977, 1976a, 1976b), typically did not ask for police intervention. Fewer than 10% had direct experience with the police. Of those who did have contact with the police, most felt the police could stop the assault only temporarily. The women frequently did not ask for police help again, as they felt things got worse after police contact. A recent study by the U.S. Commission on Civil Rights confirmed these findings.[2]

The available information describing acute battering incidents comes from battered women. The batterers seldom provide their versions, and other people rarely are around to observe the battering incidents. Gelles (1974) has suggested that, in fact, the presence of another person drastically alters the nature of violence in a couple. The few batterers interviewed have been unable to describe much about what happened to them during this second phase. According to reports from battered women, only the batterer can end the second phase. Their only option is to find a safe place to hide from him. Why he stops the assault also is unclear. Perhaps he becomes exhausted and emotionally depleted. Battered women describe acute battering incidents that have no grounding in reason. It is not uncommon for the batterer to wake the woman out of a deep sleep to begin his assault. If she answers his verbal harangue, he becomes even angrier with what she says. If she remains quiet, her withdrawal enrages him. She gets the beating no matter what her response is. The woman's screaming and moaning may excite him futher, as may her attempts at self-defense. Many women have their arms twisted and broken when they raise them to ward off blows. Severe injuries also occur if they fall or are pushed against objects in the room. The violence has an element of overkill; i.e., the man cannot stop even if the woman is severely injured.

Battered women describe each acute battering incident in minute detail and with considerable objectivity. Many of the women report not feeling their injuries while they are being inflicted. They describe concentrating on getting it over quickly with as little damage as possible. They allow themselves to feel their rage at this time and sometimes fight back. Although they may be severely beaten by the time phase two is over, most women are grateful for its end. They consider themselves lucky that it was not worse, no matter how serious their injuries. They often attempt to deny the seriousness of their injuries by refusing to seek immediate medical treatment. Sometimes this is done to appease the batterer and make certain phase two really is finished and not just temporarily halted.

PHASE THREE

The ending of phase two and movement into the third phase of the battering cycle is welcomed by both parties. Just as brutality is associated with phase two, the third phase is characterized by extremely loving, kind, and contrite behavior from the batterer. He knows he has gone too far and tries to make it up to her. It is during the third phase of the cycle that the battered women's victimization becomes complete.

This phase of the battering cycle immediately follows the second and is characterized by calm. The tension that built up in phase one and was released in phase two is gone. It is in this third phase that the batterer consistently behaves in a charming and loving manner. He is usually sorry for what he has done in phase one and phase two and generally acknowledges his contriteness to the battered woman. He begs her forgiveness and promises her that he will never do it again. His behavior is described as typical of a little boy who has done something wrong; i.e., he confesses when caught in the act and then cries for forgiveness. The batterer believes he never again will hurt the woman he loves. Since he is somewhat aware that she really did not deserve his violence, the batterer believes he can control himself. He manages to convince all concerned that this time he means it; he will give up drinking, dating other women, visiting his mother, or whatever else affects his internal anxiety state. His sincerity is believable.

The battered woman wants to believe that she will no longer have to suffer abuse. His reasonableness supports her belief that he really can change, as does his loving behavior during this phase. She convinces herself that he can do what he says he wants to do. It is during phase three that the woman gets a glimpse of her original dream of how wonderful love is. This is her reinforcement for staying in the relationship. The traditional notion that two people who love each other will overcome all kinds of odds against them prevails. The battered woman chooses to believe that the behavior she sees during phase three signifies what her man is really like. She identifies the "good man" with the man she loves. After all, he is now everything she ever wanted in a man. He is seen as strong and dependable, as well as loving.

Since almost all of the rewards of being married or coupled occur during phase three for the battered woman, this is when it is the most difficult for her to make a decision to end the relationship. It is also the time during which helpers usually see her. When she resists leaving the relationship and pleads that she really loves him, she bases her reference to the current loving, phase three behavior rather than the more painful phase one and two. She hopes that if the other two cycles can be eliminated, the battering behavior will cease, and her idealized relationship will remain. If she has been through several cycles previously, the notion that she has traded her psychological and physical safety for this temporary dream state adds to her own self-hatred and embarrassment. Her self-image withers as she copes with the awareness that she is selling herself for the few moments of phase three loving. She becomes an accomplice to her own battering.

The length of time that this phase lasts is not yet known. It seems that it is longer than phase two but shorter than phase one. Neither is there any distinct end to this phase. Most women report that before they know, the calm, loving behavior gives way to little battering incidents again. The phase one tension building occurs, and a new cycle of battering behavior begins.

It is at the beginning of this phase, immediately following the acute battering incident, that we have been most likely to make contact with battered women. This is when they are most likely to flee or seek out safety. My research project allowed me to meet several battered women immediately after hospitalization for severe physical injuries received during the acute battering incident. The change in women I visited daily in the hospital was dramatic as they progressed from the end of phase two into phase three of the battering cycle. They all went from being lonely, angry, frightened, and hurting women to feeling happy, confident, and loved within a few days. Initially, they were realistic in assessing their situation. They accepted their inability to control the batterer's behavior. They were experiencing their anger and terror, which helped motivate them to consider making important changes in their situation.

Each of these women was convincing in her desire to stop being a victim until the batterer arrived. I would know when he had made contact with her by the profusion of flowers, candy, cards, and other gifts in her room. By the second day the telephone calls or visits intensified, as did his pleas to be forgiven and promises never to do it again. Usually he engaged others in this fierce battle to hold on to her. His mother, father, sisters, brothers, aunts, uncles, friends, and anyone else he could commandeer would call and plead his case to her. They all worked on her guilt. They told her she was his only hope, and without her he would be destroyed. They questioned what would happen to the children if she took their father away from them. Never mind that the role model a batterer and a battered woman sets for them is emotionally crippling. Although everyone acknowledged his fault in the battering, she was being held responsible if he were punished. Since most battered women seem to hold traditional values about love and marriage, they are easy prey for such guilt trips about breaking up a happy home—even if it's not such a happy one. Marriage is forever, she is told, and she believes it.

He's sick and needs help, is another message, the implication being that if she stays with him, he'll somehow get help. During the intense persuasion everyone really believes all these statements. The truth is, however, his chances of seeking help are minimal if she stays with him. It seems that the most successful motivation for a batterer to seek help is for the woman to leave him. He thinks therapy will help him get her back.

Other battered women often recount similar stories to those of the hospitalized women. Their reward for accepting the abusive violence is the period of calm and kindness. For some women, though, it is not all glowing. One woman said she dreaded this phase because her man attempted to make her feel better by buying extravagant gifts they could not afford. If she tried to return the gifts, he rapidly became abusive again. If she kept them, she worried about how they would pay for them. Inevitably, she had to work harder to earn more money or face repossession proceedings. Thus, she had no calm respite—she was being battered during phase three also.

SPECIFIC TREATMENT ALTERNATIVES

INTERDEPENDENCE

In designing treatment alternatives for battered women, stopping the battering is the immediate concern, but the long-term expected outcome is economic and psychological interdependence. To be interdependent means to be capable of either independent or dependent behavior within a relationship as appropriate. Each person in the relationship can provide strength (independence) which the other can lean upon (dependence); while, at the same time, the person who is independent can depend upon the other for certain needs.

Most people value independence without accepting the fact that dependence is also mentally healthy, providing there is respect and trust in the relationship. A mutuality exists within the relationship that relies upon flexibility rather than fixed roles. If the man is unemployed, it is acceptable to depend upon the woman's salary. If the woman, or the man, chooses to keep house and depend upon the spouse's salary, that also is acceptable. Although the term inter-dependence usually is used in the context of emotional feelings, it also can apply to economic status. In an interdependent relationship, the woman needs a skill that enables her to be economically independent at any time. She must be capable of standing alone and meeting her needs economically as well as emotionally. She must be free to choose to enter a relationship, rather than believing it is her only alternative.

Most relationships that involve battered women are not interdependent on both emotional and economic levels. The woman becomes the victim because of her extreme dependence upon the batterer. She does not believe that she can be a totally independent person.

Interestingly enough, neither does the batterer believe he can stand alone. A bond seems to exist between the couple that says, "We may not make it together, but alone we'll surely perish." Both typically are traditionalists, who fear the religious, social, emotional, and economic ramifications of divorce. Death is a more acceptable alternative. It is essential to understand this conviction when working with the troubled couple. The woman sees death as the only way out of her situation, either the batterer's death or her own. The batterer similarly would rather die or kill her than voluntarily leave. The dilemma that this causes is enormous, as the best treatment alternative for the battered woman is to get out of the battering relationship. To end her victimization, she must leave and never return. Other treatment alternatives which will be discussed here may eventually be useful over a period of time. *At the present time, however, the most effective alternative for the battered woman is to end her relationship with the batterer.*

The three major issues involved in the design of treatment alternatives for battered women are safety, the criminal justice system, and psychotherapy.

SAFETY

The treatment alternatives that deal with battered women's needs for safety span most of society's public and private institutions. They touch upon the need for safe hiding places for battered women and their children, a fair law enforcement and criminal justice system, emergency medical services, responsive social service departments, job protection, vocational training/education for women and children, and a community support system that provides physical and psychological assistance. Awareness of the need to provide for battered women's safety has been growing in this country and Europe. Expanding alternatives represent a beginning of social awareness that battered women have been victimized by an indifferent society as well as by their men.

REFUGES, SAFEHOUSES, AND SHELTERS: THE ENGLISH MODEL

Safehouses, refuges, shelters, and other hiding places have been the cornerstone of treatment alternatives for battered women. Erin Pizzey founded the first known refuge in England in 1971. She established Chiswick Women's Aid[3] as a meeting place for women who wanted to talk. The house was donated by the local housing council. Almost immediately women who were being beaten and could not return home came for safety and refuge (Pizzey, 1974). The need for such places of refuge evidently is extraordinary as every refuge that has opened in England, Wales, Ireland, and Scotland, and then throughout Europe and the United States, immediately has overflowed capacity. Chiswick Women's Aid has grown from one house to a network of more than 25 houses.

Other refuges developed simultaneously throughout the British Isles. Although they all used Chiswick as their model, many modifications were made. Almost all the English refuges are now coordinated through the National Women's Aid Federation[4], a central agency supported by government and local funds. By September 1976, 98 different groups were operating 75 refuges. Although two national groups compete for funds in Britain, all refuges cooperate in helping a battered woman find appropriate assistance. Refuges or similar facilities also exist in the Netherlands, West Germany, France, and the United States, but none has developed an extensive network like the English one.

All refuges or safehouses provide some assistance, even if it is only a safe place to sleep. Other services may include medical help and rehousing. In England, nationalized medical service provides assistance for those women and children who need physical attention; however, psychotherapy is not as routinely available in England as it is in the United States. The usual stay in an English refuge is six to 12 months; however the housing shortage in England may force battered women and their children to remain in the refuge for longer than they would need to otherwise. It takes from six months to over a year to get women rehoused by local housing councils. If a woman is from another council's jurisdiction, rehousing may take several years. Newly arrived women thus have the benefit of assistance from women who have been in refuge for different lengths of time.

Most of the differences between refuge models are in the degree of community that is established amongst members. The major issue for most safehouses and refuges is deciding how much independence or responsibility to demand from battered women upon their arrival.

Chiswick was founded on a total therapeutic community model. Women there are initially housed in a crisis-oriented receiving center. The telephone number and address of the refuge are widely known. An open door policy exists; no battered woman or child is ever turned away. This policy results in chaotic, overcrowded conditions but undoubtedly saves lives. Irate batterers have arrived only to be scared away by the large number of people in the refuge.

When a battered woman arrives at Chiswick, she is greeted by a reception group of staff and members of the house. She is given some personal belongings if she has brought none and is allocated a bed and a place to store her things in a dormitory-style room. If she has children, she is given the option of having others in the house share the responsibility of caring for them. Because refuges have little money, self-help is a necessity. All meals, chores, and finances are the responsibility of the collective group. Independence is encouraged by slowly assuming responsibility for oneself and others in a sheltered and protective environment.

Once in this safe atmosphere, the women begin to determine their own needs. Women learn that they can trust others to help them and that they can be successful in helping others. The environment has all the elements necessary to foster the development of interdependence. Critics of this approach stress that just because the philosophy is hypothetically sound, there is no reason to believe that the presence of these elements will indeed meet the long-term goals of battered women. At best, they say, it provides short-term safety; at worst, it encourages further dependence, as the battered women are not forced to accept power over their own lives.

Women are encouraged to leave the crisis house for one of the second-stage houses as soon as possible. Second-stage houses also are managed communally, but every woman is expected to share equally in the process. These houses are located throughout London, its suburbs, and in several other cities. The largest, a former hotel, houses 80 women and children; while smaller ones have an average capacity of around 20. Battered women and their children are eligible to receive financial support under the social security system and may remain in the house until they are ready to leave. They either must provide their own new housing, or they must wait their turn on the housing council list. Some women chose to continue to live indefinitely in this communal style. For these women, a third-stage housing arrangement has been established. Here there is less mobility, and residents have more of a sense of permanence.

Other refuges established in England as well as in this country do not accept the Chiswick model for total communal living. They support a greater degree of independence, both initially and throughout the battered woman's stay. These other refuges are smaller than Chiswick, with 12 to 20 women and children the usual size. Camden refuge, a member of the National Women's Aid Federation, does not encourage community responsibility for children, finances, or meals. Each woman has her own closet in the kitchen to store food which she purchases out of her own social security allowance. At Camden, it is considered important to encourage independence in food shopping, meal preparation, and budget control. Women are encouraged to learn from one another, but this is not done systematically. A paid house mother is hired to help the process along.

Swindon refuge encourages independence immediately by insisting that women learn how to cope with the bureaucracy by applying for their own social security benefits. The local committee sets up strict house rules which all women are expected to follow. These rules include required house maintenance chores and regulation of visitors, especially men. Other refuge support groups have left house management strictly up to the women residents. In one group, the members exercised their decision-making rights by voting to withhold their rent payments to the refuge. This put the support committee in a dilemma. They had a group of battered women who were independent enough to challenge authority, but they also were faced with having to close the house if they could not get their rent. For further descriptions of various British refuge groups, see a narrative summary prepared by Fields and Kirchner (1976); Pizzey's (1974) and Martin's (1976) books; Flax, Walker, and Schreiber's (1976) presentation to the American Psychological Association; and

Stafford's (1976) presentation to the American Sociological Association.

AMERICAN REFUGES

The development of refuges, or safehouses, as they are beginning to be called in the United States, is in its infancy compared to the progress in England. Women's groups around the country have provided temporary safehousing for battered women on an informal basis. National Organization of Women (N.O.W.) chapter headquarters, women's resource centers, and feminist bookstores have been the most reliable sources for locating individual homes where battered women and their children could seek temporary shelter and safety. Untold numbers of battered women have sought safety in motel rooms or friends' and family's homes. Some of these groups and other local groups have provided counseling for battered women and their families. New programs are developing, some under the Victim/Witness Assistance program funded by the Law Enforcement Assistance Agency (LEAA). Safehouses are now available in many major metropolitan areas.

The importance of the safehouse movement is that it provides a sense of community and a support system for battered women. As soon as they walk through the door they are no longer helpless victims. They learn that they do have power over their own lives, that other people care enough about them to take risks to help them, and that society's institutions can be of assistance. This support is felt no matter what the organizational structure of the refuge. Through modeling techniques, battered women learn to try different life-styles that other women have adopted. They learn by watching the staff and other members. Battered women typically have been isolated from other people. The sharing of commonalities and differences among themselves helps offset their deprivation. They experience the benefits of being able to make the system work and eventually learn how to do it themselves. They learn better parenting skills through direct staff intervention or by contact with others who have different discipline techniques or ways of demonstrating their love for their children. They must learn to think, act, and love themselves yet still have some dependence upon group support. Women who remain in safehouses until they feel comfortable rarely engage in another battering relationship. About 50%

of women who stay longer than one week in a safehouse will not return to live with their batterers. Personal observation indicates that the percentage rises dramatically if the safehouse remains open to women who return home and then want to come back to the refuge. This may occur three or four times before the battered woman is able to leave permanently. These women may need to experience the inevitability of the battering cycle several times before they accept their inability to control it.

LIMITATIONS OF SAFEHOUSES

There are some definite limitations to the refuge or safehouse concept. First, it provides an artificial sense of community that does not exist outside of itself. Many women cannot cope with the real world unless they have such a support system. Time has not allowed the development of such a natural support network, although some groups have begun the process; e.g., Women's Advocates in St. Paul, Minnesota; Rainbow Retreat in Phoenix, Arizona; and Bradley Angle House in Portland, Oregon. Many groups that have not been able to afford to operate safehouses have concentrated on strengthening potential support systems within the community. These natural support systems will be discussed further.

Another drawback to safehouses is their limited potential for educational or vocational training. Some houses have made arrangements with local schools or job training programs, but most have their hands full coping with basic physical and emotional needs. Although women from many different social, cultural, educational, and economic levels use the safehouses, unless they have job skills before they enter, they probably will not be self-supporting when they leave. Without the potential for economic independence these women will be at the mercy of the state or another man.

The children of battered women provide still another problem in safehouses. Women who turn to refuge most often have adolescent children who have begun protecting their mother from the batterer's violence. The second most likely time for a battered woman to leave is when there are several children under the age of five. Most of these children have lived under stress and fear for long periods before being taken from their homes to a strange place where they must relate to many strange people. They have learned to expect and accept violence, even if they themselves have never been the direct target of the abuse. Many children show evidence of emotional disturbance because of their violent homes. Some also have serious learning problems. While refuges have attempted to provide care for infants, preschoolers, and school-age children, it is not enough. The withdrawn children are usually overlooked. Space is a problem for younger children who need a place to run and play. Other children, especially the adolescents, engage in various acting-out behaviors that make communal living in cramped quarters a horror. They often destroy the few meager furnishings. Adolescent boys can be as violent as their fathers and often find willing younger versions of their mothers in the adolescent girls. The theory that an abusing family begets a new generation of abusers is painfully witnessed in these houses. Much time, energy, and money are spent trying to reverse the trends and prevent these children from perpetuating violence.

Crowding is another problem in safehouses. Refuges are filled with so many people that the noise level is often deafening. There is no privacy and not much room for individuality. Most houses are in physical disrepair due to overuse. Washing machines, if they exist, are often broken, as are other appliances which simply cannot stand the wear they are given. More critically, disease is widespread. Colds, stomach ailments, and other contagious diseases run rampant through houses where sick members cannot be isolated. Finances make it impossible to staff the houses with doctors and nurses, so professionals must donate their time. As dismal as this picture may sound, it is crucial to understand that both here and in England women have chosen to live in a safehouse rather than return to a quiet, clean, spacious, disease-free home with a batterer in it.

A further limitation to the safehouse or refuge movement is the lack of facilities for men. The batterer is left alone unless he comes after his woman. He then may be turned over to law enforcement authorities. If the batterer simply would cease his erring ways after his victim leaves home, this would not be a concern to those interested in helping women. But, this is not the case. It is more likely that he either will become psychotic, seriously depressed; or, even worse, he will find another woman to batter. It is unfortunate that most of these men do not get any treatment, as it is they who create the victims. In several refuges, however, batterers have been involved in treatment. Rainbow Retreat in Phoenix states that 60% of the men participate in group, family, or individual therapy.

Chiswick has set up a house where the men can live or come for group meetings. Although neither refuge reports the same kind of excitement and success with men as they do with women, the initial steps have been taken.

Safehouses are expensive and difficult to operate. Staff turnover is high, as they are typically underpaid and overworked. Most refuges give the staff several days off per month to rejuvenate. Funding is a constant problem. Support groups become tired, and they change frequently. All refuge members become saddened when a former member or child is killed, an event that happens far too often. They assume guilt, feeling if only they had done better, she might have stayed. The battered woman is most apt to remain in safety if she has suffered through several battering cycles, accepts the inevitability of further violence, and is prevented from having contact with the batterer in the calm, loving phase three cycle. All of the difficulties in operating the safehouse disappear when a battered woman shakes off her victim mantle. These successes make the many problems seem surmountable.

OTHER SOURCES OF SAFETY

There are also many natural support systems within the community that can provide a measure of safety for battered women.

Hospital Emergency Rooms. Hospital emergency rooms commonly treat battered women who have suffered physical trauma. As would be expected, the staff in most hospital emergency rooms sees battered women immediately following the phase two acute battering incident and as they move into the loving behavior of phase three. Without knowledge of the phase one tension building behavior, the staff members see only a small part of the cycle. Most emergency rooms are staffed by doctors who rotate every six weeks. Typically, they do not have time to question the origin of injuries, even if they are suspicious. Nurses have the most continuity with repeat patients and are most likely to spot battered women, especially after some awareness training. If a nurse suspects battering, the woman's chart should be tagged to alert other staff members. Suspicious cases should be treated in a specific manner. First, the woman should be examined and interviewed alone. She should be asked directly if her injuries were the result of a beating. Once she is confronted directly, it is difficult for her to conceal battering unless she is terrified. Whether or not she admits to being abused, she should be given the telephone numbers of the nearest helping agency, preferably one specifically dealing with victimization of women. I have known battered women who have kept such a telephone number hidden for six or more months before they used it. If she does admit to being battered, all the details of the incident should be entered on her chart. Her own words should be used whenever possible. Descriptive behavior rather than impressions or interpretations should be noted. This may be valuable legal evidence.

Whenever possible, a battered woman should be admitted to the hospital. She usually is physically and emotionally exhausted, and hospitalization can hasten her healing process. It also provides a safe refuge temporarily. During hospitalization, both the battered woman and the batterer are forced to deal with the serious consequences of the violence. If they prefer to deny and minimize her injuries, hospitalization helps prevent them from doing so. The battered woman has time to think and decide on a course of action without the batterer's attempts at loving contrition. Although most women return to their homes after hospital treatment, for many it is the first step to independence.

Private Physicians and Clinics. Private physicians and clinics see a smaller number of battered women following a phase two explosion. Many women report being too ashamed or frightened to confide in a family doctor; they prefer the anonymity of large hospital emergency rooms. Private physicians generally see battered women during the tension building first phase of the battering cycle. As the tension causes anxiety, women request medication to help them feel calmer, to sleep, to relieve backaches and other stress symptoms. Many battered women are considered hypochondriacs because they visit their doctors so often; yet, they have few other sources of professional assistance. It is less of a risk to see the doctor for physical complaints than for psychological ones. Hilberman (1977) reports a group of rural battered women who sought services from the comprehensive health clinic without their batterer's knowledge at great risk to themselves. They received supportive counseling and medication to relieve stress symptoms and facilitate sleep.

Many battered women come to the attention of medical personnel during pregnancy. They usually seek routine obstetrical care which provides some continuity with a clinic or medical staff. For yet unexplained reasons, the batterer usually either becomes more physically abusive to the woman during pregnancy, or he stops all battering behavior. The escalated violence often takes the form of prenatal child abuse with repeated blows to the woman's protruding stomach. Sometimes abortion results. Sexual mutilation is also more frequent when a battered woman is pregnant. If the batterer's pattern is to cease his abusiveness, the woman may choose to become pregnant frequently to prevent violence. Unfortunately, the presence of infants or young children seems to increase the batterer's jealousy of their time demands on the woman. Obstetricians and nurses may be able to provide preventive assistance to battered women before an acute battering incident occurs by documenting details in her records.

Company Medical and Counseling Departments. Company medical and counseling departments are another natural community resource that can help provide safety and help for battered women. Many batterers are well known to their wive's coworkers. Such a man may hang around the woman's office without much reason, usually not making much trouble for her until near the final stages of phase one behavior. The battered woman sometimes will seek counseling or medical help through her company so that the batterer does not know she has done so. Lack of sleep and anxiety often hamper her efficiency. If she can get sent home on sick pay, she often uses the time to try to reduce the tensions that have been building. Often a battered woman stays absent for several days following an acute battering incident. If she has been injured, she waits until makeup can cover the bruises. She often sees the company physician to check for broken bones, especially broken ribs, for which she can put off treatment about four days until the pain worsens.

Some large companies have programs for battered women employees. For example, one company physician has studied the battered women syndrome. This doctor will place such a woman on disability if her medical condition warrants it and will suggest referral sources for psychotherapy. The woman can remain on disability with full pay and all medical expenses covered until her psychologist feels she is ready to return to her job. This type of program assures battered women job protection while giving them time to cope with their crises, including the option of going into hiding for a short period of time.

Social Service Departments. Social service departments also can provide immediate safety for battered women. One method would be to declare battered women a class of citizens who need immediate financial support. This action would make all women, regardless of income level, eligible for temporary social service assistance. The money enables the battered woman to seek new living quarters if she wishes to leave home. Some states will grant a double rent payment to the battered woman if she is on public assistance and already has paid rent in the marital residence on the first of the month and needs to seek safety elsewhere later in the month. States could be reimbursed for such assistance under Title XX of the Social Security Act. Battered women thus would not need to feel financially trapped in their relationships.

Social service departments also can encourage welfare workers to detect and report instances of battering among their clients. Many social workers report that they knew their clients were being beaten, but they did not know what to do about it. They should be required to document details in their case records and make appropriate professional referrals.

Social service departments or state health departments are usually the designated state agencies to gather statistics on epidemiological matters such as incidence of venereal disease and child abuse. It is suggested that they also be required to keep anonymous statistical data on incidence of battered women. Privileged communication status could be granted to those required to report suspected cases to protect them from legal liability. The risk of requiring names is too great at this time. A bill being drafted in Colorado would require the state social service agency to provide protection for battered women. Similar legislation is being proposed in other states.

Other natural support systems that can provide safety for battered women exist in communities. The potential for religious leaders to help is not yet known. Legal assistance will be discussed in the following section.

THE CRIMINAL JUSTICE SYSTEM

Any discussion of safety for battered women must include the criminal justice system. The police and the courts are not protecting this class of assault victims adequately. In New York City, a class action suit has been filed on behalf of 12 battered women against the New York City Police Department, the Probation Officers, and

Clerks of the Court. The suit requests a declaratory judgment which would force the defendants to perform their duties adequately to protect the battered women.[5] The major issue in this case is the provision of temporary restraining orders upon request and need.

Inadequate protection for battered women is not unique to New York City. Battered women everywhere do not receive protection under the law. Married battered women do not even have the benefit of the law in most states. A thorough review of the law on this subject can be found in Martin (1976). A recent Denver study citing violation of the civil rights of battered women has been released by the U.S. Commission on Civil Rights. The major issues for battered women in the criminal justice system are prompt police protection, rights of arrest, equalization in obtaining and enforcing restraining orders, and the legal ramifications of fault divorces.

POLICE PROTECTION

Police protection[6] is considered inadequate not only by battered women but also by batterers and the police themselves. Recent FBI statistics (Martin, 1976) indicate that answering domestic violence calls can be duty of the most hazardous sort for police. Police are called most frequently during the phase two acute battering incident. Experience has proved that intervention during this explosive phase will be most successful if it separates the man and woman. It is necessary to prevent the man from committing further violence and to provide safety for the woman. The most effective intervention by police would be to treat the domestic violence call as an assault and to arrest the batterer. Furthermore, the police should sign the complaint. The state, represented by the police, then is responsible for pressing charges, not the battered woman. It is unrealistic to expect the victim to sign a complaint and press charges when she is given no protection from further assault. Most police officers will lose interest in protecting the battered woman if she repeatedly drops charges. They interpret her reluctance as a desire to remain battered, rather than fear of the consequences of pressing charges.

In treating battering as an assault case, police should include both married and unmarried relationships. Police need the further right to request a temporary restraining order, as they may in many states in child abuse cases. Finally, police should be given responsibility for enforcing restraining orders. The issuing court should send copies of the order to the local law enforcement agency, rather than requiring the victim to show the order to the police. In areas where police and LEAA programs interact, battered women usually receive more protection because police have better training, and more referral sources are available. Although police may log in their domestic violence calls, the data are largely irretrievable. Such data should be available to document the scope of the battered women problem.

RESTRAINING ORDERS

Restraining orders are the legal profession's second most potent technique in dealing with offenders, arrest and prosecution being the first. Each state has its own method for obtaining such an order. A temporary restraining order usually is issued first. It becomes permanent unless the assailant shows cause why it should not. The judge, in effect, orders the batterer to stop his assault and to stay away from the battered woman's home. If the couple is not married and does not own joint property, the order is issued quite simply upon evidence of violence. If the couple is married, however, judges are reluctant in most states and forbidden by law in others to enjoin a married man from using his property. Unless divorce petitions are filed, most married women have extraordinary trouble getting a temporary restraining order. Some attorneys do not find restraining orders particularly useful, as they feel the batterer will not obey them. Disobeying a restraining order usually results in a contempt citation and an arrest order. The inequities and hardships experienced by battered women in obtaining such relief need legislative attention.

LEGAL RIGHTS IN DIVORCE ACTIONS

Legal rights in divorce actions also need to be considered. Many states still provide for fault divorces using desertion as grounds. Battered women who leave their husbands to seek safety must be exempted from a potential desertion charge. Documentation from any of the previously mentioned support groups or individual attorneys is needed. Battered women also need to know their rights in any potential divorce action. Many women are ignorant of property distribution and child custody laws. Legal Aid services across the country are providing excellent legal defense for some

battered women. Private attorneys need to follow suit. Psychotherapists and other helpers also need to be familiar with local laws so
they can better assist their clients.

PSYCHOTHERAPY MODALITIES

In a country such as the United States where there is a kind of
reverence for the practice of psychotherapy, it is not surprising that
battered women have sought the services of psychotherapists. As is
true of other helpers, psychotherapists, including psychiatrists,
psychologists, social workers, and psychiatric nurses, have been
inadequate in helping battered women. These women report that
most therapists refuse, directly or indirectly (usually by omission), to
deal specifically with acute battering incidents. They concentrate
instead on the psychological consequences presented. It is to be
expected that women who have been abused repeatedly have enough
psychological symptoms to keep a therapist busy. Many psychotherapists interviewed have admitted not realizing that their client
was being brutally beaten over long periods of time.

Battered women have related stories of being treated as though
they engaged in "crazy" behavior. Many have been institutionalized
involuntarily. In some cases, they were given so many shock
treatments that their memories were impaired permanently. These
women were diagnosed as paranoid, evidenced by their suspicious-
ness and lack of trust of people they feared might say the wrong
thing to their batterers. In a paranoid way, they concealed their
actions, wrote and stashed away secret messages on tiny pieces of
paper, and they constantly worried about manipulating other
people's behavior so as not to upset the batterer. Others were treated
for serious depression, which no doubt served to protect them from
the constant level of stress in their unpredictable lives. For too many,
their justified and perhaps motivating anger was mellowed by
indiscriminate use of tranquilizers.

Many battered women's coping techniques, learned to protect
themselves from further harm, have been viewed as evidence of
severe intrapsychic personality disorders. My pilot research project
(Walker, 1976a, 1977) has yielded data indicating that battered
women suffer from situationally imposed emotional problems due to
their victimization. They do not choose to be battered because of

some personality deficit but develop behavioral disturbances because of the battering. A proposal for further systematic research into battered women's personality has been submitted to the National Institute of Mental Health (Walker, 1976b).

Psychotherapy generally has emphasized the value of keeping families intact whenever possible. In dealing with battered women, however, breaking apart the family should be encouraged whenever possible. The major difficulty is that most battered women want the therapist to stop the batterers from abusing them, but they do not want to break up the relationship. Psychotherapy modalities that strengthen the battered woman's successful coping strategies while helping her overcome her powerlessness have proved effective. Supportive psychotherapy during the separation and divorce period has proved successful. Rarely do women who have received such therapy get involved in another battering relationship. Although the kinds of psychotherapy modalities vary in technique and scope, the goals remain constant. Current behavior is the focus, although exploring the past is sometimes helpful in interpreting present problems. It is important to clarify the ambivalent feelings of the battered woman. They center around issues of love/hate, anger/passivity, rage/terror, depression/anxiety, staying/leaving, omnipotence/impotence, security/panic, and others. A combination of behavioral, insight-oriented, feminist therapy has proved the most effective therapeutic approach. Although the different therapeutic modalities are numerous, those with the best reported success with battered women to date are crisis intervention, individual psychotherapy, group psychotherapy, and couples therapy.

CRISIS INTERVENTION

Crisis intervention techniques are often very appropriate for intensive therapy after an acute battering incident. Battered women or the batterer individually are concerned enough about their lack of control to want to understand and change their behavior. Crisis therapy usually focuses on a specific critical incident. The goal is to teach the client how to resolve possible future crises by applying conflict resolution techniques to the present one while motivation is very high. In using crisis therapy with battered women, it is important to label the women battered. The use of denial is a typical coping mechanism that prevents them from considering action. The women and men should be seen individually unless, in the judgment of the therapist, there is little likelihood of further battering. The therapist should not expect much trust initially. Battered women are similar to rape victims in that they respond more easily to a female therapist who is trained to understand the effects of such victimization. It is important to help the battered woman follow through whenever possible but also to understand and accept her ambivalence about making positive changes in her life. Although some battered women are ready to utilize crisis therapy, most need more time.

INDIVIDUAL PSYCHOTHERAPY

Most women who seek a therapist do so during the first phase of the battering cycle. They recognize the rising tension and feel the inevitability of the forthcoming battering. They usually believe that if they could rid themselves of provocative behavior, their batterers would become model phase three men. They ask the therapist to teach them new techniques to cope with the battering behavior. The battered women who seek therapy often do so at great personal risk. Most do not dare tell their men they are in therapy initially, although they eventually do. They sometimes assume another name to preserve anonymity, and invent excuses to account for their movements during the therapy sessions.

The battered woman who comes to the therapist during phase one is usually trying to cope with her feelings of guilt, anxiety, and anger. Ther therapist can help her express her guilt by having her recount the details of battering incidents in which she could not stop her own battering. A feminist therapy approach, which tries to separate the woman's personal issues from common issues shared by other victimized women, may be effective. It is necessary to confirm society's lack of adequate help for her but also to be encouraging about the potential for change. Control of anxiety may be accomplished through relaxation training, hypnosis, or recommending that the battered woman join a health club to focus on positive body feelings. It also is important to help the battered woman recognize and control her anger. She should be encouraged to experience anger each time it occurs, rather than suppressing it and releasing it all at once, perhaps triggering an acute battering incident.

The realities of present alternatives and future goal planning are explored in individual therapy. The battered woman needs to recognize concrete steps she can take to improve her situation. If her goal is to remain with the batterer, even temporarily, then therapeutic goals toward strengthening her independence within the relationship become important. Career goals need to be explored. Reinforcing the positives in the battered woman's life, using successive approximations from minimum to maximum independence, is important. Individual therapy concentrates on the present but may use the past to promote understanding of the current situation. The therapy is more action oriented than analytic, as unstructured psychoanalysis is too risky. As therapy progresses, other adjunctive therapies can be recommended, e.g., assertiveness training, parent education, vocational counseling, and couples therapy.

GROUP PSYCHOTHERAPY

Group psychotherapy is another therapy format for battered women. It has some benefits over individual therapy. Battered women are usually isolated and rarely meet other battered women. They have few friends in whom they can confide. A group composed of all battered women can be an extremely therapeutic experience. Such a group combines the best of the consciousness raising groups with the expertise of a therapist who is familiar with group process. A number of agencies are conducting women's groups for victims. One of the most successful programs is in Seattle.[7] Two women psychotherapists, Karil Klingbeil and Vicki Boyd, who previously were responsible for rape victim services, began a group for battered women. These women were identified either in a predominantly lower income hospital or in a mostly middle income Health Maintenance Organization. The group of 12 women and two highly skilled therapists meet weekly. The women derive a sense of strength from all of the group members that is difficult to provide on an individual basis. Therapy is action oriented with a focus on moving toward changing behavior. Most of the women have been seriously physically battered when they first come to the group. The therapists take an aggressive role in encouraging women to prosecute when appropriate. They already have established an advocates division to help the women victims use the criminal justice system. This is necessary to help them overcome the immobilization that their terror brings. As women witness others successfully making changes, they are more likely to try themselves. There is often a risk factor for therapists who lead these groups. Some batterers have unleashed their rage on the therapists. The Seattle group was held at knifepoint for several hours before being released. Another group had a car driven through its front door. Other terrorizing threats have been reported.

COUPLES THERAPY

Couples therapy is the therapeutic technique that most psycho-therapists, other helpers, and battered women count on to make everything better. Battered women feel that if they can get their men to participate in therapy, then they will stop their abusive behavior. This assumption is not necessarily true. Very few traditional couples therapy techniques apply to battering couples, unless the therapist wants to spend time teaching these couples how to fight better. Nonfighting techniques need to be stressed instead. Most couples in a battering relationship have extremely poor communication skills. Their relationship has unusually strong dependency bonds that need to be broken. It is therefore more important to work with the two individuals in the relationship, rather than deal with the relationship itself. Ultimately, the goal is interdependence.

Recognizing the need for new treatment techniques for couples therapy, Mort Flax, a psychologist, and I developed a procedure that has been successful in limiting the severity of battering incidents, although it has not eliminated them altogether (Flax, 1977; Flax and Walker, forthcoming; Walker and Flax, 1977). The procedure is based on the cycle theory of battering and utilizes a communication training approach developed by Weiss, Hops, and Patterson (1973).

No game playing concerning the reasons the couple is in therapy is allowed. The man is labeled a batterer; the woman, a battered woman. Male and female cotherapists work with the batterer and the battered woman, respectively. Initially the men and women work separately, and the couple lives apart. After a short period, they are allowed to move back together, and they begin joint therapy sessions. The issues discussed deal with strengthening each individual so the relationship becomes free of all coercion. The couple learns how to ask for what they want from one another without being limited by often erroneous assumptions. They are taught to recognize their own behavior patterns in their unique battering cycle so they can become aware of the danger points. Contingency reinforcement management procedures are employed, as are individual reinforcers for battering-free time periods. Natural reinforcers are strengthened. Therapy time is spent strengthening the positives and dissecting the negatives to prevent explosions in the future. Behavior rehearsals and role playing on videotapes often are used.

Although problems exist with this type of therapy, couples benefit. They attend regularly, and life is better for them. The women do not work as rapidly toward independence as they do in individual or group therapy, but they lose the pervasive terror that immobilized them, and they learn to express anger more constructively. The men learn to be more assertive, too, asking directly for what they want without having to threaten a woman if they are not satisfied. As difficult as it is, couples therapy is a workable treatment alternative for battered women and their partners.

CONCLUSIONS

Battered women have been identified and offered therapeutic alternative choices only recently. The modalities discussed are only a beginning. The goal is to promote interdependence so that psychological and physical battering behavior ceases. The most effective means to reach this goal is for the couple to separate. Other treatment alternatives provide some relief. Women who are battered are victims. As these women learn that being battered is no longer necessary, they will demand and receive services from treatment alternatives.

NOTES

1. A copy of the report on the Domestic Violence Research Project is available from Dr. Jeanie K. Meyer, Operations Resource Unit, Kansas City Police Department, 830 Argyle Building, 306 East 12th Street, Kansas City, MO 64106.

2. This study is available from the U.S. Commission on Civil Rights, Women's Rights Division, Washington, D.C. 20425. They have also produced a documentary movie based on this research study.

3. Chiswick Women's Aid, 369 Chiswick High Road, London, W4, England.

4. National Women's Aid Federation, 51 Chalcot Road, London, NW1, England.

5. A copy of the complaint is available from Marjory D. Fields, Managing Attorney – Matrimonial Unit, Brooklyn Legal Aid Services, 152 Court Street, Brooklyn, N.Y. 11201.

6. The term police may be synonymous with a local law enforcement agency.

7. More information is available from Karil Klingbeil, M.S.W., Social Service Director, Harborview Medical Center, 325 Ninth Avenue, Seattle, WA 98104, and Vicki Boyd, Ph.D., Psychologist, Group Health Collective, Seattle, WA.

REFERENCES

BROWNMILLER, S. (1975). Against our will: Men, women and rape. New York: Simon and Schuster.

FIELDS, M.D., and KIRCHNER, R.M. (1976). "Summary of English and Scottish shelters." Unpublished paper.

FLAX, M.L. (1977). "Couples therapy with battered women and their partners." Paper presented at the Colorado Women's College Conference on Battered Women, Denver, March 31.

FLAX, M.L. and WALKER, L.E. (forthcoming). "Conjoint marital therapy with battered wives and their spouses."

FLAX, M.L., WALKER, L.E., and SCHREIBER, K.J. (1976). "The battered women syndrome." Symposium presented at the American Psychological Association Convention, Washington, D.C., September 3.

GAYFORD, J.J. (1975). "Wife-battering: A preliminary survey of 100 cases." British Medical Journal, I (January): 194-197.

GELLES, R.J. (1974). The violent home: A study of physical aggression between husbands and wives. Beverly Hills, Calif. Sage.

HILBERMAN, E. (1977). "Sixty battered women: A preliminary survey." Paper presented at American Psychiatric Association Convention, Toronto, May 5.

MARTIN, D. (1976). Battered wives. San Francisco, Calif.: Glide.

PIZZEY, E. (1974). Scream quietly or the neighbors will hear. England: Penguin.

Select Committee of Parliament (1975). Report on violence in marriage, Session 1974-1975, Vol. I and Vol. II. Her Majesty's Stationery Office, 49 High Holburn, London WC1V, England.

STAFFORD, J. (1976). "Battered women and the National Women's Aid Federation." Paper presented at the American Sociological Association Conference, New York.

STRAUS, M.A. (1976). "Sexual inequality, cultural norms and wife-beating." In J.R. Chapman and M. Gates (eds.) Women into wives: The legal and economic impact of marriage. Sage Yearbooks in Women's Policy Studies, Vol. 2. Beverly Hills, Calif.: Sage.

WALKER, L.E. (n.d.). Battered women. New York: Harper & Row (in preparation).

——— Battered women and learned helplessness (in preparation).

——— (1977). "Who are the battered women? Frontiers: A Journal of Women's Studies, (May).

——— (1976a). "Battered women: Hypothesis and theory building." Presented at American Psychological Association Conference, Washington, D.C., (September).

——— (1976b). "Battered women syndrome study." Grant Application submitted to National Institute of Mental Health.

WALKER, L.E., and FLAX, M.L. (1977). "Psychotherapy with battered women and their partners." Presented at the Conference on Violent Crimes Against Women, University of Washington, Seattle, May 2.

WALKER, L.E., FLAX, M.F., FIELDS, M.J., and LEIDIG, M.W. (1977). "The battered women syndrome revisited." Symposium presented at the American Psychological Convention, San Francisco, August 29.

WEISS, R.L., HOPS, H., and PATTERSON, G.R. (1973). A framework for conceptualizing marital conflict, a technology for altering it, and some data for evaluating it. In L.A. Hamedynak, L.C. Hanty, and E.J. Mash (eds.), Behavior change: Methodology, Concepts and Practices. Champaign, Ill.: Research.

7

THE PROSTITUTE AS VICTIM

JENNIFER JAMES

Prostitution is often referred to as a "victimless crime" or a "crime without a complainant." These terms are used to characterize crimes, such as vagrancy, gambling, pornography, and prostitution, in which typically none of the involved citizens files a complaint with the police. Because the prostitute and her customer are involved in a mutually agreed upon relationship, neither party feels any need for the services or interference of the authorities—in contrast to the relationship between a burglar and his home-owner victim, in which the latter is quite clearly an involuntary participant in the interaction. Those who refer to the prostitute as a victim do so in a nonlegal sense. She is seen as a victim because of her life-style, her "immorality," or "degradation," or the presumption that she is exploited by pimps or others.

Many of those who view prostitutes as the victims of prostitution base their judgments on assumptions about the individual psychology—or pathology—of prostitutes. As Stein (1974:21-22) said about her attitude at the beginning of her study of call girls,

> I kept looking for signs that the women were really miserable or neurotic or self-destructive. I wanted them to be that way. I think I wanted call girls to be "sick" because I believed that anybody—at least any woman—who sold sexual access ought to be sick.

The plethora of myths about prostitutes, prostitution, and the effects of prostitution on its practitioners is an inevitable result of prostitution's illegality. Prostitutes are labeled as criminals, forced to lead undercover lives that are far removed from and inaccessible to "respectable" members of society. Aside from the customers (men who usually are far more interested in their own immediate needs and desires than in investigating the life-style of the prostitute, who may have a considerable psychological investment in maintaining their fantasies about prostitutes, and who, in any case, are unlikely to broadcast widely their experiences since they are committing an illegal act by patronizing a prostitute) the only other members of "respectable" society who ordinarily have contact with prostitutes are police officers and other members of the criminal justice system. In other words, police and jail records have been until recently our only source of "hard data" on prostitutes and prostitution. This is certainly a limited source of information, and one that raises an interesting possibility. Rather than being the victims of prostitution itself, prostitutes may be the victims of the laws against prostitution and the ways in which they are enforced.

DISCRIMINATORY LAW ENFORCEMENT

Violations of the prostitution statutes account for approximately 30% of most women's jail populations. Convicted prostitutes serve long jail sentences compared to other misdemeanants such as shoplifters or those involved in larceny or assault. The judicial attitude represented by these sentencing patterns has no justification when considered in reference to the traditional legal concerns of danger to person or property loss. Nor does the large number of women arrested for prostitution (33,306 in 1975, according to the Uniform Crime Reports of 1976) indicate the commitment of the criminal justice system to an effective, realistic campaign to eliminate prostitution. Each act of prostitution, after all, requires at least two participants: a seller *and* a buyer. Despite this incontrovertible fact, the arrest rate for customers is only two for every eight prostitutes arrested (Uniform Crime Reports, 1976). It has been estimated by Kinsey and others (1953) that about 20% of the male population has some contact with prostitutes. There are obviously many more customers than prostitutes, and yet the prostitutes seem to bear virtually the entire weight of legal reprisals. Since the prostitution laws in almost every state are neutral on their face, holding the prostitute and the customer equally culpable, the figures prove that prostitutes are the victims of discriminatory law enforcement.

CLASS DISCRIMINATION

The traditional justification for discriminatory enforcement of prostitution laws was stated by Davis (1937:752):

> The professional prostitute being a social outcast may be periodically punished without disturbing the usual course of society; no one misses her while she is serving out her term—no one, at least, about whom society has any concern. The man [customer], however, is something more than a partner in an immoral act; he discharges important social and business relations. . . . He cannot be imprisoned without deranging society.

This argument assumes a class difference between prostitutes and their customers: customers are middle- or upper-class "pillars of society"; prostitutes are lower class "lumpenproletariat." While we may doubt that law enforcement should discriminate on the basis of class, the characterization of customers as middle class implied by Davis is accurate: most customers are middle class, married, white, professionals, or businessmen who live in the suburbs. The class of prostitutes, however, is not as easily categorized. For example, in one study (James, 1976a)[1] including 136 streetwalkers, 64% of the subjects reported their childhood family's income as middle or upper class. It is social mobility, as effected by societal application of the "deviant" label, that makes the common assumption of "prostitute = lower class" near absolute in fact. As Davis further stated, "The harlot's return is not primarily a reward for abstinence, labor, or rent. It is primarily a reward for loss of social standing." Benjamin and Masters (1964:93) also noted that "The economic rewards of prostitution are normally far greater than those of most other female occupations" in large part because the prostitute is paid not only for providing a service but also for incurring a loss of social status. The statistics on prostitutes' class standing as measured by income, education, and so on, are not at issue here. We are merely pointing out that, by "working the streets" as a prostitute, a woman becomes defined by the larger society as "lower class" and thus gains all of the liabilities pertaining to that social status. No parallel social process exists to label customers as deviant, and their higher-class status is therefore not affected by their illegal participation in prostitution.

The accepted status of customers, as opposed to that accorded to prostitutes, tends to protect these men from the possibility of involvement in the criminal justice system. Judging by the arrest statistics, the majority of customers seem to be either invisible to the police or else above the law. The latter is, of course, more likely, especially since "Agencies of social control do not operate with impunity; they must protect themselves from public reprisal and antipathy" (Kirk, 1972:24). Any attempt to routinely arrest, process, and label a large proportion of a politically powerful class (middle-class white males, in this case) can lead only to "organizational strain and trouble" (Chambliss, 1969:21). Harassment and labeling of social outcasts, on the other hand, has always been considered a reasonable way to gain public approval and support. It has been reported that 70% of the women who are now inmates in American prisons were initially arrested for prostitution, indicating the possible importance of prostitution law enforcement as a labeling device and of the jail experience as an introduction to other crime:

> The adolescent girl who is labeled a sex offender for promiscuity . . . may initially experience a conflict about her identity. Intimate association with sophisticated deviants [in jail] , however, may provide an incentive to learn the hustler role . . . and thus resolve the status anxiety by gaining prestige through association with deviants, and later, experimentation in the deviant role. [Davis, 1971:305]

Finally, in considering the possible class differential between prostitutes and their customers it must be remembered that women in this society traditionally have no class standing of their own: they are considered to belong to the class of their closest male associate (father, brother, husband, or lover). The illegal, "deviant" status of prostitution means that the circle of those with whom a prostitute can form close associations is arbitrarily limited to a very small number of men, virtually all of whom are, or are considered to be, lower class. (This point will be amplified later in this chapter when we discuss the relationship between prostitutes and pimps.)

NATURE OF LAWS

A second justification for discriminatory enforcement of prostitution laws is implicit in the nature of the laws themselves. The control of overt prostitution is achieved in the United States through two main types of laws, those against loitering with the intent to commit an act of prostitution and offering or agreeing to an act of prostitution. The most common enforcement procedures involve the use of police officers as decoys. The officer behaves as he assumes a customer would behave and, when approached by a suspected prostitute, elicits evidence of intent. The prostitute is arrested if she mentions money and sexual service in her verbal exchange with the officer. These arrest techniques frequently involve the officer in the possibility of entrapment and questionable sexual exchanges. Some jurisdictions use civilian agents who complete acts of sexual intercourse before the arrest is made. These agents view themselves as protecting society by committing immoral acts for moral reasons. The use of female agents to solicit and arrest customers is rare because it requires a violation of appropriate behavior for women and an "unfair" use of female sexuality to entrap men. In most states, customers are rarely, if ever, arrested. A woman who has once been convicted of offering/agreeing, regardless of the circumstances, is subject to future arrests under loitering statutes as a "known prostitute." (A "known prostitute" is a woman who has been convicted of an act of prostitution within the past year.) If she is seen in the area "known to be inhabited by prostitutes" she may also be arrested for loitering. Loitering laws are frequently used by enforcement agencies to control individuals labeled as deviants.

It obviously is easier to arrest prostitutes—at least, street-walkers[2]—than to arrest their customers. The location of the streetwalker's place of business in itself makes her an obvious target. Men may walk the streets freely wherever and whenever they wish; a woman downtown late at night with a male escort is ipso facto suspect. George R. Cole (1972:97) reports that a police expert, in delineating for police officers the "subjects who should be subjected to field interrogations," included "unescorted women or young girls in public places, particularly at night in such places as cafes, bars, bus and train depots, or street corners." Unescorted men or young boys in public places were not included in this list of suspect persons. Moreover, it is considered acceptable behavior for men to initiate conversations—including conversations with overt or covert sexual content—with female passers-by. This last point leads us to a discussion of *why* prostitutes have been made the victims of discriminatory law enforcement, aside from the argument of what is most convenient for the police.

CUSTOMERS

In this society, there are some behaviors which are considered acceptable for men but not for women, e.g., standing on a street corner alone at night or soliciting sexual conversations with strangers. Prostitutes are women who are simultaneously rewarded and punished for choosing to earn their living through patterns of behavior that are unacceptable for members of their sex. In other words, prostitutes are the victims of sex-role stereotyping. The sexual needs of customers are loosely defined as normal, except for those of a small percentage of "freaks" or perverts. In fact, the customers of prostitutes and their activities as such have enjoyed a long tradition of "normality." Even during periods when intensive official attempts to end the business of prostitution were underway— see descriptions by Anderson (1974) of Chicago, 1910-1915, and by Holmes (1972) of nationwide efforts at about the same time— customers' needs were accepted as "inevitable." At most, the men were chided for risking venereal disease and implored to practice self-control. Today, men who purchase the services of prostitutes are still considered normal (nondeviant), even though their actions may be seen as unpalatable, or even immoral, according to the personal standards of the observer. Customers of prostitutes are, of course, acting outside the law, but where the law and the accepted male sex role come into conflict, the norms of sexual role playing overshadow the power of the law to label deviance. Men are expected to have a wide variety of sexual needs and to actively seek fulfillment of those needs. As part of that search, men are allowed to illegally purchase the sexual services of women with relative impunity, as arrest statistics demonstrate.

A review of the acceptability of men's reasons for visiting prostitutes can be couched only as an impression of common attitudes. Having quantity in sexual partners has long been a praised accomplishment for men in many social groups. Although some restraint may be considered important after marriage, the attitude clearly is that a man who has been with many women has positive status. The epithet of the "Don Juan" or "stud" does not carry the connotation that "whore" or "promiscuous" does for women. The male "need" for sexual variety, a common subject in the commercial media and in sexual-joking behavior, and the desire for sex without emotional involvement are both frequently expressed as common, acceptable male sexual behavior, while they are both strongly rejected for women. Men with these desires and "needs," as well as traveling salesmen, convention attenders, participants in stag parties, and so forth, are all considered "natural" customers of prostitutes. The provision of sexual services to males by women is, in contrast, clearly labeled deviant. Males break few social rules in patronizing a prostitute; females break almost all the rules in becoming prostitutes. Streetwalkers, in particular, place themselves at the wrong end of the whore-madonna spectrum: they accept money for sex, they are promiscuous, they are not in love with their customers, they are not subtle, and they engage in "abnormal" or deviant sex acts—acts which "respectable" women are not expected to accept (e.g., anal intercourse). As mentioned earlier, even the streetwalker's place of business is a violation of her sex role.

Most importantly, however, the independent, promiscuous, overt sexuality of the prostitute challenges the traditional assumption that female sexuality is entirely dependent upon, and awakened only by, male sexuality. As Davis (1937) stated, "Women are either part of the family system, or they are prostitutes, members of a caste set apart." Unregulated sexuality is accepted from males; from females, however, whose sexual stability is the sine qua non of our family concept, ultrafamilial sex threatens the basic structures of society. So threatening is the idea of female sexual independence, that we have laws defining juvenile women who engage in sexual intercourse without official permission as deviants "in danger of falling into habits of vice." Because women and their sexuality are tied so closely to the family structure—that is, to a long-term relationship based on a complexity of economic, emotional, and sexual expectations dictated by law and custom—sexual interactions between male and female social equals are commonly more or less channeled and controlled by these social expectations. Prostitutes are not considered to be the social equals of their customers, however. As we have seen, customers are primarily middle or upper class, and prostitutes are considered to be lower class. Customers do not usually see prostitutes as being potential members of that section of womanhood to whom they may have to relate according to the prescribed roles of the family system, and they are therefore able to interact with prostitutes in a much freer way. Gagnon and Simon (1973:230) stated that,

Since many of the organizing constraints on sexual activity are related to maintenance of the family and its future, the contact with the prostitute is significant, because it allows sexual expression without such controls on behavior.

It is true, of course, that the female sex role followed by nondeviant, nonprostitute women also consists in large part of barter transactions.

Non-deviant male and female expectations concerning how women use [their] sexuality, and the exploitation of sexuality to achieve gain otherwise unavailable all add up to a routine exchange of sexual favors for pay. . . . The distinction between prostitution and the mundane characteristics of the female sex role simply are not as distinct as one might hope [Rosenblum, 1975:182]

The point we are making here is that the less overtly pragmatic sexual transactions a man enters into with a nonprostitute are likely to involve or lead to a variety of consequences which may be legally, "morally," or emotionally binding. Moreover, the variety of sexual services a man can obtain from a nondeviant woman is likely to be smaller than that possible with a prostitute; and once a man enters into a long-term relationship with a woman, he has in a sense recognized her as his social equal and thus must "pay" more (e.g., a house, a car, clothes, and so on) for the same sexual service.

When the effects of sex-role stereotyping are taken into account, we can see that the perceived difference in class between the prostitute and her customers has a larger function than simply protecting the latter from social and legal labeling. One aspect of this function, for example, is that "many a client [customer] is sexually neutral or impotent with his wife and erotic or potent with a woman he can safely degrade—usually a prostitute" (Esselstyn, 1968:130). This supposed inferiority of the prostitute may be a matter of her presumed lower-class status alone, or it may include recognition of her "deviant" label: some men desire the excitement of sexual relations in an illegal, or "I'm OK, you're deviant," situation (James, 1976b).

More importantly, however, the perceived interclass nature of prostitution is an expression of the middle-class man's need for liberation from the sex-role stereotyping of his class. The accepted range of male sexual behavior in our society is considerably wider than the accepted behavior conventions of the middle class—and especially of middle-class women. Women defined as lower class, then, and particularly those who have been "set apart" by the label "deviant," must serve as substitutes for the middle-class women so firmly restricted by their class-related sex-role proscriptions. Prostitution allows men "to regress to an 'Id' state of complete freedom from all restraints of civilization and acculturation" (Winick and Kinsie, 1971:97), to move briefly in to the deviant subculture, secure in their class-guaranteed ability to return to 'normality.' " As noted by Gagnon and Simon (1973:231),

> The frequency of contacts with prostitutes by males at conventions and in other situations that are separated from the home suggests the loosening of social controls that are [sic] necessary for such contacts to take place.

The more highly restricted female sex role contains almost none of the sexual motivations and behaviors allowed to the male; nor does it allow a woman to serve as a professional accompanyist for those men who would rent her participation in sexual activities. Rather than stating, then, that a prostitute is a deviant human being and a prostitute's customer is a normal human being, it is actually more exact—and more telling—to say that a prostitute is a deviant *woman* and her customer is a normal *man.*

The puritan aspect of middle-class society means that the full acting out of the male sex role by middle-class males requires the existence of prostitution. As a result, the male need for purchased female sexual service is, and long has been, accepted as "inevitable" and therefore not to be punished. To have laws against prostitution almost seems to imply that some aspects of the male sex role itself are intolerable—or at least dangerously at odds with the conventions of middle-class society. Women are daily jailed, stigmatized, and exiled from "decent" society for thier ability to recognize and deal with this conflict between male sexual needs and male social ideals.

ECONOMIC DISCRIMINATION

Far from being limited to the traditionally "private" sector of sexual behaviors, sex-role stereotyping has a pervasive influence in many public aspects of our society, including the economic system. Money-making options are still quite limited for women, especially for un- or low-skilled women. Recognition of this basic sex inequality in our economic structure helps us understand prostitution as an occupational choice for some women, rather than as a symptom of the immorality or deviance of individuals. There is evidence that some women, in choosing the occupation of prostitution, are reacting to their victimization by this sex-based economic inequality. Pomeroy (1965:175), for example, studied 175 prostitutes, up to 93% of whom were motivated by economic factors; he noted that "the gross income from prostitution is usually larger than could be expected from any other type of unskilled labor." Benjamin and Masters (1964:93) were also aware of this sex-based economic differential and its relationship to prostitution: "The economic rewards of prostitution are normally far greater than those of most other female occupations." According to Esselstyn (1968:129), "women are attracted to prostitution in contemporary America because the income is high and because it affords an opportunity to earn more, buy more, and live better than would be possible by any other plausible alternative." Davis (1937:750) summed up the economic pull of prostitution: "Purely from the angle of economic return, the hard question is not why so many women become prostitutes, but why so few of them do."

Some researchers claim to find an abnormal, perhaps even neurotic, materialism among prostitutes. Jackman et al. (1967:138), for example, state that:

> The rationalization by prostitutes violating social taboos against commercial sex behavior takes the form of exaggerating other values, particularly those of financial success, and for some the unselfish assumption of the financial burden of people dependent upon them.

However, as Greenwald (1970:200) more accurately points out,

> Economic factors helped to mold the entire society, the family structure, and therefore the very personalities of these girls [call girls] . . . the girls were caught up in the worship of material success.

In what way is the economic motivation of these women different from that of men who strive to attain a position on the executive level so that they can afford "the good life" and support the people dependent upon them? The majority of Americans, it would seem, share the desire for financial success. Prostitutes are women who, usually with good cause, see prostitution as their only means for moving from a three- to six-thousand-a-year income to the gracious living possible with $50,000 a year. It is important to note that this view of prostitutes contradicts the traditional stereotype of prostitutes as wretched creatures forced into prostitution by extreme economic deprivation. In one recent study of 136 streetwalkers (James, 1976a), 8.4% of the subjects claimed to have started prostitution because of economic necessity, while 56.5% were motivated by a desire for money and material goods—a desire which, due to sex-based economic discrimination, they saw no way to fulfill other than by prostitution. A typical comment by a streetwalker in that study referred to "the excitement of buying whatever you wanted without asking anybody . . . of having big sums of money that you never had before." Once accustomed to a higher income, as another subject of that study noted, "It would be pretty hard to go back to less money."

A person's choice of occupation is not limited solely by external realities. One's self-image plays an important part in one's perception of possible alternatives. If a man believes himself to have a "poor head for math," he will probably not be able to visualize himself attaining great success as a physicist. Women as a whole suffer from an especially narrow self-image in terms of occupational choices because of sex-role stereotyping. Traditionally, women's roles have been those of wife and mother, both of which are exclusively biological and service roles. The emphasis on service carries over into the definition of "new" traditional women's roles, such as teaching children, serving food or drink, and secretarial work. The importance of physical appearance in many of these occupations reinforces women's self-image as physical/biological objects, limited to the confines of their sex-role stereotype at work as well as at home. As Rosenblum (1975:169) argues, "Prostitution utilizes the same attributes characteristic of the female sex role, and uses those attributes towards the same ends. . . ." In other words, prostitution is a very natural extension of the female sex role into the occupational arena.

Some researchers (e.g., Esselstyn, 1968) believe that certain occupations lead women easily into prostitution. These occupations are those that adhere most closely to the traditional female service role, often emphasizing physical appearance as well as service. Clinard (1959:228) comments that "Quasi-prostituting experiences, such as those of a waitress who, after hours, accepts favors from customers in return for sexual intercourse, may lead to prostitution." It is not unusual for a woman who is required by her employer to flirt with customers and "be sexy" to find that the men with whom she must interact in business transactions relate to her as a sexual object or potential sex partner. Once she has been cast in this role of sex object, she may decide to make the best of a negative situation by accepting the "favors"—or the money—men are eager to give her for playing out the implications of the role. Again, these low-status service occupations are among the few occupational alternatives available to un- or low-skilled women.

INDEPENDENCE AND EXCITEMENT

Another possibility excluded by the traditional female sex role is financial independence. In a sense, then, a financially independent woman is a "deviant" woman. These roles are beginning to shift and broaden now, but there are still virtually no occupations available to un- or low-skilled women which allow the independence or provide the adventure of prostitution. Rosenblum (1975:177) states that the "specific precipitating factors" which cause women to choose prostitution as a profession "can be identified simply as independence and money." Data from the recent study (James, 1976a) mentioned earlier, support the assertion that independence is highly valued by many of the women who choose prostitution. When asked "Why did you leave home?" the largest category of responses by the subjects in that study was "desire for independence," and the second largest category was "dispute with family," which may also imply a desire for independence from the strictures of family life. Another question in that study, "What are the advantages of being a prostitute?", also revealed the value that independence has for these women. Although the economic motivation overwhelmed all other categories in the first responses, in the second responses, independence had first place. The search for an independent life-style can lead a young woman into a situation in which she sees prostitution as her only alternative: "It [her entrance into prostitution] was actually caused because I ran away [when I was] too young to get a job. So I either had the alternative to go back home or to prostitute. So there was no way I was going to go back home, and so I turned out [became a prostitute]." Davis (1971), Benjamin and Masters (1964), and Esselstyn (1968) also specifically mention independence as a motivating factor in the choice of prostitution.

For many women, the "fast life" of prostitution represents more than simply economic independence unobtainable within the conventions of the "straight" world's female sex role. The life-style of the prostitution subculture has itself proved attractive to a large number of women over the years. "Fondness for dancing and restaurant life" and the "tendency to vagabondage" comprise over one fourth of the "immediate causes of prostitution" listed by Kemp (1936:190). In tabulating "the factors in becoming prostitutes" of three groups of prostitutes, Pomeroy (1965:184) found 3% to 19% influenced by their perception of prostitution as "an easy life," 12 to 24 percent by the "fun and excitement" they found in the "fast life," and 14 to 38 percent by the fact that prostitution enabled them to meet "interesting people." Gray, in a study examining "why particular women enter prostitution" (1973:401), reported that "many of the respondents . . . felt intrigued by the description [by prostitutes] of prostitution which appeared exciting and glamorous . . . the initial attraction for the girls in this study was social as well as material" (pp. 410-411). Benjamin and Masters (1964:107) state that the life-style inherent in identification with the prostitution subculture continues to be a strong attraction after women have committed themselves to the profession: "There is an abundance of evidence that on the conscious level it is the *excitement* of the prostitute's life, more than any other single factor, which works to frustrate rehabilitation efforts." These excerpts from interviews with street-walkers (from James, 1976a) illustrate some of the attractions of prostitution: "The glamour side . . . being able to be in with the in crowd . . . you really feel kind of good because you meet people who say, I wish I was like you—have diamond rings, a pocketful of money, and go out and drink"; "To see if I can get away with it before I get caught: a game, like"; "You don't have certain hours you have to work. You can go to work when you want, leave when you want . . . you don't have a boss hanging over you, you're independent"; "It's really kind of fun . . . it's a challenge."

The preceding discussion provides a substantial explanation of why some women choose prostitution rather than the economic dependence of the traditional wife's occupational role—as defined by the female sex-role—even when both options are available to them. Neither marriage nor extralegal monogamy provides or allows for the economic independence, the excitement, the adventure, or the social life available through prostitution. The basic fact of sexual objectification (exchanging sexual services for financial support) may be the same in either case, but, for many women, prostitution has benefits that outweigh the privileges—and limitations—of "respectable" women's roles. Winick and Kinsie (1971:75) refer to a rehabilitation program for prostitutes in Japan in the 1950s that included such traditional women's activities as arts and crafts and homemaking. The program failed, they report, because the prostitutes were simply not interested. As Greenwald discovered (1970:202), most prostitutes feel "overt hatred of routine, confining jobs." The traditional female occupations, including that of housewife, can be seen as among the most "routine, confining jobs" in this society, and thus present limited temptation to women who value the relative freedom of the "fast life." To sum up this section of our discussion: prostitution is one way for women to reject their victimization by our sex-biased economic system by choosing an independent and exciting, albeit "deviant," occupational lifestyle.

PIMPS

Thus far we have examined prostitutes as the victims of discriminatory law enforcement, sex-role stereotyping, and economic discrimination. Now we will take a look at prostitutes as victims of those who are traditionally assumed to be their primary oppressors: pimps. A common myth in this society pictures prostitutes as defeated women cowering under the coercion of brutal pimps. Kemp (1936:214), for example, stated that "in many cases friendship with a pimp may be considered the immediate cause of a woman's becoming a harlot. It is the man who leads her on." However, "friendship" and "leading on" are not necessarily coercive, and Kemp earlier (p. 190) stated that the influence of a pimp was the "immediate cause of prostitution" for only 8.3% of prostitutes. Gray (1973:412) found that the influence of pimps, when it was a factor, "was generally minimal." Data from the James (1976a) study showed a somewhat larger role for pimps in recruiting women for prostitution. It should be noted, however, that the influence of "girlfriends" was more than equal to the influence of pimps, that more than twice as many women reported choosing prostitution solely on their own initiative, and that our field experience leads us to agree with Gray that the pressure applied by pimps in recruiting women is generally minimal. One woman described her entrance into prostitution this way: "The only reason I got started was because of my old man's suggestion, because otherwise I don't think—maybe I would have, later. I liked the money; it was easy money."

Women in this society are socialized to feel they need a man to take care of them, to "take care of business," to "complete" them, to love them, to make a home with them; this is part of the traditional female sex role. Prostitutes are no exception to this rule. "Well, everybody wants a man," said one streetwalker. "You can get lonesome," explained another; "even though they laugh and say, if you're with that many men how can you get lonesome. But believe it or not, it's just like getting up at 8 o'clock in the morning, going to work, and coming home at 5 o'clock in the evening; it's just something you do to survive and that's it. There's no feelings involved." For many of these women, a relationship with a pimp means "just knowing that you have somebody there all the time, not just for protection, just someone you can go to." Because of their involvement in a deviant life-style, however, prostitutes must share their lives with men who understand the dynamics and values of their deviant subculture—men who will accept their violations of the traditional female sex role. Any man who lives with a prostitute will be called a pimp, although usually the only factors that distinguish a prostitute-pimp relationship from that of a "normal" marriage relationship, aside from the illegality of both roles, are the woman's status as sole "breadwinner" and, often, the man's overt maintenance of two or more similar relationships simultaneously. It has become obvious that physical male abuse of females in marital relationships is common. As is true throughout society, women's socialized need for men is reinforced by the fact that a woman's status is determined by that of her man. A prostitute who can achieve a relationship with a "high class" pimp raises her standing in the subculture of prostitution. This rise in status pays important dividends in her interactions with other members of the subculture: "If you have a pimp, other guys on the street, they kind of leave you alone." Thus, confounding the scenario of the coercive pimp, one can often find prostitutes actively seeking to attach themselves to those pimps whose patronage they feel will be most beneficial.

Of course, not all prostitute-pimp relationships are desirable models of human social interaction. Some pimps are physically abusive, just as some husbands are. Perhaps prostitutes who experience abuse from their pimps are in a better position than nonworking wives with abusive husbands, in that prostitutes are financially more independent. On the other hand, prostitutes—whether they are married to their pimps or not—are likely to be taken less seriously by authorities, such as police, to whom they turn for help. This lack of respect and concern on the part of law enforcement personnel towards prostitutes also prevents prostitutes from seeking legal help when they are abused or assaulted by customers, which is not an uncommon occurrence. Faced with the attitude that she was "asking for it," or at least "had it coming to her," a prostitute who reports abuse from a customer or her pimp to the police is liable to feel more victimized by the discrimination of the legal system than by the violence of individual men (James, 1973).

REVIEW OF THEORIES

There is yet another way of looking at prostitutes as victims. Rather than seeing them as simply victims of prostitution itself and of societal reactions to prostitution, one can ask whether prostitutes are women with histories of victim experience that influenced them in their choice of occupation and life-style. We have seen that prostitution is an aspect of, not a contradiction to, the female sex role as it exists in this society; and yet the choice to prostitute is obviously heavily loaded with negative valuations, according to the judgment of the majority culture. What, then, determines which individual women will act out the prostitution components of the female sex role? What factors enable certain women to accept the deviant status conferred upon them by their choice of prostitution? Scores of researchers, theorists, and moralists have published their opinions on what is "wrong" with prostitutes, individually and as a class. At the end of the last century, for example, Lombroso (1898) cited physiological abnormalities and deficiencies as the cause of all female crime, including prostitution. Another researcher (Kemp, 1936), as late as 1936, stated that "from 30 to 50 percent of all prostitutes must be classed as feeble-minded." More recently, these discredited theories have been replaced by psychological evaluations of prostitutes, which are more "modern" sounding, if not necessarily more valid. "Latent homosexuality" has been seen as a main spring of prostitute motivation by some (e.g., Greenwald, 1970; Maerov, 1965; Hollender, 1961). Since homosexuality, like prostitution, is popularly considered deviance, the temptation to put all the "bad eggs" in one theoretical basket is perhaps understandable. There are no hard data, however, linking homosexuality, whether latent or overt, with female prostitution. Some researchers believe many prostitutes have an oedipal fixation. Winick and Kinsie (1971:83), for example, see prostitution as atonement for guilt produced by incestuous fantasies. This theory is impossible to disprove, since we cannot accurately measure the incidence of incestuous fantasies. On the other hand, it is impossible to prove their theory, or to prove that it applies more to prostitution than to other occupations. "Money is heavily loaded with all kinds of psychological conflicts. In our civilization, among many other things . . . it symbolizes the will to power and the ensuing unconscious guilt of having taken the father's place," Choisy states (1961:1). Perhaps every women, prostitute and business executive alike, who desires economic independence is acting out oedipal fantasies. It seems unlikely, however, that many women are motivated solely or primarily by such a tenuous subconscious factor in making their occupational choice. Again, the literature provides virtually no hard data to justify including this theory among the significant prostitute motivating factors.

The myth that women become prostitutes because they are "oversexed" has been countered by the discovery that most prostitutes see their sexual activities with customers as purely business and usually get no sexual pleasure from them. Unfortunately, an opposite myth also exists: that of "the invariably frigid prostitute" (Maerov, 1965:692). Responding to this myth, Pomeroy (1965:183) reports that the 175 prostitutes he studied "were more sexually responsive in their personal lives than were women who were not prostitutes." As noted earlier, emphasis on physical appearance is an important aspect of the female sex role. "Movies, television, popular literature and, particularly, advertising make it seem that the cardinal sin a woman can commit is to be unattractive" (Greenwald, 1970:201). Some researchers believe, with Greenwald, that prostitutes are motivated by the need to prove their attractiveness through sexual contact with many men. Taking the theory a step further, Winick and Kinsie (1971:35) state that

> many prostitutes apprehended by the police tend to be overweight and short. They often have poor teeth, minor blemishes, untidy hair, and are otherwise careless about their personal appearance. Docility and indiffer-

ence are common. This leads one to conclude that such women may feel inadequate to compete in more traditional activities and thus more readily accept a vocation that involves the sale of something they may not value highly.

Winick and Kinsie do not seem to consider the fact that a large percentage of the prostitutes apprehended by the police are "hypes"—drug addicts working as prostitutes to support their habit—who form a special, lower class in the hierarchy of the "fast life." In any case, since it is demonstrably true that the majority of "unattractive" women do not become prostitutes, and since it is a matter of personal opinion what percentage of prostitutes is "unattractive," the importance of the Winick and Kinsie statement quoted above lies in its assumption that women's "traditional activities" are those which emphasize physical appearance. This assumption is very pervasive throughout society and is a major influence for women in the development of self-image—and self-image is always a factor in the individual's choice of occupation. Perhaps we could find women who became prostitutes because their "attractiveness" rating was not high enough for them to gain employment as receptionists or cocktail waitresses. On the other hand, prostitutes generally make more money than waitresses or receptionists, regardless of physical appearance, and the economic motivation may be statistically far more important than the psychological one presented by Greenwald and Winick and Kinsie. The last of these common psychological theories about prostitutes pictures them using their profession to act out their hostility toward men. Looking at this objectively, it would seem equally valid, except for the illegality of prostitution, to suggest that some women become elementary schoolteachers in order to act out their hostility toward children. Perhaps this motivation is real for some women, both teachers and prostitutes, but documentation is scarce.

Moving on from theories based on psychological evaluation, we will now consider some theories based on hard data about prostitute's lives—data obtained from prostitutes themselves. The James (1976) study and a few other recent studies indicate that the factors which enable some women to accept the deviant status inherent in prostitution can be tentatively identified as exposure to the prostitution life-style, certain patterns in child/parent relationships, and perhaps patterns of negative sexual experiences that lead to the development of a self-concept including a high degree of sexual self-objectification. The last two of these three factors can be seen as evidence that prostitutes are women with histories of victimization.

CHILD/PARENT RELATIONSHIPS

Parental abuse or neglect is widely considered a typical childhood experience of women who become prostitutes. Kemp (1936), Choisy (1961), Maerov (1965), Jackman et al. (1967), Esselstyn (1968), Greenwald (1970), Davis (1971), and Gray (1973) all mention unsatisfactory relationships with parents as a fact of life for these women. Whether the condition is simple neglect-by-absence or outright physical or psychological abuse, the result is generally considered to be alienation of the child from the parents and a consequent inability—greater or lesser, depending upon the circumstances—of the child to adequately socialize the conventional mores of "respectable" society. Data from the James (1976) study seem to reaffirm the prevalence of parental abuse/neglect experience among prostitutes. The mean age at which the women in that study left home permanently was 16.25 years. As previously mentioned, "dispute with family" was one of the major reasons given by these women for leaving home, and physical and emotional abuse also was a significant factor in separating many of them from their families. Of the 136 prostitutes in the James study, 65.4% had lived apart from their families for some period prior to moving out permanently, and 70.4% reported the absence from the family of one or more parents—most often the father—during the subject's childhood. Neglect, rather than abuse, was the pattern for the majority of James' subjects, although abuse was reported by a significant number. Some typical comments about relations with parents were: "We had a lack of communication problem, me and my parents, for a long time. I didn't even know how to approach them. I was scared to talk to them, because every time I did something wrong, they'd yell at me." "My mom didn't let us go out with boys. We were at home and always working. If anyone called up, we got cursed out and then a beating." "I felt isolated, and that's why I ran away. I just felt that my mother didn't care." "My step-father, it's been negative since he's been around . . . He hits me till I'm all stiff." One apparent area of neglect on the part of parents of women in this study was sex education. Compared to the 31 to 34 percent found by other researchers (e.g., Wittels, 1951; Sorensen, 1973) among normal female populations, only 15.4% of these prostitutes had learned about sex from their parents.

SEXUAL HISTORY

This lack of parental guidance may help to explain why many prostitutes apparently are more sexually active at an earlier age than the majority of women in the United States. A full 91.9% of the prostitutes in the James study, for example, were not virgins by the age of 18 (including 23% who had experienced intercourse by the age of 13 or younger), compared to the 74.9% of the black subjects and 19.9% of the white subjects studied by Kantner and Zelnick (1972). Although information on sexual experiences prior to first intercourse was not elicited through the questionnaires used in the James study, extensive interviews of the subjects in that study revealed a pattern similar to the one found by Davis (1971:301) in her study of 30 prostitutes: "The 'technical virginity' pattern typical of the middle-class female was not in evidence here. First sexual contacts typically involved sexual intercourse. . . ." More than one third of the subjects in the James study reported that they had no further sexual relationship with their first intercourse partner, while other studies have found 10 to 15 percent of their samples in this category (e.g., Eastman, 1972). That the superficial, nonemotionally charged nature of the first sexual intercourse of many of these women initiated a series of such encounters is supported by the fact that the mean number of private (not-for-profit) sexual partners of young adult subjects in the James study was 23. Making this figure even more significant is the fact that the mean number of persons with whom these subjects felt they had developed a "significant relationship" was only five.

Societal reactions to juvenile female sexual activity may be an influence on some women's entrance into prostitution, especially for those young women who are more sexually active and less discrete than the majority of their peers, as seems to be the case with many prostitutes. "At what number of lovers is a girl supposed to lose the status of a decent person?" asks Choisy (1961:1). Carns (1973:680) explains: "a woman's decision to enter coitus . . . implies that she is creating for herself a sexual status which will have a relatively pervasive distribution . . . she will be evaluated downwardly. Such is the nature of the male bond." Girls learn early society's moral valuation of their sexuality. For example, in discussing her childhood sex education, one streetwalker stated, "I think the basic theme of the whole thing was that it was a dirty thing but that it was a duty for a woman to perform, and if you fooled around, you were a prostitute." Female promiscuity, real or imputed, virtually guarantees loss of status in the majority culture: "I got pregnant and kicked out of the house and school." "I was accused of being promiscuous while I was still a virgin. They did that because I used to run around with a lot of guys." The labeling implied by such loss of status may be an important step in the process by which a woman comes to identity with, and thus begins to see as a possible alternative, a deviant life-style such as prostitution. For its youthful victims, the labeling impact of such status loss must strongly affect the development of an adult self-image. These women may attempt to rebuild their self-image by moving into a subculture where the wider society's negative labeling of them will not impede their efforts toward a higher status, although that status itself will be perceived as negative by the wider society.

However negative the long-term effects of juvenile promiscuity on a woman's social status, the short-term effects of contra-normative juvenile sexual activity may often appear quite positive to the young woman involved. Young women suffering from parental abuse or neglect, a common pattern for prostitutes, may be especially susceptible to the advantages of what Greenwald (1970:167) calls "early rewarded sex—that is, . . . engaging in some form of sexual activity with an adult for which they were rewarded. [These women] discovered at an early age that they could get some measure of affection, of interest, by giving sexual gratification." This type of positive sexual reinforcement, particularly when coupled with the cultural stereotype of women as primarily sexual beings, may cause some women to perceive their sexuality as their primary means for gaining status: "Sex as a status tool is exploited to gain male attention" (Davis, 1971:304). Since all women in our culture must somehow come to terms with the fact that their personal value is often considered as inseparable from their sexual value, it is not uncommon for female adolescents to use "sex as a status tool" through makeup, flirting, dating, petting, and so forth. Prostitutes, however, more often skip over the usual preintercourse socio-sexual activities in favor of an active and more-or-less promiscuous intercourse pattern. Victimization results when "there is a 'drift into deviance,' with promiscuity initially used as a status tool, but later becoming defined by the individual as having consequences for the foreclosure of alternative career routes" (Davis, 1971:300).

INCEST AND RAPE

There is some evidence (e.g. James, 1976c) that prostitutes are women who have also been the victims of less subtle negative sexual experiences. Specifically, the James study showed that prostitutes are disproportionately victimized by incest and rape compared to normal female populations. The only study populations with father-incest rates comparable to James' are those selected from the specialized samples of police reports or the case loads of child-protection agencies (e.g., DeFrancis, 1969). The effect of incest on the child involved is virtually unknown. Some researchers, e.g., Jaffee et al. (1975:691), prefer not to comment: "little is known of the physical and emotional effects of incest." Ferracuti (1972:179) states that "it is hardly proved that participation in incest . . . results in psychological disturbances." He notes, however, that "Frequently [victims of incest] become sexually promiscuous after the end of the incestuous conduct." DeFrancis (1969) found guilt, shame, and loss of self-esteem to be the usual reactions of child victims of sex offenses. These feelings often led to disruptive, rebellious behavior, and some older (i.e., adolescent) victims later became prostitutes. Sexual abuse "continued over a long period of time," as is usual with incest, was found by Gagnon (1965:192) to be "extremely disorganizing in its impact" on the victim. Weiner (1964:137) echoes Ferracuti in stating that "girls who begin incest in adolescence frequently become promiscuous following termination of the incest." In an earlier James study (1971) that included 20 adolescent prostitutes, a full 65% of these young subjects had been the victims of coerced sexual intercourse, with 84.7% of these experiences occurring while the subject-victim was aged 15 or younger. Over half (57.4%) of the prostitute population in James's later study had also been raped, and 36.2% of the women in this sample were multiple rape victims.

It is not possible, of course, to conclude that, because certain study populations of "deviant" women were disproportionately victims of rape and incest, these sex-related abuses were therefore the cause of deviance. On the other hand, the overfrequent victimization of these women, particularly in youth and childhood, is a fact—just as their status as "deviants" is a fact—and should not be lightly dismissed. We realize that incidences of sexual victimization such as incest do not occur in a social "vacuum" and are virtually always surrounded by a complexity of causal, mitigating, or aggravating factors. In fact, a large proportion of the available research on incest—like the majority of studies of other more common types of sexual experiences—focuses primarily on the family background of the victim-subject. Study of the *causes* of sexual behaviors and experiences should not be our only concern, however. What we want to emphasize here is the importance of evaluating the *effects* of certain sexual patterns and experiences on the life of the individual. A simultaneous evaluation of cause and effect would be the ideal, but such an evaluation is beyond the scope of this chapter. We second DeFrancis (1969:225) in his assertion that

> it would be valuable to conduct a longitudinal study to determine more accurately what the long-term effects are on a child victim of sexual abuse. There are many conjectures which should be tested. Does exposure to sexual abuse lead to prostitution, as so often asserted? Does it lead to delinquency; to promiscuous behavior; to confusion of sexual identity; or to marital problems? We know that serious family dislocations, impairment of interfamily relationships and emotional disturbance are some of the immediate consequences of sexual abuse, but how permanent or far reaching is this impact?

Another conjecture can be made on the effect of sexual abuse: early, traumatic sexual self-objectification may be one factor influencing some women toward entrance into prostitution or other "deviant" life-styles. Sexual self-objectification is experienced by all women in this society to some degree, due to the simultaneous cultural adoration and vilification of the female body and its sexuality (the familiar madonna-whore spectrum). It seems possible, however, that to be used sexually at an early age in a way that produces guilt, shame, and loss of self-esteem on the part of the victim would be likely to lessen one's resistance to viewing one's self as a salable commodity. The relationship between early sexual history—especially incidences of sexual victimization—and adult deviance needs, and deserves, further study.

CONCLUSION

There is no obvious victim in a typical act of prostitution. Willing seller meets willing buyer, and both parties receive some gratification from the encounter: money, on the one hand, and sexual and/or psychological satisfaction on the other. It is when we examine the entrance of women into prostitution and when we review the enforcement of anti-prostitution laws that we find elements of victimization coming into focus. Because prostitution is an expression of deviance from the traditional female sex role and therefore entails ostracism from the status and privileges of "respectability," entrance into the profession is typically preceded and facilitated by an inadequate parent/child relationship and the development of a negative or sexually objectified self-image. These personal factors are then compounded by sex-role stereotyping and sex-based economic discrimination. Only widespread changes in socio-sexual attitudes will effect changes in these patterns of victimization and their relationship to prostitution. In regard to victimization of prostitutes by discriminatory law enforcement, however, change is more readily available.

Most other countries have stopped trying to end prostitution and instead made various less-abusive legal arrangements for its regulation. In West Germany, for example, prostitution is considered a social necessity, and the government supports the building of pimp-free prostitution hostels where prostitutes can live and work in comfortable rooms with access to shopping centers, recreational facilities, and mandatory health inspection. The Netherlands use zoning laws to prevent street solicitation from offending the general public. A total of 100 member nations of the United Nations have eliminated the crime of prostitution and have abandoned experiments at regulation (United Nations, 1951). The criminal laws in those countries seek instead to control public solicitation and to discourage the pimps and procurers who live off the earnings of prostitutes.

Decriminalization would seem the least abusive method of dealing with prostitution in the United States. Decriminalization differs from legalization in that, instead of creating more legal involvement, it removes prostitution from the criminal code entirely. An ideal approach would be to put all sexual behavior in private between consenting adults outside the purview of the law, but this ideal must be balanced by the reality of public expediency. Failing the ideal, then, options for controls would depend upon the communities' concern about the overtness of sexual activities, the possible disease problems, business and zoning regulations, and age of consent. Taxation, health, and age requirements can be approached in a number of ways. The least abusive to the individual woman would be to require a small-business license and a health card. Prostitutes would obtain a license much as a masseuse does; her place of business would have to conform with zoning requirements; she would be required to report her income, be of age, and keep her health card current. Violations would mean revocation of the license and would be handled by a nonpolice agency. Regulations such as the above would, of course, still limit personal freedom in a purely private area. The nonlicensed prostitute could still be prosecuted, although she would be served a civil citation rather than a criminal one. Decriminalization, with some restrictions, is regarded as a provisional solution to victimization of prostitutes by the criminal justice system only while efforts are made to change the more fundamental causes of prostitution itself. As long as we retain our traditional sex-role expectations, however, we will have prostitution. As long as women are socialized into the traditional female role and see their alternatives limited by that role, prostitution will remain an attractive occupational option for many women. It is within the power of our legislatures to lessen the victimization of prostitutes as prostitutes, but to eliminate the victimization of prostitutes as women will be a longer, far more difficult struggle.

NOTES

1. Ongoing research (1974-1977) includes a sample of 240 female offenders, 136 of whom have been identified as prostitutes. This research is funded by the National Institute on Drug Abuse, No. DA0091801, "Female Criminal Involvement and Narcotics Addiction."

2. Attempts are occasionally made to arrest women who work in houses or massage/sauna parlors, but arrest figures on these women are less than 5% of the total. Their prostitution is at least partially hidden by the offering of other, more legitimate services. Subtle prostitutes found on all social levels, e.g., call girls or conventioneers, are rarely arrested because they cause no direct affront to the public. Their sexuality is not explicit in their behavior.

REFERENCES

ANDERSON, A. (1974). "Prostitution and social justice." Social Service Review (June): 203.

BENJAMIN, H., and MASTERS, R. (1964). Prostitution and morality. New York: Julien Press.

CARNS, D. (1973). "Talking about sex: Notes on first coitus and the double sexual standard." Journal of Marriage and Family, 35:677-688.

CHAMBLISS, W. (1969). Crime and the legal process. New York: McGraw-Hill.

CHOISY, M. (1961). Psychoanalysis of the prostitute. New York: Philosophical Library.

CLINARD, M. (1959). Sociology of deviant behavior. New York: Rinehart.

COLE, G.R. (1972). Criminal justice: Law and politics. New York: Duxbury Press.

DAVIS, K. (1937). "The sociology of prostitution." American Sociological Review, 2:744-755.

DAVIS, N. (1971). "The prostitute: Developing a deviant identity," pp. 297-322 in J. Henslin (ed.), Studies in the sociology of sex. New York: Appleton-Century-Crofts.

DeFRANCIS, V. (1969). "Protecting the child victims of sex crimes committed by adults." P. 215 in final report, American Humane Association, Children's Division. Denver, Colorado.

EASTMAN, W. (1972). "First intercourse: Some statistics on who, where, when, and why." Sexual Behavior, 2:22-27.

ESSELSTYN, T.C. (1968). Prostitution in the U.S. Annals of the American Academy of Political and Social Sciences, (March):123-125.

FERRACUTI, F. (1972). "Incest between father and daughter." Pp. 169-183 in H. Resnik and E. Wolfgang (eds.), Sexual behaviors: Social, clinical, and legal aspects. Boston: Little, Brown.

GAGNON, J. (1965). "Female child victims of sex offenses." Social Problems, 13:176-192.

GAGNON, J., and SIMON, W. (1973). Sexual conduct. Chicago: Aldine.

GRAY, D. (1973). "Turning-out: A study of teen-age prostitution." Urban Life and Culture, (January):401-425.

GREENWALD, H. (1970). The elegant prostitute. New York: Ballantine.

HOLLENDER, M.H. (1961). "Prostitution, the body and human relatedness." International Journal of Psychoanalysis, 42:404-413.

HOLMES, K. (1972). "Reflections by gaslight: Prostitution in another age." Issues in Criminology, (Winter):83.

JACKMAN, N., O'TOOLE, R. and GEIS, G. (1967). "The self-image of the prostitute." Pp. 133-146 in J. Gagnon and W. Simon (eds.), Sexual deviance. New York: Harper & Row.

JAFFE, A., DYNNESON, L. and TEN BENSEL, R. (1975). "Sexual abuse of children." American Journal of Disabled Children, 129:689-692.

JAMES, J. (1971). "A formal analysis of prostitution." Final report to the Division of Research, State of Washington Department of Social and Health Services, Olympia, Washington.

――― (1973). "The prostitute-pimp relationship." Medical Aspects of Human Sexuality, (November):147-160.

――― (1976a). "Motivations for entrance into prostitution." In L. Crites (ed.), The female offender: A comprehensive anthology. University of Alabama Press (in press).

――― (1976b). "Normal men and deviant women." Unpublished manuscript.

――― (1976c). "Early sexual experience and prostitution." The American Journal of Psychiatry (in press).

KANTNER, J., and ZELNIK, M. (1972). "Sexual experience of young unmarried women in the United States." Family Planning Perspectives, 4:9-18.

KEMP, T. (1936). Prostitution: An investigation of its causes, especially with regard to heriditary factors. Copenhagen: Levin & Munskgaard.

KINSEY, A., POMEROY, W. MARTIN, C., and GEBHARD, P. (1953). Sexual behavior in the human female. Philadelphia: Saunders.

KIRK, S. (1972). "Clients as outsiders: Theoretical approaches to deviance." Social Work, (March): 24.

LOMBROSO, C. (1898). The female offender. New York: D. Appleton.

MAEROV, A. (1965). "Prostitution: A survey and review of 20 cases." Psychiatric Quarterly, 39:675-701.

POMEROY, W. (1965). "Some aspects of prostitution." Journal of Sex Research, (November):177-187.

ROSENBLUM, K. (1975). "Female deviance and the female sex role: A preliminary investigation." British Journal of Sociology, 25(June):69-85.

SORENSEN, R. (1973). Adolescent sexuality in contemporary America. New York: World.

STEIN, M.L. (1974). Lovers, friends, slaves. New York: Putnam's.

Uniform Crime Reports (1976). Crime in the United States. Washington, D.C.: United States Government Printing Office.

United Nations (1951). International Convention for the Suppression of the White Slave Traffic. United Nations Publishing.

WEINER, I. (1964). "On incest: A survey." Excerpta Criminologica, 4:137-155.

WINICK, C., and KINSIE, P. (1971). The lively commerce. New York: New American Library.

WITTELS, F. (1951). Sex habits of American women. New York: Eton.

8

SEXUAL HARASSMENT:
WOMEN'S HIDDEN OCCUPATIONAL HAZARD

L A U R A J. E V A N S

> It didn't matter that I was there for six months and that he knew I had only
> taken the job on the condition that I be promoted at the first opening. If
> I wasn't going to sleep with him, I wasn't going to get my promotion. It
> made me feel powerless and dehumanized. I can't tell you how it affected
> me.[1]

Is this woman's story an unusual example of the office fun-and-games gone wrong? Did she just happen to run in to the rare employer who takes unfair advantage of his economic power? After all, sexual advances toward women on the job are usually trivial events that most women are flattered by and any woman can handle—right? On the contrary, this story is typical. Sexual harassment cripples many women's careers and is a serious barrier to all women's hopes for job equality.

Much of the information in this chapter is based on research and other activities undertaken by Working Women United Institute.[2] The Institute has uncovered and documented the widespread prevalence of sexual harassment. A 1975 survey by Working Women United (WWU, a now defunct grass-roots organization which was based in Ithaca, New York) set a working definition for the problem as "any repeated and unwanted sexual comments, looks, suggestions or physical contact that you find objectionable or offensive and that causes you discomfort on your job."[3] From the results of this preliminary survey and a "Speak Out on Sexual Harassment" held in May 1975, it was possible to isolate some of the forms sexual harassment takes. They include the following: (1) constant ogling and leering at a woman's body, (2) constantly brushing against a woman's body, (3) forcing a woman to submit to squeezing or pinching, (4) catching a woman alone for forced sexual intimacies, (5) outright sexual propositions, often backed by the threat of losing a job or a promotion, (6) forced sexual relations (Nemy, 1975).

Perhaps the most dramatic result of the WWU survey was the confirmation of earlier empirical observations on the extent of the problem. Of the 155 respondents, 70% said they had experienced sexual harassment on the job.[4]

Subsequent surveys confirm the WWU finding that sexual harassment is the common lot of working women.

1. Nine thousand readers of *Redbook* responded to a questionnaire on sexual harassment on the job published in the magazine (Redbook, 1976). Eighty-eight percent said they had experienced sexual harrassment on the job (Safran, 1976).

2. The United Nations Ad Hoc Group on Equal Rights for Women surveyed all women employed at the U.N. Forty-nine percent said sexual pressure exists on the job (NYU Law Review, 1976:149).

3. A class at the University of Texas at San Antonio interviewed 401 working women. *All* had suffered sexual harassment at work (Carey, 1977).

PATRIARCHAL MYTHS VS. WOMEN'S REALITY

Only within the last two years has sexual harassment of working women been openly discussed. Like many other women's issues, the reality of sexual harassment has been obscured by popular myths that contradict women's actual experience.

Among the most prominent myths about sexual harassment are these: women enjoy it, it's trivial and unimportant, it only happens to women in low-status jobs, and it's easy for a woman to "handle."

Underlying these myths is the assumption that sexual attentions to a woman—no matter the time, place, circumstances, or by whom—are flattering because they indicate that men find her attractive, and she is, therefore, more of "a woman," more "feminine," and more "desirable." A part of this is that men are trained to take the sexual initiative, and exercising it is a test of manhood.

Unfortunately, women have been socialized to assess their personal worth by their desirability to men and are trained to receive men's advances gracefully, regardless of their own personal feelings.

Not only are these attitudes and socialization detrimental to women's self-concept, but, on the job, where the appropriate role is

that of *worker,* this attitude is in direct conflict with the demands of
the job. This conflict plays itself out whenever men in the office
continue to treat women as sex objects rather than as workers, and
women workers (all 38 million) are left to cope with the repercussions.

As we look at the myths, we must examine them in the context of
society's values and the sociopolitical fact that men have a monopoly
on power in the work force as well as in the larger society, while women
are dependent, individually and collectively, on men for their
livelihood.

MYTH 1: SEXUAL HARASSMENT IS FUN

Many men are unable to understand why women find sexual
advances and innuendos on the job upsetting. They often see
behavior that women characterize as harassment as "just good fun"
or even "complimentary." The myth is that any "normal" woman
welcomes and is flattered by sexual attention in *any* form.

Women's real feelings about sexual harassment are, in fact, quite
different. In WWU's survey, 81% of the women reported feeling
angry when confronted with sexual harassment, 50% reported feeling
upset, 24% were frightened and 23% felt guilty. (Percentages add up
to more than 100 because of multiple answers.) Specific effects
women reported included: (1) feeling powerless or trapped, (2)
becoming self-conscious about their appearance, (3) feelings of defeat
and diminished ambition, (4) decreased job satisfaction and impair-
ment of job performance, and (5) physical symptoms such as nervous
stomach, migraines, and loss of appetite.

> The end of the evening would draw near, he'd find some excuse for me to
> stay. Usually I had to stay if I wanted to get paid, and believe me, tips
> there weren't enough to live off so you needed your paycheck. I didn't
> care for that silly game at all and that's when I started aching when I had
> to go in there every week. I'd get sick to my stomach, I'd get headaches
> and customers noticed a difference in me. [WWU, 1975]

Seventy-five percent of women surveyed by *Redbook* said they
found uninvited sexual attentions embarrassing, demeaning, or
intimidating.

MYTH 2: SEXUAL HARASSMENT IS TRIVIAL

Sexual harassment is often seen as a trivial issue, and it is most often men who see it this way. Many men do not understand the pressure and conflict involved for women who must confront unwanted sexual advances on the job. It is particularly hard for men to imagine the seriousness of sexual harassment on the job because it doesn't happen to them.

Most women feel differently; their experience has taught them otherwise. Ninety-two percent of the respondents to the WWU survey considered sexual harassment a serious problem for working women.

The economic effect of sexual harassment on working women is anything but trivial. Some women leave jobs because they face persistent sexual harassment; others are fired because they refuse to be sexually cooperative. Nearly half of the women surveyed by *Redbook* said that they themselves or a woman they knew had quit or been fired because of sexual harassment (Safran, 1976). In the U.N. survey (NYU Law Review, 1976), 21% of the women who said that sexual pressure existed on the job also said that they had experienced it in connection with promotion. All of this contributes to the cycle of downward mobility, unemployment, and poverty among women.

Destruction of working women's ambition, confidence, job satisfaction, and performance is another outcome of supposedly trivial sexual harassment.

> That job was really important to me. I'd poured my life into it. But this guy refused to believe that I really didn't want to date him. He just kept after me and kept after me. Finally I had to quit. I'd poured all my hopes and ambitions into a career in that field and it was years before I could try again. [Nemy, 1975]

> And the fact that I had to leave and he wouldn't let me keep my job without sleeping with him just made me so disappointed and apprehensive that I haven't even looked for another job. It's to the point where I can't take it anymore.

> I'd been trying to get a job as a filmmaker for years. It's practically an all male field; nobody would even look at my work. Finally I got an offer on the condition that I go away with this guy for the weekend. What amazed and frightened me was that I actually considered doing it! I wanted the job so badly. I said no, but I couldn't take it anymore. I gave up.

When a woman's sexuality is the basis for evaluating her work, the message is that the quality of her work is unimportant and that her only real responsibility is to satisfy male sexual desires. If this were an attitude she met with rarely, it might be easier to combat. But it is not. It's an attitude she has faced all her life, and it may have made her hesitant and anxious about entering the work force in the first place.

Sexual harassment is also frequently thought of as funny. Until recently, the only consistent reference to sexual harassment of working women was found in male humor as in cartoons showing a secretary clutching her steno pad and racing around a desk one step ahead of her boss. If sexual harassment on the job is as trivial and funny as some men claim, one wonders why women who resist harassment are punished so severely. The answer, of course, is that it is not trivial. At stake are traditional male and female roles. A woman who resists sexual harassment refuses to play her assigned role as passive sex object and is likely to feel the full weight of the male power structure come down upon her.

MYTH 3: SEXUAL HARASSMENT ONLY AFFECTS WOMEN IN LOW-STATUS JOBS

Women as well as men often believe that sexual harassment afflicts only women in powerless, low-paying, low-status jobs. Many women find out otherwise, as one university professor, speaking of her own experience, said:

> I believed at one time that educated women, women who worked as professionals, women who worked as equals with men, were exempt from the kind of sexual harassment that we're talking about. Over the last five years I found out that this is not true.

The previously cited survey provides some evidence that women in so-called low-status jobs such as waitresses and clerical workers are more likely to be sexually harassed than women in other job categories. Since one third of all working women are in clerical jobs and another third in sales and service jobs (Kihss, 1977), most working women fall into this vulnerable category.

Although some women may be more vulnerable to sexual harassment than others, no woman is immune, and a prestigious position is no sure protection. Take the case of a 40-year-old bank vice president:

> I was hit from all directions at once with several important bank clients
> offering me their business on the condition that I go out with them. I was
> responsible for keeping and building up these large accounts. If they pulled
> out, my career was finished. [Bralove, 1976]

This woman managed to fend off her clients and still keep their
business and her job, but many, even when backed by high-status
jobs, are not so lucky. An example is a market analyst who was
recruited away from her old company only to discover that her new
boss required that she be pinchable and available. She refused and
found herself looking for work (Christensen, 1975).

Job status may have some effect on the type of harassment a
woman is likely to face. In the WWU survey, women who
experienced physical harassment had a median salary of $92/week,
while women whose harassment was purely verbal had a median
salary of $121/week.

Whatever status a woman may have achieved in the work force,
the function of sexual harassment is to remind her of male
prerogatives and of her inferior and dependent position. It may be
true that the expression of sexual harassment is more subtle in higher
status jobs, but in all cases the message is the same. "You're not my
equal. Don't compete. Stay in your place. Your real value is your
body."

MYTH 4: SEXUAL HARASSMENT IS EASY FOR WOMEN TO HANDLE

After her boss chased her around his desk and ripped off her
clothes, a Florida secretary decided to retain an attorney. The
attorney laughed at her story, telling her that she was a big girl now
and should handle the situation herself (Peterman, 1975). The
attorney's attitude reflects the myth that women can handle sexual
harassment with ease. Men are unwilling to take responsibility for
their harassment of women and, by accepting this myth, place
responsibility for sexual harassment on their victims. Thus, it is up to
women to control their harassers; men don't have to control
themselves. Although social conditioning has taught women to
accept this responsibility, many are beginning to question it. The
idea that any mature woman should be capable of handling sexual
harassment is one of the most destructive myths about this problem.
In fact, a woman faced with sexual harassment on her job is in a
double bind. There is often no way she can handle the situation
without hurting herself.

Most women first attempt to handle sexual harassment at work by ignoring it and hoping their harasser will desist. But, according to the WWU survey, in 75% of the cases where a woman ignored the behavior, it either continued or got worse. In addition, many women reported being punished for not responding. One fourth of the women who said they ignored sexual advances reported unwarranted reprimands, sabotage of their work, and other forms of retaliation.

The next step, confronting the harasser directly, is often ineffective, as many men don't take a woman's protest seriously.

> My boss decided that it was more convenient to slide past me in order to get the mail in the boxes and he would slide past and put his hand on my behind or put his arm around me. When he started it I would jokingly say, "Please don't do that. It really bothers me. Cut it out! Watch your hands!" He just kept it up, he thought I was being funny.

> One day we were sorting mail and he slid past me, put his arm around me, put his hand on my behind. I drew a line around myself and I said, "Anything inside this circle is mine. Don't touch it! It's mine. Leave me alone!" That to him was a big joke. Nothing I ever said made any difference.

If a woman does succeed in convincing her harasser that her protests are serious, she is open to retaliation. After the mailroom worker quoted above asserted herself, her boss put a letter in her personnel file criticizing her job performance.

When keeping silent becomes too great a strain and protesting to one's harasser has failed, a woman must decide whether or not to carry her protest further. In the WWU survey, only 18% of the women who said they were harassed complained about it through established channels. The reasons given by the rest of the women for not complaining were the following:

1. Fifty-three percent said they felt nothing would be done. (Unfortunately, they're right. In over half the cases where the victim did complain, nothing was done.)

2. Forty-three percent felt their claims would be treated lightly or they would be ridiculed.

3. Thirty percent feared they would be blamed or would suffer some repercussions if they complained. (These women are right, too. In one third of the cases where the victim complained, negative repercussions resulted.)

Another reason for not complaining is a feeling of guilt. Women are made to feel responsible for their own victimization by being told that, when a man approaches them sexually, they must have been doing something to provoke him. A 16-year-old model whose boss attacked her in her dressing room said, "I didn't say anything because I thought no one would really believe what had happened, that somehow I must have fostered it. I felt really disgusting and ashamed."

If a woman lodges a formal complaint, and it is taken seriously, she may be labeled a troublemaker and be punished while her harasser is protected. For example, the final episode in the mailroom worker's story came when she told the personnel department that her boss was harassing her. The personnel department threatened her with a libel suit and gave her four months to either find another job within the company (all jobs were then frozen) or quit. She quit.

Another women tells the story of complaining first to her boss who was harassing her, then to his boss, next to the ombudsman (whose attitude was "behave professionally and everything will work out just fine"), and finally to the director of personnel. *She* was transferred to another department. Her conclusion: "Somehow it always works out that the woman has to leave. This man is still on his job and nobody, nobody ever suggested that maybe he should leave."

We know of only one case in which the harasser was punished. The man in question was fired, apparently because the company wanted to get rid of him anyway. The women who complained about his behavior were all let go, too. The man found a better job for higher pay. The women weren't so fortunate (Peterman, 1975).

As we have seen, there are no really workable options for any woman faced with sexual harassment. A few economically secure women have the option of leaving, but many women need a job so badly that they must submit to sexual advances from an employer or supervisor. These women have no options at all; for them, sexual harassment becomes economic rape.

> Within my first month as a waitress, it was made clear to me that if you are "friendly" enough, you could have a better situation, better hours, better everything. If you're tricky enough, you just dangle everybody, but it reaches a point where it's too much of a hassle and you quit and take something else. But when you have children and no support payments, you can't keep quitting.

Sexual harassment, then, is not easily handled, nor is it appropriate that women be expected to handle it. It presents a real threat to economic security and traps women in a role conflict with all its resultant anxiety and stress. Any woman who buys the myth that she can handle sexual harassment is likely to feel guilty for *her* failure, not realizing that the deck is stacked against her.

SEXUAL HARASSMENT AND PUBLIC POLICY

Until recently the battle against sexual harassment was fought—when it was fought at all—in private. Now the issue is being contested in two public arenas: the unemployment insurance system, and the federal courts. However, the same myths that women run up against in the private sector confront them again in public policy.

SEXUAL HARASSMENT AND UNEMPLOYMENT INSURANCE

A person who voluntarily leaves her job is eligible for unemployment benefits only if she can establish good cause for quitting. Among the reasons accepted by state unemployment agencies are intentional harassment—such as constant nagging, false accusation, or repeated insinuations by an employer that an employee is dishonest—and any condition that endangers an employee's physical or mental health. However, women who leave because of sexual harassment will have a hard time convincing the agency that they left for good cause. Even though many state agencies agree in the abstract that sexual harassment is sufficient reason for quitting, the individual referees who examine claims often bring to their work the same attitudes about sexual harassment that left the woman no alternative but quitting in the first place.

A case in point is the story of one of the founders of WWUI. Before considering her story, bear in mind that the Director of the Unemployment Insurance Division of the New York State Department of Labor has stated that sexual harassment *is* good cause for quitting. "If true," he said, "we would pay benefits without question. But it's one of the toughest cases to handle. It's a question of credibility. Where we have witnesses, we would tend, without question, to throw the case to the claimant" (Nemy, 1975).

After eight years as an administrative assistant at an eastern university, the woman in question quit her job because repeated sexual harassment by a male professor had made her so anxious she was suffering severe neck and arm pains that doctors and physio-therapists had been unable to alleviate.

Before quitting, she tried in many ways to "handle" the situation. She avoided the professor, even using the stairs instead of the elevator because she knew of at least one instance when he had molested a woman in the elevator. She wore slacks every day to prevent him from staring at her legs. She told her secretary not to leave her alone with him. On several occasions she complained to her supervisor about the professor's behavior toward her and other women. The supervisor said, "Mature women should know how to handle situations like that," and suggested they "try not to get into these situations." The woman made four attempts to transfer, all fruitless.

After two years of harassment, her distress was so great that she quit even though she was due for a raise in two weeks and was the sole support of two children. Her neck and arm pain vanished immediately. When she applied for unemployment benefits, a hearing was held before a referee to determine her eligibility. At the hearing, two other women corroborated her testimony, and even her supervisor reluctantly admitted that she had been harassed and that he had done nothing about it.

The referee denied the application for benefits on the grounds that her reasons for leaving were "personal and noncompelling" (Heins and Horn, 1975). In making his decision, the referee said the woman should have requested a transfer before leaving, ignoring the evidence that she had made such a request four times. He criticized her for not complaining to the professor himself, ignoring the fact that the professor had the power to terminate her employment and that she resisted him in every way emotionally and economically feasible to her. In his findings of fact, the referee avoided the subject of sexual harassment altogether and spoke of the woman's "antipathy" toward her superior rather than his harassment of her, thereby shifting blame to her. Nowhere in the entire record was the persistent sexual harassment of her and other women questioned. It was merely downplayed and treated as something they should have taken care of themselves.

In a California unemployment case, a woman charged that her employer had persistently harassed her. He talked about his wish to have sexual contact with her, patted her on the behind, made comments to friends and customers on her figure, and implied to them that she was a loose woman and would do anything with anybody. She quit, but returned to work when he agreed to change his behavior. He didn't keep his bargain, and she quit again (California, 1975a). Her application for unemployment benefits was denied by a referee who saw her problem as "working with a group of men whose speech standards were not of the highest." During the hearing he asked the woman if she didn't think that "today's modern world requires that females in business and industry have a little tougher attitude toward life in general?" (Rosenberg, 1975). The County Commission on the Status of Women intervened on the woman's behalf, and the referee's ruling was eventually reversed by an Appeals Board (California, 1975b).

Truly, as New York's Director of the Unemployment Insurance Division said, "It's a question of credibility." Unfortunately, women often have no credibility with the men judging their cases, even when the evidence backs them up.

To counteract the male bias operating in unemployment insurance agencies, WWUI helped to develop legislation now before the New York State legislature. The bill specifically states that harassment on the basis of sex is good cause for leaving one's job. Similar legislation has been introduced in California and Wisconsin.

SEXUAL HARASSMENT AND THE COURTS

Recently, the issue of sexual harassment on the job has been brought before the courts by women claiming that such harassment is a form of sex discrimination and is denying them equal terms and conditions of employment in violation of Title VII of the 1964 Civil Rights Act. Title VII provides:

> It shall be an unlawful employment practice for an employer—(1) to fail or refuse to hire or to discharge any individual or otherwise to discriminate against any individual with respect to his compensation, terms, conditions, or privileges of employment, because of such individual's race, color, religion, sex, or national origin; or (2) to limit, segregate, or classify his employees or applicants for employment in any way which would deprive or tend to deprive any individual of employment opportunities or otherwise adversely affect his status as an employee, because of such individual's race, color, religion, sex or national origin.

The Equal Employment Opportunity Commission (EEOC), the agency charged with enforcing Title VII, has taken the position that sexual harassment *is* sex discrimination under Title VII, but too many of the courts that have heard sexual harassment cases have disagreed.

The basic issues in the judicial controversy are brought out in the first sexual harassment case to come before the courts (Corne and DeVane v. Bausch and Lomb, Inc., 1975a). In 1974, two Arizona women filed a complaint alleging sex discrimination in employment, charging that their supervisor made repeated verbal and physical sexual advances toward them and that the company knew about the situation but did nothing to stop it. As a result, the two women felt compelled to resign their positions as clerical workers.

The EEOC sided with the two women and filed an amicus curiae brief in their behalf, arguing that sexual harassment was covered by Title VII on the grounds that

> Toleration of his conduct constituted a term and condition of their employment. . . . No more irrational, or unwarranted, a condition of employment than that alleged in this case can be imagined. Women employees, in order to be productive workers, must be allowed to enjoy their employment as men do, free of unsolicited verbal and physical sexual advances directed toward them simply because of their sex. And, as plaintiffs contend, the choice between frequent unsolicited sexual advances and being employed has a significant and clearly unwarranted effect on employment opportunities. . . . For if Title VII does not provide such elementary protection against sexually motivated conduct, its promise to women is virtually without meaning. [Corne, 1975b]

The U.S. District Court for the District of Arizona dismissed the women's case. The court found that the supervisor's behavior did not fall within the type of conduct that Title VII brands as sex discrimination because the acts had no relationship to the nature of employment and because the alleged harassment might be directed at males as well as females. The court reasoned that it could not be said that women as a category were discriminated against by sexual harassment, only that some women belonged to the category of sexually harassed people. Since men might also belong to this category, it could not be considered a protected category under Title VII. To put it differently, the court found that, theoretically, both men and women can be sexually harassed, thus the category cannot be said to be defined *primarily* by gender, and, therefore, sexual harassment is not discrimination on the basis of sex and is not actionable under Title VII.

A federal district court in New Jersey took the same view. In Tomkins v. Public Service Electric and Gas Company (1976a), a secretary charged that her supervisor took her out to lunch, ostensibly to discuss her promotion. While there, he attacked her and threatened her. She reported the incident to company officials only to find herself demoted and eventually fired. The Tomkins court held that sexual harassment does not constitute sex discrimination under Title VII. The court stated,

> In this case the supervisor was male and the employee was female. But no immutable principle of psychology compels this alignment of parties. The gender lines might as easily have been reversed or even not crossed at all. While sexual desire animated the parties, or at least one of them, the gender of each is incidental to the claim of abuse. [Tomkins, 1976c]

No more facetious reasoning can be found than this. To disallow a claim of discrimination on the grounds that someday the roles may be reversed would ban all discrimination suits from the courts. Blacks may someday discriminate against whites, but that possibility has not prevented the courts from holding that the current situation is illegal and from upholding Title VII with regard to race.

A contrary conclusion on the applicability of Title VII to sexual harassment was drawn by a Washington, D.C., Federal District Court in Williams v. Saxbe. The court ruled that the retaliatory actions of a male supervisor, taken because a female employee declined his sexual advances, constituted sex discrimination within the meaning of Title VII[6] because

> A finding of sex discrimination under Title VII does not require that the discriminatory policy or practice depend upon a characteristic peculiar to one of the genders. That a rule, regulation, practice, or policy is applied on the basis of gender is alone sufficient for a finding of sex discrimination. [Williams, 1976]

A second issue in dispute is whether or not a company is responsible for the actions of its supervisor. The Corne (1975a) court ruled that the supervisor was merely satisfying a personal urge rather than carrying out a company policy, and, therefore, Bausch and Lomb could not be held to have practiced sex discrimination.

As the Tomkins court later pointed out, this decision flies in the face of precedents established by comparable race and religious discrimination cases. In such instances, companies have been held responsible when their supervisors' personal prejudices affect employees.

It's clear that Title VII is being disparately enforced. Title VII is meant to apply equally to all the categories it includes—race, color, religion, sex, and national origin. If a supervisor uses racial epithets or interjects impermissible racial stereotypes into the work environment because these are his personal views, the company is held responsible. Yet some courts have chosen to apply a different standard when impermissible sexual stereotypes are interjected into the work environment.

The theme that sexual harassment is a personal problem runs through many of the court decisions. The Tomkins court said,

> Title VIII . . . is not intended to provide federal tort remedy damages for what amounts to physical attack motivated by sexual desire on the part of a supervisor and which happened to occur in a corporate corridor rather than a back alley. [Tomkins, 1976c]

In Barnes v. Train, a Washington, D.C., federal district court held,

> This is a controversy underpinned by the subtleties of an inharmonious personal relationship. Regardless of how inexcusable the conduct of the plaintiff's supervisor might have been, it does not evidence an arbitrary barrier to continued employment based on plaintiff's sex. [NYU Law Review, 1976:150-151]

Ms. Barnes's job was abolished because of her refusal to engage in sexual relations with her supervisor. It is hard to think of a more "arbitary barrier" to employment.

The Corne court raised another revealing side issue. In its opinion, the court expressed concern that a decision for the women would create a "potential federal lawsuit every time any employee made amorous or sexually oriented advances toward another and the courts would be burdened" (NYU Law Review, 1976:151).

This idea has appeared in several other Title VII decisions. In the case of Miller v. Bank of America, a California District Court ruled against a woman who claimed her supervisor promised her a promotion if she would be sexually cooperative and caused her dismissal when she refused. The Miller court said that the idea that sexual harassment was actionable under Title VII was "ludicrous" and went on to say, "It is conceivable, under plaintiff's theory that flirtation of the smallest order would give rise to liability" (U.S. Law Week, 1976:1039).

The Tomkins court also worried about this point:

If the plaintiff's views were to prevail, no superior could, prudently, attempt to open a social dialogue with any subordinate of either sex. An invitation to dinner could become an invitation to a federal lawsuit if a once harmonious relationship turned sour at some later time. [1976c]

Two threads run through these statements. One is that women are petty creatures who, if given the opportunity, will bring a lawsuit any time an employer asks one of them out to dinner. This is a rather remarkable conclusion considering that none of the women in question was in court because she had been asked to dinner. Each was there because she lost her job for refusing to have sexual relations with her supervisor. The other thread is that women are vicious and would falsely accuse an employer "if a once harmonious relationship turned sour." This recalls the often-heard assertion that a rape victim is just a woman who changed her mind. The desire of the courts is to protect men from the hypothetical vengeance of women, even though the evidence before the courts concerns the very real vengeance of men upon women who have refused them. In sexual harassment, as in rape, the courts protect men from their victims.

A more positive view of the applicability of Title VII to sexual harassment cases was taken recently by the U.S. Fourth Circuit Court of Appeals in Richmond, Virginia. In this case, a lower court ruled against a woman who charged that she was fired because she refused to engage in sexual relations with her immediate supervisor. The Court of Appeals overturned the lower court's ruling and held that the woman has the right to sue her former employer for damages under Title VII. She is now suing for one million dollars (Majority Report, 1977).

However, the effectiveness of Title VII litigation as an avenue for relief in sexual harassment cases is uncertain for the immediate future. The "positive" decision in Williams (1976) is being appealed, and the recent Fourth Circuit decision, which recognized the right to sue for sex discrimination in a sexual harassment case, is narrow and not definitive. [7] Most decisions in these cases have failed to find sexual harassment as a cause of action. All of these negative decisions could be appealed to the Supreme Court, but there is little ground for optimism about the results.

WWUI is concerned that Title VII litigation in the area of sexual harassment proceed cautiously. To pave the way for reversing adverse decisions, groundwork must be laid carefully. Developing the idea that sexual harassment is a form of sex discrimination can be done both by developing data about its incidence and impact and through serious public education efforts to change prevailing attitudes. Until this groundwork is laid, administrative approaches through such vehicles as unemployment insurance, workers compensation, personnel policies, and unions will continue to provide greater potential for relief. A national network of attorneys and litigants would contribute to the development of legal strategies for eliminating sexual harassment. Activists and researchers involved in the issue have cited the need for a dialogue on litigative approaches and WWUI has undertaken the development of such a network.

TOWARD A DEFINITION OF
SEXUAL HARASSMENT ON THE JOB

Sexual harassment is a complex, subtle, deeply rooted problem that arouses emotion and controversy. Thus far the presentation of the issue in public discussions and in the courts has been limited mainly to the most clear-cut examples of on-the-job sexual assault and situations where advancement or continued employment are contingent upon complying with sexual demands. However, it is clear that the problem reaches beyond these examples. In its broadest sense, it starts at the employment interview when an arbitrary "standard of desirability" is applied to the women applicant, a standard that weeds out older and less conventionally attractive women. Although women's personal space and privacy are not recognized by the law, harassment—even on the visual or verbal level—can be viewed in this broad sense as an invasion of privacy and personal space. In addition, there is evidence that these pressures damage women's mental health, self-image, job satisfaction, and career mobility.

There is a need for more discussion and exploration of the subtle, ambiguous aspects of sexual harassment.[8] There are, however, some questions that continually arise in discussions about this problem.

(1) What about harassment of men?

If sexual harassment is viewed as an abuse of power rooted in both the greater status of men relative to women and men's social conditioning to seize the right of sexual initiative, then it becomes highly unlikely that the perpetrators of sexual harassment will be women. Because of their social conditioning, women are not comfortable in the role of sexual initiator. In fact, the research of WWUI has not uncovered a single incident in which a man has been sexually harassed, as defined in this paper, by a woman.

Is it possible, then, that men could be sexually harassed by other men? Another man may have the requisite social conditioning and the power in the work place to make such advances. In addition, because of the fear of homosexuality, men can be expected to perceive advances by men as harassment. However, if we look at the social realities, it is unlikely that homosexual harassment on the job would occur frequently. Because homosexuals are not protected against employment discrimination, the risk of making such advances is too great.

So, while it is possible in principle for men to be the victims of sexual harassment, it is unlikely in fact. Raising this question would seem to be an attempt to divert attention from the stressful, traumatic effect of sexual harassment for women.

(2) What about women who use sex for advancement?

Although we cannot deny that some women may *try* to use their sexuality to advance in their jobs, the continued concentration of women in lower echelon, dead-end jobs demonstrates the futility of this method of getting ahead. On the whole, women do not get advancement by using sex or by any other means. Statistics indicate that complying with sexual demands does not result in deserved promotions, much less undeserved ones. And it would probably be more correct to say that a woman who "slept her way to the top" was forced to comply with unfair demands because of her sex rather than that she took unfair advantage of her sex.

The idea that working women use sex to get ahead is a way to deny the accomplishments of the few women who have managed, through hard work and superior qualifications, to advance. What is really being said is that they couldn't have gotten there on their own professional merit.

(3) Don't some women provoke sexual harassment?

Saying that women provoke sexual harassment is a way of making the victim responsible for the crime. Only in crimes against women is the possibility of provocation thought to absolve the perpetrator from responsibility for his attack. A man displaying a big bankroll or wearing an expensive suit may be robbed; nobody would think that the robber should go free because he was provoked by the sight of money or alerted by the victim's manner of dress.

The idea that women must take care not to provoke men is an attempt to limit women's freedom. It works, too. The majority of the women who answered *Redbook's* survey said they adopt a cool, guarded attitude on the job in order to protect themselves. Fifteen percent said they protect themselves by dressing with "extreme modesty" (Safran, 1976).

REMEDIES

Women have just begun to fight sexual harassment, and their effort is being launched on many fronts through legislation, litigation, government agencies, unions, and women's organizations.

In spite of the biased records of the courts and unemployment agencies, some women have managed to break through antiwoman prejudice in these systems. It requires a great deal of perseverance, however, because women seem to lose the first round. Any women taking a sexual harassment claim to an administrative agency such as an unemployment insurance office should be careful to state her case in a way that cannot be construed to disqualify her for benefits, and she should expect to appeal what may well be a negative decision at the first level. In federal courts, the chances of success are even slighter, and sound legal advice should be sought before initiating any action. Legislative reform has been initiated in several states, and it is hoped that this will eventually give women the needed statutory support.

Unions can also be used to attack sexual harassment. For example, the Screen Actors Guild in Los Angeles and in New York City set up a morals complaint bureau designed to arbitrate such charges. The Guild has also written into its contract a prohibition against conducting job interviews outside the office (Bralove, 1976).

Some state and city human rights commissions have included sexual harassment as a form of sex discrimination. After the issue was brought up in hearings held by the New York City Human Rights Commission, the Commission began writing clauses guarding against "violations of sexual privacy" into all of its affirmative action agreements.

CONCLUSION

If, as preliminary evidence indicates, the average American working woman experiences sexual harassment at some point in her working life, the perpetrator must be the average American working male. The numbers of women reporting harassment are just too large for sexual harassment to be the work of a few misfit males. This means that sexual harassment is not an aberration; rather, it is an expression of the prevailing male view of women. Men who have grown up with the attitude that a woman is to be taken seriously only as a wife, mother, and sex partner don't change their attitudes just because the woman in question happens to be working with them. When women enter the work force, they challenge male stereotypes about women's proper roles. Sexual harassment acts as a weapon used to remind working women of their "proper role." Only by exposing sexual harassment and stripping away the myths that hide it can women hope to win their battle for equal employment.

As long as women are forced to contend with sexual demands on the job, the idea of equal opportunity will remain a fantasy.

NOTES

1. This and other personal testimony (except where noted) comes from the first "Speak Out on Sexual Harassment of Women at Work," held May 4, 1975, in Ithaca, New York, under the auspices of Working Women United.

2. Working Women United Institute is an independent research/action/resource center of national scope devoted to the needs and problems of women who work outside the home. The Institute is committed to reaching women of all racial, ethnic, and economic backgrounds and to furthering the goals of equal employment opportunity, decent working conditions, and full involvement of women in decisions affecting their working lives. Its first major undertaking has been a project on sexual harassment on the job. For more information contact Working Women United Institute, 593 Park Avenue, New York, NY 10021.

3. Since that time it has become clear that further scientific research is needed. An important finding of this preliminary survey is that there is no common definition of the term sexual harassment; such a common definition would be an important factor in future public policy decisions in this area. Future WWUI research will isolate the objective parameters of sexual harassment on the job and yield information about where and to whom it is most likely to occur, its consequences, and effective strategies for terminating it.

4. The 155 respondents ranged in age from 19 to 61 years of age and came from two groups: women who attended the WWU-sponsored "Speak Out on Sexual Harassment at Work," held in Ithaca, N.Y., and women members of a civil service employee's union in Binghamton, N.Y. The women who came to the Speak Out were acquainted with the issue of sexual harassment beforehand, while the women from the civil service union were unfamiliar with the issue, although not, as it turned out, with the practice.

5. Victims of sexual harassment can also go to court and charge their harassers with assault and battery or sue for damages if the circumstances warrant. Few women do so, probably because many are reluctant to press a personal charge.

6. The Williams court also said that a finding of sex discrimination under Title VII could be made if a heterosexual female harassed male employees or if a homosexual harassed employees of the same sex but not if a bisexual harassed employees of both sexes.

7. At this publication, the Third Circuit Court of Appeals has ruled favorably in the Barnes appeal, holding sexual harassment actionable under Title VII. This decision is encouraging legal strategists to think more positively about the possibility of Title VII cases.

8. WWUI intends to conduct further research into the issue of sexual harassment on the job, as well as other issues of concern to working women, and to translate its research results into a form to be used to change public policies and to be used by working women in efforts to organize for better working conditions.

REFERENCES

BRALOVE, M. (1976). "A cold shoulder: Career women decry sexual harassment by bosses and clients." The Wall Street Journal, (January):1, 15.

California Unemployment Insurance Appeals Board (1975a). Decision of the referee, case #SJ-5963. Sacramento, Calif.

——— (1975b). Benefit decision, case #75-5225. Sacramento, Calif.

CAREY, S. (1977). "Sexual politics in business." San Antonio, Texas.

CHRISTENSEN, K. (1975). "Sexual harassment—The quiet job threat." Chicago Daily News, (August 20):33, 38.

Corne and DeVane v. Bausch and Lomb, Inc. (1975a). U.S. Court of Appeals for the Ninth Circuit, No. CCA 75-1857. Appellants' opening brief, Heather Sigworth.

——— (1975b). EEOC's Amicus Curiae brief.

HEINS, M., and HORN, S. (1975). Brief on behalf of claimant appellant in the matter of the claim of Carmita Wood for unemployment insurance benefits. Itaca, N.Y.

KIHSS, P. (1977). "Women's wages fall even farther behind." New York Times, (April 3):35.

Majority Report (1977). "Suing her way up." (March 5):4.

NEMY, E. (1975). "Women begin to speak out against sexual harassment at work." The New York Times, (August 19):38.

NYU Law Review (1976). "Comment: Employment discrimination–Sexual harassment and Title VII." 51(April):148-167.

PETERMAN, P. (1975). "Sex and the working girl." St. Petersburg Times (September 12).

Redbook Magazine (1976). "How do you handle sex on the job: A Redbook questionnaire." 146(January):74-75.

ROSENBERG, R. (1975). "A woman must persevere in battle against sexism." Santa Clara Sun, (August 20):6.

SAFRAN, C. (1976). "What men do to women on the job: A shocking look at sexual harassment." Redbook Magazine, 148(November):149, 217-223.

SILVERMAN, D. (1977). "Sexual harassment: Working women's dilemma." Quest: A Feminist Quarterly, 3(Winter):15-24.

STESSIN, L. (1977). "Should guruism be grounds for dismissal?" The New York Times, (March 27):2.

Tomkins v. Public Service Electric and Gas Co. (1976a). U.S. District Court, District of New Jersey, Civil Action No. 75-1673. Amended complaint.

––– (1976b). Memorandum in opposition to motion for protective order.

––– (1976c). Opinion.

The United States Law Week (1976). "Isolated sexual advances no ground for Title VII claim." 45 (September 14):1039, 2135.

Williams v. Saxbe (1976). United States District Court, District of Columbia, Civil Action No. 74-186.

Working Women United Institute (1975). Sexual harassment on the job: Results of a preliminary survey. Ithaca, N.Y.: Author.

––– (1976). Transcript of Speak Out on Sexual Harassment of Women at Work held May 4, 1975. Ithaca, N.Y.

9

WOMEN'S HEALTH:
THE SIDE EFFECTS OF SEX BIAS

JULIA GRAHAM LEAR

A recent issue of *Daedalus* (1977) took the pulse of American medicine and found it "Doing Better and Feeling Worse." A similar diagnosis could be made of the impact of medicine on American women: the statistics say women's health status is improving; the literature says we are increasingly dissatisfied with the cost, availability, and quality of medical services.

The more obvious health indicators suggest American women should be particularly pleased with their benefits from medicine. In 1974, life expectancy at birth for the average American woman was 76.7 years, an increase of 2.6 years over that in 1960. The infant mortality rate in 1973 was 17.7 per 1,000, down from 26.0 per 1,000 in 1960. Thanks to recent Supreme Court decisions, women now control their own fertility, and they have dropped the national birth rate from 23.7 live births per 1,000 in 1970 to 15.0 live births per 1,000 in 1974.

Despite these encouraging health statistics, other evidence suggests that women neither receive the health care they need nor are happy with the health care they get. *Item:* Abortions are no longer illegal in the United States, but they are unobtainable in large sections of the country. In 1975, abortions were not performed in 82% of *public* hospitals. *Item:* Women make up 41% of the United States work force, but the Occupational Safety and Health Administration, which is responsible for setting safety standards for the work place, has issued draft standards for lead exposure levels that will not protect the health of pregnant workers. *Item:* Provision of care by primarily male physicians has so alienated some women that women's clinics and self-help groups have sprung up across the country. At a grassroots level, thousands of women are exploring alternatives to the current modes of health care delivery.

Parallel to the emergence of women-managed health services has been the development of a feminist critique of American medicine. Health professionals and writers such as Doris Hare, Helen Marienskind, Barbara Ehrenreich, Phyllis Chesler, and Mary Howell have probed the structures of the health system, from training of providers to delivery of services, and laid bare the system's insensitivity to women's concerns. One landmark study (Howell, 1972) examined the educational experience of women medical students and documented the hostility and lack of support these women encounter. Another study (Scully and Bart, 1973) exposed the attitudes toward women evidenced in obstetrics and gynecology textbooks. Yet another study (Chesler, 1972) assessed the psychic damage to women by sex bias and the pernicious impact of Freudian analysis in encouraging subservient roles for women.

The cumulative result of the past 10 years of feminist writings on American medicine and women has been a long list of problems women have encountered in receiving appropriate medical care or attempting to participate in the medical care delivery system.

Until recently, there has been a tendency to ignore this catalogue of complaints as a women's issue, one not seriously related to questions of health policy and fundamental problems of the medical care system. Establishment policymakers especially have tended to dismiss the critiques of women health writers as based on radical, biased research. However, the growing numbers of complaints and their substantiation in nonfeminist sources appear to be "mainstreaming" women's charges against American medicine. For example, in 1976 the U.S. General Accounting Office confirmed that sterilizations had been performed by Indian Health Service physicians without the knowledge or consent of their patients. The *Journal of Dental Education* (Rosenberg and Thompson, 1976) found that male faculty and students in dental school perceive women students as deviants and assume they will practice neither full time nor as many years as their male colleagues. And in April 1977, Assistant Secretary of State Patsy Mink joined two other women in filing suit against the University of Chicago and Eli Lilly and Company for having been used in a drug test without their knowledge or consent. The drug they were administered, DES, has been proven to increase the risk of vaginal cancer in the daughters of DES recipients and to increase the risk of sterility in their sons.

These confirmations from well-accepted individuals that women experience serious deficiencies in their medical care provide some hope that future attempts to reform the health care system may address the special health concerns of women. However, since these concerns have not been addressed by health policymakers in the past, some skepticism is in order regarding the likelihood that they will be dealt with in the natural course of things.

To assure that women's needs are met by future health policies, feminists must undertake concerted efforts to explain women's problems within the current health system and point out how these problems relate to other systemic difficulties. That is the purpose of this paper. The first section of this chapter will explore the interrelationships between the feminist critique of American medicine and broader assessments of the system. The second section will describe in some detail the major problems women have identified as presenting particular difficulties for them. The third and final section will examine some of the reasons why medicine and health practitioners appear insensitive to women's concerns.

CRITIQUE OF AMERICAN MEDICINE

There is a consensus that the problems of American medicine fall into three broad categories (Fuchs, 1974): inadequate access to care, excessive cost of care, and inappropriate quality of care. Each of these problems has been recognized as a national health issue requiring some form of redress. What is less commonly recognized is that each of these problems has special implications for women that must be dealt with if the nation is to respond effectively and completely to access, cost, and quality of health care concerns.

AMERICAN MEDICAL SYSTEM AND WOMEN

The current health care system in the United States is inaccessible for many, too expensive, and does not always deliver high quality care. Women and men alike bear the burden of these deficiencies. However, because women have a different physiology from men, use the health care system differently, and are perceived differently by physicians, the problems of the health care system impact in different ways on women and on men. To assure that health care reform is directed toward the needs of women as well as the needs of men, it is vital to examine where the health care system fails to serve women.

WOMEN'S ACCESS TO CARE

Women's problems in access to health care begin at the very beginning—in the way access is measured. To evaluate medical care, need must first be established. Basic access studies being done by the National Opinion Research Center at the University of Chicago do not attempt to separate women's need for general primary care from their need for and access to gynecological care. Questionnaires used to determine need and physician utilization ask people to identify their primary care provider. The respondent selects one, not two, providers. Not surprisingly, 49% of the women (like 49% of the men) identify a general practitioner or internist as their primary care provider. However, since it is known that many general practitioners and internists do not practice office gynecology, this questionnaire does not identify whether all women's primary care needs are being met. The policy implications of this situation are clear. If access studies do not attempt to measure women's unmet medical care needs, it is unlikely that programs designed to meet those needs will be implemented.

Despite the lack of measurement of women's unmet medical care needs, evidence exists that there are several areas where unmet need and lack of access to care are overwhelming. Two of these areas are inadequate access to alcohol abuse research and treatment programs, and limited access to abortion services.

ALCOHOL ABUSE RESEARCH AND TREATMENT

An estimated one third of new members of Alcoholics Anonymous are women, yet only 14 of the 574 treatment programs funded by the National Institute for Alcohol Abuse and Alcoholism (NIAAA) are designed to treat women. Of 600 halfway houses in the United States, only 30 are for women. And, of 384 NIAAA-funded research projects, only 16 included women as research subjects, and only five were specifically concerned with women alcoholics. All other research projects used male subjects exclusively and were apparently predicated on the assumption that what is true of male alcoholics is true of female alcoholics (U.S. Senate, 1976:12).

These statistics lay bare the failure of public policymakers to recognize and deal with an illness in women which is the eighth largest killer in the United States today. Not only have public health authorities failed to provide access to treatment programs for women and to support continuing research on female alcoholics, but private physicians have also failed to identify alcoholism as a life-threatening disease for women. According to Antonia D'Angelo, board member of the National Council on Alcoholism, "Many physicians and psychiatrists are not able to recognize or treat alcoholism and often prescribe prescription drugs to women to try to alleviate their problems, which promotes the vicious cross-addiction problems for women" (U.S. Senate, 1976:11).

Although there is little hard data, one survey of physician offices in Omaha, Nebraska, showed that only 14% of the women alcoholics who presented themselves for treatment identified alcohol as the problem. Other medical or emotional problems were cited as the reason for the visit (U.S. Senate, 1976:231). This being the case, physicians' sensitivity to the possibility of alcoholism may be the key to identification and treatment of alcoholism. Unfortunately, this sensitivity runs counter to the societal myth that most alcoholics are men and that all female alcoholics are irresponsible women with loose morals. According to Gaines (U.S. Senate, 1976:119), "The role of women in our society, whether black or white, has been equated with wife and mother. The female alcoholic is seen as a special threat, as Joan Curleen points out, 'no one likes to believe that the hand that rocks the cradle might be a shaky one.' "

While all alcoholic women have problems obtaining diagnosis and treatment, certain communities of women have particular difficulties. Black women, for example, have been found to have higher abstinence rates and heavier drinking rates than white women (U.S. Senate, 1976:121). The lesbian community, like its male counterpart, suffers enormous alcoholism rates. One study (Fifield, 1975) estimates that 25 to 35% of the lesbian community is alcoholic. Although the causes of alcoholism are generally recognized as complex, lesbians have the additional problems of coping with their life-style in a hostile society and dealing with the tradition of the lesbian bar (U.S. Senate, 1976:133).

A possible breakthrough in public realization of female alcoholism came in 1976 with the passage of Public Law 94-371, the Comprehensive Alcohol Abuse and Alcoholism Prevention, Treatment, and Rehabilitation Act Amendments of 1976. This legislation provides that grant applications for treatment and prevention services for women should receive special attention in the grant review process. The amendments also require state alcoholism agencies to identify the needs of alcoholic women and to describe ways for their programs to meet these needs. While effective funding and implementation of the purposes of the act are yet to be accomplished, the lack of services for women alcoholics has been identified as a public concern.

ACCESS TO ABORTION SERVICES

Fundamental to woman's autonomy is her ability to control her body. It is on the issue of access to abortion services that the issues of women's health care and women's rights most clearly intersect. In 1971 in *Roe* v. *Wade* and *Doe* v. *Bolton,* the Supreme Court held that states may not prohibit abortions nor may they make the procedural regulations applying to abortions so onerous that the right to an abortion is effectively denied. Yet in 1975, according to a study by the Alan Guttmacher Institute (1976), women could not obtain safe, legal abortions in many parts of the country.

Access to abortion is concentrated in the largest urban areas. A map of the United States showing counties in which at least one abortion provider has been identified (Alan Guttmacher Institute, 1976) shows that abortion services are concentrated on the east and west coasts. For women in the Rocky Mountain states, the Midwest, and the South, obtaining an abortion will require the ability and money to travel long distances. In six states, for example, no abortions were performed in nonmetropolitan areas. These states were Arizona, Louisiana, Minnesota, Mississippi, Nebraska, and Rhode Island. Eight states—Massachusetts, Missouri, Nevada, Oklahoma, South Carolina, Texas, West Virginia, and Wisconsin— reported fewer than 100 abortions in their nonmetropolitan areas.

Because fertility studies have shown that the incidence of unwanted and mistimed births does not vary significantly by geographic area (Alan Guttmacher Institute, 1976), the absence of abortions in large parts of the country is related not to religious beliefs or cultural attitudes but rather to the unwillingness of the health care system to provide services to women. Thus the Guttmacher Institute study estimated that in 1975 approximately 260,000 to 770,000 women who needed abortions were unable to receive them.

Despite the Supreme Court ruling that pregnant women have a right to choose abortion, a majority of hospitals in the United States have refused to make this surgery available. In 1974 and early 1975, only 27% of non-Catholic private hospitals and 18% of public hospitals reported any abortions. The refusal of public hospitals to permit abortions is the primary reason why women and young girls in rural areas do not have access to abortion services. While free-standing clinics have played an increasing role in making abortions available in the United States, these clinics require a substantial population base to be economically viable. Thus, they are unable to serve sparsely populated areas.

The price of limited access to abortion services is frequently unwanted children or illegal abortions. Although the data are not complete, evidence suggests that the poor, young, nonwhite woman is most likely to bear the burden of limited access. For example, the Center for Disease Control reported that 80% of the deaths from illegal abortions were nonwhite women. Logic suggests that the poor who are the greatest users of public hospitals suffer most from the refusal to perform abortions. Logic also suggests that teenagers are particularly affected by the need to travel to obtain abortions

While abortion services are currently limited because hospitals and their medical staffs will not provide them, abortions may be curtailed in the future by limitations on public financing of abortions. In 1976 the United States Congress adopted the Hyde Amendment which prohibits the Department of Health, Education, and Welfare (DHEW) from using its funds to provide abortions except where the life of the mother would be endangered by carrying the baby to term. In 1976 an estimated 300,000 abortions, or one third of all legal abortions, were paid for by Medicaid. The Hyde Amendment, which with-stood a court challenge, was reintroduced in the Congress in 1977 and adopted. Both President Jimmy Carter and Secretary of Health, Education, and Welfare Joseph Califano have made clear their personal opposition to abortion and their support for efforts to terminate financial assistance for abortion services. The right of poor women to equal access to the health care system apparently has not won the support of health policy leaders in Washington.

QUALITY OF MEDICAL CARE

As urgent as access-to-care issues are, quality-of-care problems have evoked the strongest feelings among health consumers. The society-wide debate over medical quality includes a range of charges against the health care system. It is argued that Americans are overoperated upon, overprescribed with undertested drugs, and generally victimized by a medical approach to health maintenance. To this catalogue of complaints, those who have examined the impact of the health care system on women have added additional charges of malpractice. Among these are charges that women have been overemphasized in contraception, underprotected on the job, overtreated during pregnancy, and misinformed in treatment of mental or emotional disorders, and that problems of major propor-tions, such as teenage pregnancy, have been ignored by health professionals and policymakers alike.

WOMEN AS PATIENTS

The most troubling charge regarding women and medicine is that physicians diagnose and treat women inadequately because male physicians hold biased perceptions of women (Corea, 1977). Ehren-reich (1974) reviewed nearly two centuries of physician dominance of health care and argued that women have been victimized by a medical "science" that attributes all their disorders to malfunctioning of the reproductive tract or that dismisses women generally as being fundamentally silly or neurotic.

The mythology that has focused on links between a female's personality and her reproductive organs appears to have made a profound impact on the clinical treatment of women. Haller (1977) has charted the waxing and waning over the years of gynecological fashions that have included painful, damaging, and pointless procedures involving the vagina, clitoris, uterus, and various points in between. That female surgery has been in vogue a long time is evidenced by a remark from Kime (1892) that he would rather take his chances as a "moonshiner in the mountains of East Tennessee than be a uterus in New York" (Haller, 1977:31). Eighty years later the uterus is still in jeopardy. A 1970 study (Bunker) found that in the United States the hysterectomy rate per 100,000 was twice that found in England and Wales. More recently, a sociologist studying ob/gyn residency programs at two hospitals found that residents had a sales pitch developed to convince their patients to part with their uterii. This pitch was based on the not-uncommon theme in obstetrics and gynecology today that removal of the uterus guards against cancer of the uterus. What the sales pitch did not say is that the death rate from cancer of the uterus is less than the death rate from complications due to hysterectomies (Corea, 1977).

Other indications of physician antifemale bias or disregard for women is seen in traits attributed to women by Freudian analysis, failure to inform women in drug tests or sterilization procedures, and references to women in medical literature, both professional writings and those designed for lay persons. Consider the implications of the 1970 gynecology textbook quoted by Scully and Bart (1973) which directs the medical student that he or she should advise the bride "to allow her husband's sex drive to set their pace and she should attempt to gear hers satisfactorily to his" (Novak, Jones and Jones, 1970).

That women are seen as unreliable testifiers to their own health status and as prone to psychosomatic illness was explored by Lennane and Lennane (1973). A similar study (Hare, 1974) suggested that if a woman is sick and no physiological malfunction is apparent, she is likely to be told that "it is all in her head." Hare describes an article that appeared in the *British Medical Journal* describing a syndrome called Iceland disease. This disease produces numerous discomforts but does not give evidence of physiological disorders. The authors of the article conclude that since the vast preponderance of victims of this disease are women, the cause of the disease is probably mental rather than physical (Hare, 1974:2224).

Hare suggests some other possibilities of differential treatment for men and women. She points out that prior to federal legislation underwriting the kidney machine use, there is some evidence that men were favored patients for the machine. In 1971 she found that 65% of the 5,000 patients on chronic dialysis were male. As the mortality rates for men and women from kidney failure were not dissimilar, this 2:1 ratio was not anticipated. Prior to federal funding for the renal dialysis program, persons eligible for the machines were selected on the basis of criteria established and applied by a hospital committee. It is possible that the availability for men of free care through the Veteran's Administration hospital system or the application of an economic worth criteria might have contributed to the skewing of the sex ratio of patients using the kidney machines.

While federal funding for renal dialysis units (kidney machines) has reduced the probability that women will be denied access to the machines due to inability to pay or low economic worth, the new drive to contain hospital costs may lead to limited use of expensive medical machinery or laboratory tests. If choices must be made about who will receive expensive, possibly life-saving, treatment, they come down to deciding who shall live. What is the value of a female life as compared to a male life? What has been the value assigned in the past? What will be the value assigned in the future? What decisions will be made when a woman lies unconscious in an emergency room?

The foregoing paragraphs have suggested some of the medical care implications of attitudes toward women that are prevalent in our society. The following paragraphs will examine more closely some specific medical problems for women that have been either ignored or unsatisfactorily addressed by the health care system.

OCCUPATIONAL HEALTH

Women are 41% of the labor force. The majority of these women are of child-bearing age. Under Title VII of the Civil Rights Act of

1964, women have a legal guarantee against job discrimination. They do not, however, have a guarantee to a safe work environment. Pregnant women are not considered entitled to a healthy work place.

On-the-job dangers to women and their health have been catalogued recently in a number of excellent publications. Corea (1977), Hricko and Brunt (1976), and Hunt (1975) all describe current information that focuses especially on the impact of toxic-substance exposure on women's reproductive capacity. Among the findings they report are the following:

Anesthetists and operating room nurses in European studies suffer 38% and 30% miscarriage rates, respectively. These rates compare to a 10% miscarriage rate among general-duty nurses. An American study cosponsored by the American Society for Anesthesiology confirmed the higher miscarriage rate and also found a threefold increase in birth defects among children of nurse anesthetists. The American study also indicated that women in the operating room suffered an increased risk of cancer and liver and kidney disease. Male operating room personnel showed no demonstrable increase in cancer but were at greater risk than the general population for liver disease. The wives of operating room personnel also gave birth to children with an abnormally high number of birth defects.

Atomic workers and others exposed to radiation demonstrate substantially increased risks of cancer. Research indicates that radiation levels that may not be harmful to an adult may have numerous deleterious effects on unborn children. These effects include leukemia and increased risk of brain damage. Current exposure standards set by the Nuclear Regulatory Commission and the Energy Research and Development Administration exceed the safety level for fetuses (Krekel, 1976).

Estrogen manufacturers, male and female, suffer reproductive tract disorders. Men are reported suffering from enlarged breasts and decreased libido. Women are reported experiencing heavy bleeding during their menstrual periods and psotmenopausal irregular heavy bleeding.

These data suggest that substantial numbers of the working population are at risk because they labor in hazardous conditions. Many of these workers suffer increased hazards because they are pregnant.

Adoption of the Occupational Safety and Health Act in 1970 offered a new opportunity for women to secure the right to work in a safe environment. The 1970 legislation establishes that employers should maintain work places that are free from recognized hazards. The Occupational Safety and Health Administration (OSHA) in the Department of Labor has been charged with setting and enforcing standards. The National Institute for Occupational Safety and Health, DHEW, is responsible for conducting research necessary to determine safety levels for worker exposure to various hazardous substances.

While understaffing and underbudgeting have prevented both agencies from effecting the purposes of the act, the primary block to effective enforcement appears to be attitudes among government agencies as to what constitutes a safe work place for women. In 1976, for example, OSHA issued draft standards for the lead industry which permit worker exposure above the level determined safe for pregnant workers. As of this writing, final regulations have not been issued but it appears clear that a pregnant worker or a worker who might be pregnant will not be considered entitled to work in a "high risk" environment. For some workers this may mean being forced to choose between termination of pregnancy or leaving the job and suffering the economic consequences of unemployment.

TEENAGE PREGNANCY

Teenage pregnancy is a major public health issue. Surveys suggest that 80% of such pregnancies are unwanted. Since unwanted children are likely to be the victims of child abuse, these children are likely to grow up physically and emotionally deprived. Because teenage mothers are likely to be poor, these children will also grow up in an economically deprived environment (Green and Lowe, 1976).

Statistically, children of teenage mothers suffer serious health risks. First, they tend to be premature with low birth weights. These factors contribute to mental retardation, epilepsy, and cerebral palsy. Infant mortality for children of mothers under 15 is twice that of babies born to women in thier twenties. Teenage mothers also suffer adverse health consequences, including toxemia, prolonged labor, and iron-deficiency anemia.

In 1974, 1,000,000 teenagers became pregnant; 608,000 of these teenagers had babies and an estimated 300,000 had abortions (Green and Lowe, 1976). While birth rates for women over 20 have sharply declined, the birth rates for teenagers from 15 to 19 years old have decreased only slightly, and the birth rates for teenagers under 15 have remained constant.

Increased sexual activity among teenagers and failure to use contraceptives have contributed to the growing epidemic of teenage pregnancies. Teenage failure to use contraceptives is marked. A 1971 nationwide study reported that 53% of sexually active teenagers failed to use contraceptives the last time they had intercourse. Non-use of contraceptives can only partially be related to the difficulty of obtaining contraceptives. Minors may obtain contraceptives without parental consent in 26 states and the District of Columbia. Minors can obtain abortions at their own request in 25 states and the District of Columbia (Green and Lowe, 1976).

Only in 1977 did the U.S. Department of Health, Education, and Welfare publicly indicate that it perceived teenage pregnancy as a major health problem and request public funding to initiate programs to reduce unwanted births to teenagers. However, the coupling of this initiative with the opposition from the Secretary for Health, Education, and Welfare to federal funding of abortions suggests that what teenagers may gain on the one hand may be taken away by the other.

BIRTH CONTROL DRUGS AND DEVICES

Criticism of inadequate testing of drugs and devices to control female fertility or treat postmenopausal conditions appears to head the list of complaints women have about the quality of medical care they receive in the United States. Charges of failure to request informed consent of participants in drug studies (the use of Depo-Provera; DES), deceptive advertising (Dalkon Shield), and inadequate attention to the risks for women posed by certain drugs (DES; the pill) have been primary concerns.

Depo-Provera. The case of Depo-Provera provides an instructive lesson in how the needs of health care providers and health policy-makers can operate to the detriment of female consumers.

Depo-Provera sounds like the ideal contraceptive for the illiterate, the incompetent, or women being cared for by public health officials. It is a drug administered by injection that prevents pregnancy for three months. Depo-Provera is cheap to administer, convenient for custodians of mental patients because it inhibits menstrual periods, and is a contraceptive that allows fertility control by those who provide the medical care. There is no need to rely on the patient's ability to remember to take a pill or use a diaphragm. Because of its convenience, it has been utilized in family planning clinics and mental institutions, and by private physicians. Depo-Provera is suspected of increasing the risks of sterility, cervical cancer, and breast cancer. It has not been approved by the Food and Drug Administration (FDA) for use as a contraceptive (U.S. Senate, 1973).

Why is Depo-Provera available for prescription by physicians if its use as a contraceptive has not been approved? Depo-Provera is effective as a treatment for endometrial cancer (cancer of the uterine lining), therefore the drug is available on prescription through pharmacies. There is no way to prohibit a physician from prescribing Depo-Provera for uses other than cancer treatment.

Investigational drug studies permitting the use of Depo-Provera as a contraceptive began in 1963. In 1970, injections of Depo-Provera were reported to cause breast tumors in dogs. Later tests showed that some of these tumors were malignant. Although this evidence provoked the Food and Drug Administration and its Obstetrics and Gynecology Advisory Committee to request long-term metabolic studies, the committee approved the continued human use of Depo-Provera. The reasoning behind this continued approval, as described by Dr. Charles Edwards, then director of the FDA, had little to do with drug safety: "As can be seen by review of the patient consent form, its use is intended for a very restricted patient population; i.e., those who have tried all other birth control methods without success. . . . In this group, it is felt that its known benefit outweighs its theoretical risk since no alternative therapy is available." Despite complaints from health consumer groups, Depo-Provera is still available in pharmacies and is still being prescribed for contraceptive usage.

DES (Diethylstilbestrol). DES is another drug that causes cancer. Documented evidence shows that DES causes vaginal cancer in the daughters of women who have taken DES during pregnancy. DES is also associated with cervical cancer. Because of its cancer-inducing properties, DES has been banned as a growth-promoting additive in cattle feed. DES has not been banned for use by women. In 1973 DES was approved as an emergency, morning-after, postintercourse contraceptive by the FDA.

For 30 years, from 1940 to 1971, DES was prescribed as a drug to avert miscarriages. Several million pregnant women took the drug. A reported 2.1 to 3.5 million DES daughters were born to these women. A documented 120 have developed a rare form of vaginal cancer. Ninety percent of the DES daughters are estimated to have abnormal structures in the vagina or cervix which may be precancerous. Even since the 1971 discovery that DES increased the incidence of vaginal cancer, physicians have continued to prescribe DES to prevent miscarriage. Repeated bulletins from the FDA warning physicians and hospitals about the dangers to DES daughters have failed to halt this practice. Moreover, despite the clear linkage between DES and cancer, DES continues to be prescribed to women as a morning-after contraceptive. Senate hearings in 1973 produced testimony documenting the widespread use of DES at college health services. According to those hearings, random checks of college health services indicated that little effort appeared to be made to inform the patient of DES risks or to secure a family history sufficient to determine if the patient was a DES daughter and therefore at greater risk.

Dalkon Shield. The Dalkon Shield was a health-shattering experience for women. A documented 17 women died, and many more suffered serious complications, including hysterectomies, before the shield was taken off the market.

From 1968 to 1970, the Dalkon Shield, an interuterine device (IUD), was developed and tested on 558 clinic patients and 82 private patients by Dr. Hugh Davis of Johns Hopkins University. In February, 1970, Dr. Davis published his findings on the Dalkon Shield in the *American Journal of Obstetrics and Gynecology.* The report concluded that a two-year study of this device showed a 1.1% failure rate, a rate substantially superior to other IUDs. The report did not mention either that the average test patient had worn the device for an average of 5.5 months or that Dr. Davis had told at least some of his patients to use a spermicide from the 10th to 17th days of their cycles. The report also failed to note that Dr. Davis was co-owner of the device (Dowie and Johnston, 1976:37ff).

Davis's glowing account of the Dalkon Shield experiment, together with increasing concern about side effects of "the pill," generated immediate popularity for the shield. During the next three years, an estimated 3.3 million Dalkon Shields were distributed to women in the United States and overseas.

The beginning of the end for the Dalkon Shield came in the spring of 1973 when congressional hearings on the need to regulate medical devices brought forward an army major, Russel Thomsen, who testified regarding his patients' experiences with the Dalkon Shield. Septic abortion, pelvic inflammation, serious cramping, and excessive bleeding were complications suffered by women he had fitted with the Dalkon Shield (Dowie and Johnston, 1976). Immediately, a flood of reports from concerned physicians and patients began to inundate A. H. Robins, Inc., the Dalkon Shield manufacturer, and the Food and Drug Administration. In 1974, A. H. Robins was suffiently impressed by reported deaths and complications that it withdrew the shield from the market. In 1977, the company was still negotiating with survivors of the Dalkon Shield experience regarding damages and compensation.

HEALTH CARE COSTS AND FINANCING

The escalation of health care costs is a well-documented phenomenon of the past 20 years. Over the past 10 years, especially, health care costs continually outstripped annual inflation rates. As noted earlier, in 1976 hospital charges increased 13.4% while physician charges rose 11.4%. These increases have focused attention not only on finding ways to contain rising costs, but also on alternative mechanisms for financing health care bills.

Rising costs per se have some special impacts on women. Because many women receive their primary care from two physicians, an internist/general practitioner and an obstetrician/gynecologist, women must pay for two physician visits to obtain comprehensive primary care. At least partially as a result of this pattern of physician usage, women make almost twice as many visits to physicians as men. Thus, they bear a higher percentage of the burden of health care cost inflation.

In response to increasing prices and concerns that higher prices will make health care inaccessible to many Americans, the U.S. Congress has been considering ways to help people pay their doctor bills. The alternative means of assistance being considered are all some form of national health insurance. For women to benefit fully from national health insurance, the program must be designed to respond to women's needs—needs that are not always the same as men's. Since private health insurance is frequently used as a model that national health insurance might draw upon, the following discussion of health insurance will first examine how women have been dealt with by private health insurers and then will consider some of the national health insurance issues that have direct implications for women.

PRIVATE HEALTH INSURANCE

Historically, women have paid more and received less for health and major medical coverage by private insurers than men (Denenberg, 1973). Although insurers do not classify insurance risks on the basis of race, it is still acceptable to classify individuals on the basis of sex. Under this method of classification women often pay higher premiums for more limited coverage.

Two basic health-related insurance problems for women include inadequate or nonexistent insurance for the medical expense of pregnancy and its complications and inadequate or nonexistent disability coverage for pregnancy and related costs.

Medical expense coverage for pregnancy or pregnancy-related complications is generally so minimal as to be meaningless. In some plans, maternity benefits are subject to a flat maximum payment for medical/surgical and hospital expenses. In this author's case, that maximum represented approximately 10% of actual costs for a simple delivery and two days of hospitalization. The same plan reimburses for other surgical and medical expenses on a substantially more generous basis.

Other limitations on maternity benefits include limits on the number of days allowed for hospitalization, refusal to cover maternity benefits for single women, and refusal to provide maternity benefits for dependent children (Denenberg, 1973). Some major medical insurance policies refuse to cover pregnancy and pregnancy-related complications at all.

The issue of disability benefits for women employed outside the home is currently being debated in the U.S. Congress. In December 1976, in *Gilbert* v. *General Electric,* the Supreme Court held that the exclusion of pregnancy coverage from worker disability plans was not sex discrimination and therefore was not a violation of Title VII of the Civil Rights Act of 1964. In March 1977, a bill to reverse the

Gilbert decision was introduced in both the Senate and the House of Representatives. A coalition of women's rights and civil rights groups and labor unions has maintained that providing disability coverage for hair transplants but not pregnancy does indeed constitute sex discrimination. Insurance companies and major employers are arguing that the cost of pregnancy coverage would be staggering and would force employers not to employ women. The cost of covering smokers and heavy drinkers is also staggering, but no one has suggested that they be denied coverage under group insurance packages.

NATIONAL HEALTH INSURANCE

With women's needs having fared badly under private health insurance plans, there is reason for concern over coverage of these needs under proposed national health insurance. It is generally conceded that some form of national health insurance will be designed and implemented during the Carter administration. In anticipation, numerous studies have examined the many issues that must be addressed by national health insurance. Only one author (Lewis, 1976, 1977) has discussed the implications of national health insurance plans for women's health care.

Lewis focused on six areas of national health insurance that have major implications for women: (1) eligibility for benefits, (2) scope of benefits, (3) cost-sharing formulas, (4) provider participation and reimbursement procedures, (5) delivery of medical care, and (6) accountability. Lewis's analysis of the issues and recommendations for policy are summarized below.

Eligibility

Participation in national health insurance can be made automatic for all citizens, or provisional through a financial contribution at work, or something in between. If eligibility is established via the family unit, it would mean that the three-fifths of adult American women who are wives would probably be enrolled in the national health insurance program in the dependent wife category. Enrollment in this category has several implications. First, change in marital status would disrupt coverage and might expose women to financial risk. Second, privacy of the wife's medical records would be difficult to maintain because proof of eligibility would be provided through the husband. If a woman wanted to obtain medical care without her husband's knowledge, she would be unable to do so unless she were able to pay the costs out-of-pocket. The only way to insure continuous insurance coverage for women and to protect their right to privacy would be to enroll persons in national health insurance on an individual basis.

Scope of Benefits

As noted above, private health insurance does not provide full coverage for pregnancy and pregnancy-related complications. It also may exclude coverage for single women or for insured dependent children. If women are to have equity in health insurance coverage, national health insurance should provide full benefits for pregnant women. Special health care preventive and diagnostic services for women should also be covered, including semiannual pelvic examinations, nutritional counseling for pregnant and nursing mothers, and psychiatric care for rape victims.

Cost Sharing

One means of limiting the use of medical care under national health insurance is the institution of coinsurance or cost-sharing arrangements whereby the individual pays a percentage of the cost of each visit. A variation on this cost-containment feature is a cap or ceiling on the number of visits for which a person will be reimbursed during a specified time period. Again, because most women receive their primary care from two physicians, a coinsurance mechanism that requires women to pay a percentage of each visit will be particularly onerous and may discourage appropriate visits to physicians or other health care providers.

Since some form of cost containment can be anticipated with national health insurance, the objective should be to insure that women do not have to pay more for their medical care than men do. Lewis suggests exempting women's gynecological care from cost-sharing arrangements or providing a maximum amount that all insured persons would pay out-of-pocket for medical expenses.

Provider Participation and Reimbursement

An issue of particular concern to women is which providers of medical care will be entitled to reimbursement under national health insurance. A number of professions might be entitled, including physicians, dentists, nurse practitioners, midwives, health educators, nutritionists, hospitals, health centers, and so forth. Currently, an estimated 3.5 to 4.0 million women receive care at family planning clinics and women's health centers. These centers may not now bill patients or insurers for support services. Only the physician may bill for services. Physician income must cover all support services and costs, from rent to nutrition education. An alternative arrangement would be to designate the health centers as providers and authorize the centers to bill for support services in the same way that hospitals may.

Delivery of Care Mechanisms

Most medical care in the United States is available on a fee-for-service basis from individual practitioners. Under this model, women customarily see an internist or general practitioner to diagnose nongynecological problems and a gynecologist to assess problems with their reproductive organs. This split in care, which is necessitated by internists' and general practitioners' dislike of office gynecology, could be encouraged or discouraged by the reimbursement mechanisms established under national health insurance. Some consideration should be given to designing national health insurance in such a way as to encourage the integration of women's health care.

Quality of Care

One of the most effective cost-containment mechanisms would also improve the quality of medical care for women; that is, requiring that all elective, nonemergency surgery require a second opinion. Next to abortions and tonsillectomies, hysterectomies are the surgical procedure performed most often. While some of these operations are no doubt warranted, the vast difference between the United States and Great Britain in the incidence of this type of surgery suggests that a large portion of hysterectomies may well be unnecessary.

Accountability

Lewis's final suggestion regarding national health insurance is that women must be guaranteed participation in every stage of the policymaking process. Private insurance companies are noted for their exclusion of women from the top. Denenberg (1973) reported that each of the five leading life insurance companies had only one woman among 40 or more top officers and directors. Overall, about 97½% of the insurance company boards were men. Women are also absent from the boards of the quasi-public Blue Cross/Blue Shield insurance plans. For example, in 1977 the governing boards of Blue Cross and Blue Shield in the District of Columbia had only one woman each. The total number of directors on the two boards was 41. It is difficult to believe that the absence of women at the top does not relate to insurance company practices which limit women's coverage under health insurance programs.

THE REASON WHY

The catalogue of problems outlined briefly in the foregoing pages demands some explanation. Why? Why the omission of women from occupational health programs? Why the absence of treatment programs for alcoholic women? Why the limited testing of contraceptives for women? Why the Dalkon Shield and DES daughters?

The immediate, visceral response is that this pervasive neglect of women's health needs and the inattention to hazards to their health must flow from some well-organized, deliberate plot. But it is not a plot. American medicine is too fragmented, too disorganized, and too divided within itself to orchestrate a coordinated strategy to abuse American women.

The answer to the question *why* appears to be fairly simple. Women's health problems are neglected because the people who make public health policy and who conduct medical research, educate physicians, and deliver medical care are, for the most part, men who share the biases of American society concerning women.

The absence of women at the top in the medical care system is striking. Despite the fact that women compose over 70% of health care providers, women are nowhere evident in the corridors of medical power. A review of key elements in the medical care delivery and health policy systems confirms the absence of women.

The key decision makers of the content and quality of medical care are the physicians themselves. In 1974, 10% of the physicians were female. More strikingly, only 5.6% of the internists were women, and 7.1% of the obstetrician/gynecologists were women. Although the entering medical class in the fall of 1976 was approximately 25% female, it will be seven years before this class has moved through medical school and residency programs to begin practicing medicine.

Another vital element in health policy and programs is the medical training institution. Medical schools have played major roles in shaping physician perceptions of women patients, encouraging (or discouraging) women physicians-in-training, and providing health policy leadership. Women are a small fraction of the medical school faculties and an even smaller fraction of the medical school leadership. In 1974, women constituted 3.9% of medical school faculties and 0% of the deanships (Witte et al., 1976). One study (U.S. DHEW, 1975) shows the number of women teaching full time in medical school in 1973 had actually declined 2.2% during the preceding 10 years, from 5.3% to 3.1%. During the same period the number of female physicians had increased from 14,957 to 24,354. The implications of the absence of women in medical academia are obvious. There are few role models to inspire women students. There are few teachers to assure that women receive equitable treatment. Perhaps most important, there are few female resources that can be drawn upon to assume health policy leadership positions in government.

The absence of women at the top of the federal health bureaucracy may well have its roots in the absence of women from deanships in the medical schools. DHEW draws heavily upon the medical schools for personnel to head the major federal health programs. Listings in the 1975 *Federal Directory* indicate that of 22 senior positions listed in a chart of officials in the Office of the Assistant Secretary for Health, only two positions were filled by women, the Director of Nursing Home Affairs and Director of the Office of Equal Employment Opportunity. The picture for women does not improve as one looks further down the chain of command. For example, of the 10 institutes within the National Institutes for Health, only one was headed by a woman.

At the local level, women are in an equally poor position to influence health policies or programs. As noted earlier, women constitute a fraction of the physicians in the community. With the exception of the sister-administrators of Catholic hospitals, they are also absent from administrative leadership. Nor do the policy-setting boards of trustees of hospitals have significant female representation. A Washington, D.C., study (Pear, 1977) found that at 31 area hospitals, of 640 trustees, 108 were women. Most of these women were identified as nuns who direct the Catholic hospitals or as Lady Bountifuls, wealthy contributors included for prestige and fund-raising purposes.

A role that women could and should play on hospital boards or other health policy institutions is assessing programs' responsiveness to women's concerns. For example, in the Washington, D.C., study, a black male trustee for the Prince Georges General Hospital described how he viewed his role on the board by explaining what he did when the issue was raised of affiliating the hospital to the University of Maryland Medical School. "So I raised the question, 'What is being done to assure that we will get a fairly representative number of residents and interns who are minorities and women?' . . . If we have a policy on pregnancy, unwed mothers or sterilization, what do women, especially minority women, think about it?" Too few women and men are raising these questions, and women suffer as a result.

A new opportunity for women to shape local health services has been presented by the institution of the new planning organizations, the Health Systems Agencies (HSAs). The HSAs, which are being established nationwide, are directed by governing boards whose membership must be at least 51% consumer representatives. These boards may play a key role in developing new health programs and approving changes in existing services by local hospitals. Unfortunately, women are not moving onto the HSA boards in large numbers. DHEW estimates that approximately 25% of the governing boards' membership is composed of women.

In part the solution to the absence of women from policymaking positions is to increase the number of women in medicine, hospital administration, and health planning. A more direct route, however, is to broaden the representation of health professions in the policy-making process. Currently, physicians and hospital administrators are the health care providers who sit on planning committees and governmental advisory groups or serve as health program adminis-trators. If other health care professions were represented in these activities, the role of women in policymaking would dramatically increase.

Although women make up a fraction of the physicians and hospital administrators in the United States, they represent the overwhelming majority in other health professions. For example, women are 98.5% of the registered nurses, 89% of the occupational therapists, 97.5% of the dietitians, and 70% of the medical technologists. Overall, women compose 66% of the professionals within health occupational groups (American Public Health Association, 1975b). Thus, an informed voice for women in health policy and program development could be achieved instantaneously by breaking the physician/hospital administrator monopoly on decision-making in health.

SUMMARY

This paper began with the statement that while indicators of women's health status were going up, indicators of women's feelings about the medical care they were receiving have been going down. A review of the problems that women have experienced in gaining access to care, obtaining quality care, and paying for their medical care suggests why there is increasing resentment among women toward the medical establishment. The solutions to these problems will be neither easy nor cheap. But, for their own health, women cannot afford to let their health and medical care needs be ignored or defined as exceptional and therefore outside the proper purview of public health policy.

REFERENCES

Alan Guttmacher Institute (1976). Abortion 1974-1975: Need and services in the United States, each state and metropolitan area. New York: Author.

American Public Health Association (1975a). Health and work in America: A chart book. Washington, D.C.: Author.

——— (1975b). Women in health careers. Washington, D.C.: Author.

American Society of Anesthesiologists (1974). "Occupational disease among operating room personnel: A national study." Anesthesiology, 41(4).

AUSTIN, G.B., MAHER, M.M., and LOMONACO, C.J. (1976). "Women in dentistry and medicine: Additudinal survey of educational experience." Journal of Dental Education, 40(10):11-13.

BUNKER, J.P. (1970). "Surgical manpower: A comparison of operations and surgeons in the United States and in England and Wales." New England Journal of Medicine, 282(3):135-144.

CAMPBELL, M.A. (1973). (See Howell, M.C.) Why would a girl go into medicine? Medical education in the United States: A guide for women. Old Westbury, N.Y.: The Feminist Press.

Center for Women in Medicine, The Medical College of Pennsylvania (1975). Double dynamics: Women's roles in health and illness. Philadelphia: Author.

CHESLER, P. (1972). Women and madness. New York: Doubleday.

COREA, G. (1977). The hidden malpractice: How American medicine treats women as patients and professionals. New York: William Morrow.

Daedalus (1977). "Doing better and feeling worse: Health in the United States." Proceedings of the American Academy of Arts and Sciences, Winter, 106(1):1-281.

DENENBERG, H. (1973). "Statement." Pp. 153-168 in U.S. Joint Economic Committee, Economic problems of women, Hearings, Part 1, Washington, D.C.: U.S. Government Printing Office.

DOWIE, M., and JOHNSTON, T. (1976). "A case of corporate malpractice." Mother Jones 1(8):37ff.

EHRENREICH, B. (1974). "Gender and objectivity in medicine." International Journal of Health Services, 4(4):617-623.

EHRENREICH, B., and ENGLISH, D. (1973). Witches, midwives and nurses: A history of women healers. Old Westbury, N.Y.: Feminist Press.

FIFIELD, L. (1975). "On my way to nowhere: An analysis of gay alcohol abuse and an evaluation of rehabilitation services of the Los Angeles gay community." July 10. Contract 25125. County of Los Angeles.

FUCHS, V.R. (1974). Who shall live: Health, economics and social choice. New York: Basic Books.

GREEN, C.P., and LOWE, S.J. (1976). Teenage pregnancy: A major problem for minors. New York: Alan Guttmacher Institute.

HARE, D. (1974). "The victim is guilty." Federation Proc., 35:2223-2225.

HALLER, J.S. (1977). "Abuses in gynecological surgery: An historical appraisal." Pp. 27-32 in U.S. DHEW, Women and their health: Research implications for a new era. Rockville, Md.: Author.

HEINS, M., et al. (1976). "Productivity of women physicians." Journal of the American Medical Association, 236(17):1961-1964.

HOWELL, M.C. [pseud., see Campbell, M.A.] (n.d., circa 1972). Why would a girl go into medicine. Old Westbury, N.Y.: Feminist Press.

HRICKO, A., and BRUNT, M. (1976). Working for your life: A women's guide to job health hazards. Berkeley, Calif.: Labor Occupational Health Program, Center for Labor Research and Education, Institute of Industrial Relations, University of California.

HUNT, V.R. (1975). Occupational health problems of pregnant women. University Park: Pennsylvania State University.

KIME, R.R. (1892). "What is gynecology?" Transactions, Medical Assn. of Georgia, 103-111.

KREKEL, S. (1976). Placement of women in high risk areas. Paper presented at Society on Environmental Health Conference on Women in the Workplace, Washington, D.C., June 17-19.

LENNANE, J.K., and LENNANE, R. (1973). "Alleged psychogenic disorders in women—A possible manifestation of sexual prejudice." New England Journal of Medicine, February 8.

LEWIS, D. (1976). "Principles regarding national health insurance and women's health care." Paper presented at 104th annual meeting of American Public Health Association, Miami Beach, Florida, October 18.

––– (1977). "Women and national health insurance." Medical Care, XVI, 7:549-558.

MARIENSKIND, H. (1975). "Restructuring ob-gyn." Social Policy, 6(2):48-49.

MARIENSKIND, H., and EHRENREICH, B. "Toward socialist medicine: The women's health movement." Social Policy, 6(2):34-42.

MINTZ, M. (1977). "University, firm sued over DES tests in mothers." The Washington Post, April 26:1+.

New York Times (1976). "Study finds many Indians sterilized by U.S. agency without full explanation." 126(November 23):16c.

NOVAK, E.R., JONES, G.E., and JONES, H.W. (1970). Novak's textbook of gynecology. Baltimore: Williams & Wilkens.

PEAR, R. (1977). "Well-to-do white men dominante area boards." The Washington Star, April 17:B1+.

ROSENBERG, H.M., and THOMPSON, N.L. (1976). "Attitudes toward women dental students among male dental students and male dental faculty." Journal of Dental Education, 40(10):676-680.

SCULLY, D., and BART, P. (1973). "A funny thing happened on the way to the orifice: Women in gynecology textbooks." Pp. 283-292 in J. Huber (ed.), Changing Women in a Changing Society. Chicago: University of Chicago Press.

SEAMON, B. (1975). "Pelvic autonomy: Four proposals." Social Policy, 6(2):43-47.

STERN, M.S. (1976). "Impacts of changes in physician manpower sex ratio." Journal of Medical Education, 51(December):1012-1013.

U.S. Department of Health, Education, and Welfare. Public Health Service. Health Resources Administration. National Center for Health Services Research (1975). "Women and their health: Research implications for a new era." NCHSR Research Proceedings Series, August 1-2. San Francisco, Calif. (1977). DHEW Pub. No. (HRA) 77-3138. Rockville, Md.: U.S. DHEW.

U.S. Department of Health, Education, and Welfare. Public Health Service. Health Resources Administration. National Center for Health Statistics (1976). "Health: United States 1975." DHEW Pub. No. (HRA) 76-1232. Rockville, Md.: U.S. DHEW.

U.S. General Accounting Office (1976). Federal control of new drug testing is not adequately protecting human test subjects and the public (July 15). Washington, D.C.: Government Accounting Office.

U.S. Senate. Committee on Labor and Public Welfare. Subcommittee on Alcoholism and Narcotics (1976). Hearings on alcohol abuse among women: Special problems and unmet needs. Washington, D.C.: U.S. Government Printing Office.

U.S. Senate. Committee on Labor and Public Welfare. Subcommittee on Health (1973). Quality of health care—Human experimentation (February 21, 22). Washington, D.C.: U.S. Government Printing Office.

Urban and Rural Systems Associates (1976). Exploratory study of women in the health professions schools. 10 vols. San Francisco, Calif.: Author.

WILLSON, J.R. (1971). Obstetrics and gynecology. St. Louis, Mo.: Mosby.

WITTE, M., et al. (1976). "Women physicians in the United States medical schools: A preliminary report." Journal of the American Medical Women's Association, 31(5).

WEIKSNAR, M. (1976). "To hire or fire: The case of women in the workplace." Technology Review, (October-November):16-18.

10

THE ECONOMICS OF
WOMEN'S VICTIMIZATION

JANE ROBERTS CHAPMAN

The preceding chapters show conclusively that the female victim pays an economic penalty whether she is raped, battered, or otherwise abused. It may be relatively small—missing a day from work to testify at a trial—or it may be large—weeks of hospitalization or the loss of a job. Whether large or small, the economic penalty is almost always greater for the victim than for her attacker or for society. In addition, economic factors are most often the key to a woman's initial vulnerability to physical attack, to her inability to escape from prolonged victimization, and to her lack of capacity to remedy, reduce, or avoid the consequences of victimization.

Previous chapters have described women's victimization and the treatment they receive from institutions such as the courts or health facilities. The following discussion presumes that the reader is familiar with the legal, social, psychological, and physical problems that have been presented. The purpose is to outline ways in which economic factors contribute to victimization. This chapter identifies the economic consequences of the types of female victimization that have been addressed and assesses remedies currently available to female victims.

The discussion in no way attempts to place a dollar value on human suffering. The situations of the wife who is beaten with such regularity that she no longer thinks of herself as a person, the incest victim who embarks on a lifetime of self-punishment, and the woman who is sterilized without her consent are tragedies that have more than economic consequences. But the economic factors are inter-twined with events in such a way that they are an integral part of victimization, and limited resources often constitute the crucial factor in the ability of any person to extricate herself from violent situations or to remedy the damage done by abuse.

The victims of rape, spouse abuse, molestation, and battering are predominantly women. In addition, women as a group are poorer and generally more vulnerable, economically, than men. That is, they are more likely to be unemployed or dependent, and have fewer assets (Chapman, 1976). Women are, therefore, disproportionately represented among the poor and even when employed are largely confined to low-paying jobs. Their earnings averaged less than 60% of men's in 1976 (U.S. Census Bureau).

The low economic status of women contributes to their vulner-ability to all perils, whether they be social, political, or physical, and makes them susceptible to certain kinds of crimes in the first place. Poor or elderly women with limited incomes frequently must live in neighborhoods where assaults are common. Their reliance on public transportation and, in some cases, the need to travel to and from work at night make them likely targets.

FAMILY VIOLENCE AND SEXUAL ABUSE

Some victimization is made possible or prolonged by female economic dependency. This is especially true of that which occurs within the family. A woman who is being physically abused by her husband finds it difficult to leave if she has no other source of income and limited job skills. A child being sexually abused by an adult male within her family is even more dependent. Until she reaches adolescence, it may not even occur to her that she might have an opportunity to run away or otherwise escape the abuse.

BATTERED WOMEN

The economic problems suffered by a battered woman are of two types. First are those caused by a specific crisis or attack. Second are the long-term considerations of how to survive financially if she decides to separate from her abuser.

In the short run, the physical damage may cost a great deal to repair. There are cases of women spending weeks in the hospital, losing their eyesight or incurring other permanent disabilities. Even an attack requiring considerably less medical treatment may require an employed wife to lose pay because of missed days of work while the visible signs of her attack heal.

The long-term economic predicament of a battered wife centers around survival and has been the subject of much discussion during the limited time that wife battery has been an active social issue. Del Martin (1976a), among others, has pointed out that wives most often remain in abusive situations because they cannot afford to do otherwise. Psychologists have identified additional reasons that keep women with violent men (Walker, in this volume). But, more than any other factor, the limited economic options available to women in such circumstances present the most formidable barriers to escape.

Although slightly over half of all married women are now employed, the economic reality is that a majority of wives are still dependent on their husbands (U.S. Census Bureau, 1976). Even when employed, most wives have limited earnings (either from low wages, part-time work, or both) and are ill-prepared to suddenly become sole breadwinners. This is particularly the case when there are children to support.

In marriages where the husband is violent and abusive, he also tends to isolate the wife and exert control over all aspects of her life. He frequently dominates their joint finances, leaving the wife with no access to money or other family resources. Del Martin, in a paper on the economics of wife beating, explains the plight of the wife without money:

> Many victims of wife-battering are so dependent economically they do not even have a bus token to enable them to leave. A man who beats his wife is not likely to provide her with "mad money." Many violent husbands handle all the money; sometimes they even do the grocery shopping themselves so that their wives will not have access to cash. Wives of affluent husbands are no better off. They may live in more luxurious homes and have access to charge accounts, but seldom to checking accounts. Many violent husbands take the car keys and money whenever they leave the house. [Martin, 1976a:3]

Gelles (1976) notes that educational and occupational factors affect whether a woman stays in a violent marriage: "the fewer resources a woman has, the less power she has and the more 'entrapped' she is in her marriage, the more she suffers at the hand of her husband without calling for help outside the family."

When a woman manages to escape a violent marriage, her economic problems become even more acute. She faces the immediate need to secure financial support for herself and her children. If she has not worked in some time and has limited or obsolete job skills, her earning potential may be extremely low. Her child care responsibility may further complicate her employment possibilities.

In some states, if a wife leaves the household, even to escape violent assaults, she may be found guilty of desertion and forfeit the right to alimony should she file for divorce or separate maintenance. Alimony is at best an unreliable source of income for divorced women. Available studies of judicial practices (Quedstedt, 1965:3) show that it is awarded in only a small percent of divorce cases. Child support is more frequently awarded, but, like alimony, it may not be paid. A recent study of child support found that of those women eligible to receive it, about 40% have never received even a single payment. In fact, this study revealed that if female-headed families had to rely solely on child support or alimony payments, only about 3% would be above the poverty level (Jones et al., 1977).

While a wife who leaves a violent home is likely to need immediate income, she may be far from able to go out to work. The road to psychological independence is a long one, because many abused women have been reduced to a nearly helpless state over a considerable period. In such a case, despite urgent economic need, the battered woman may not be able to support herself until a normal ego has been restored. This must be accomplished even before she can be expected to benefit from job training. The experience of the shelter movement in England has been that many battered women need to spend several years in some sort of supervised living situation (Pizzey, 1974).

Some displaced homemakers apply for welfare when they are divorced or widowed; but the battered wife living in a shelter or in someone else's household frequently cannot even seek this recourse because the Aid for Dependent Children (AFDC) regulations require that she have her own household to be eligible. In the best of circumstances, even with the capability for a rapid transition to a new life, battered women need job-related services—counseling, training, placement.

CHILD SEXUAL ABUSE

Sexual abuse, whether by strangers or relatives, can have several economic impacts on a family. In many cases, the family's initial reaction to and attempt to deal with sexual abuse is influenced by the degree of economic dependency of the mother on the father. The mother's concern over the drastic economic impact of discovery may, in fact, affect her willingness to admit that an incestuous situation exists in the household. When the father or stepfather is, as is most often the case, the abuser, discovery can mean criminal proceedings, loss of job, imprisonment, and disintegration of the family unit. Just as when a battered woman leaves a violent home, the mother then has a household to support. The family that has lost its breadwinner may be forced to rely on small, unreliable sources of income, such as child support or welfare. Women heading families divided by sexual abuse are also likely to need access to training and other services that could help them gain economic independence.

There are, of course, other economic impacts on a family, whether or not the family separates into two households. If the case enters the justice system, family members will lose time from work to accompany the child to testify or be interviewed themselves. The family frequently must bear the costs of whatever psychiatric care is needed. Victims of intrafamily sexual abuse may require lengthy psychiatric aid and access to low-cost or free mental health programs if they are to achieve a normal, productive adulthood.

Follow-up studies of incest victims have shown that the long-run consequences of incest are a propensity for the victim to abuse herself through prostitution, drug use, or alcoholism. Self-abuse of this sort frequently leads to economic deprivation and uncertainty. These adverse circumstances make it harder to secure treatment for addiction or other abuses, because the necessary programs and therapy are too costly.

HARASSMENT AND MEDICAL EXPLOITATION

SEXUAL HARASSMENT

Even when women attempt to control their lives and maintain economic independence, they do not escape the prospect of victimization, because they can be victimized by men in authority positions in the world outside their families. Chapter 8 analyzes the widespread phenomenon of sexual harassment at work. Working women face the possibility of sexual harassment from coworkers, supervisors, and potential employers. This sort of harassment in the job market is itself a form of economic exploitation, because it is accompanied by offers or withdrawals of employment, promotions, raises, transfers—all manner of financial and occupational rewards, punishments, or threats.

The prevalence of sexual harassment can be said to have an overall influence on the job status of women as a group. The anticipation of such situations and the desire to avoid them influence women's choices of occupation and work setting. For individual women who endure severe harassment, the experience may lead to unemployment and serious damage to their careers.

MEDICAL EXPLOITATION

Women are medically exploited when they receive improper or unnecessary health care. Medical care is costly, even when the treatment is needed and properly administered, but paying for improper medical treatment literally adds insult to injury. As Lear points out in Chapter 9, hysterectomies are performed at twice the rate in the United States as in England and Wales. It has been suggested that some of the operations are unnecessary, and one of the results is the cost to the patient, her insurance company, and to the premium-paying public. Improper treatment, such as over-tranquilizing, can lead to other even more expensive needs such as drug withdrawal programs or psychiatric treatment. The total cost of medical exploitation—including botched illegal abortions, unneeded surgery, overuse of drugs and other practices—has never been calculated. But it is easy to conclude that the cost is enormous, perhaps large enough to significantly influence the size and structure of the health care industry if it could be eliminated.

SEXUAL ASSAULT

A woman may have a tranquil, nonviolent marital life and a job in which sexual harassment is not a problem, yet still fall victim to a rapist.

Most rape victims must bear the substantial economic burdens from their attack alone, because there is little help from society's institutions. Five major economic consequences of a rape attack can be identified from the experiences of women victims. Not every victim experiences all of the consequences, but most experience at least some of the following:

1. The victim may miss work and, thus, lose pay because of her attack. In some cases, she will be unable to continue at her job because of her injuries or psychological trauma; in other cases, her work might put her in proximity to her attacker.

2. If the attacker remains at large and knows the victim's place of residence, she may need to move to another, more secure location. This may result in higher housing expenses as well as moving costs.

3. Rape victims may be required to pay for examination and emergency treatment, depending on hospital and insurance policies. In private hospitals, a routine forensic examination with no complications could cost up to $75.00 (Brodyaga et al., 1975:59). Abortion and pregnancy-related costs are also borne by the victim unless she can be reimbursed by her own insurance coverage.

4. A rape victim is likely to become acutely conscious of her security and many times will change to more expensive modes of transportation—from bus or subway, for example, to taxi or private car.

5. If the victim's attacker is brought to trial, she becomes the complaining witness, a necessary part of the prosecution. John Stein, in his report, *Assisting Crime Victims and Witnesses* (1977), finds that serving as a witness can be costly and that most jurisdictions are indifferent to these costs:

> Many jurisdictions provide no witness fees. Others' fees do not even cover out-of-pocket expenses, like babysitting, meals, bus fare or parking. . . . The employers of some witnesses are hostile to their employees taking time off to go to court. Being docked for lost time is common; being fired is not unheard of.

THE PROFITS OF VICTIMIZATION

The victimization of women is accompanied not only by losses to the individual victims, but also by substantial profits for another group of people. Some profits are acquired through the direct victimization of women, as in prostitution; other profits derive from vicarious victimization in pornography and advertising.

Many of the problems faced by any victim come about as a result of the indifference of the people or institutions with which she must deal. In such cases, the impact on the victim is a direct one. The impact of profit making from portrayed aggression against women is, on the other hand, diffused. It does not affect an individual in the way that a callous hospital emergency room staff would, for example. But it does reinforce the view that women are natural victims, and in doing so, has a potential impact on all who see the pornography, advertising, or films—whether they be male or female.

The fact that it is exploited for profit is only one unfortunate aspect of the women and violence theme. There are physical, mental, and social consequences more grave than the fact that some people are making money by showing women being hurt or by merchandising their bodies in violation of the law. Another distressing impact of this profit making is that these highly visible endeavors contribute to and reinforce the belief that women are innately victims and, at least part of the time, enjoy being abused.

Those entrepreneurs who make money through portrayals of violence against women have a stake in the status quo. A continuance of the view of women as victims and men as aggressors is in their financial interest. And, while the individuals involved may personally hold a variety of views toward victims of aggression—ranging from indifference to sympathy—their role in perpetuating it is an active one. They actively seek to profit from portrayals of women subjected to violence and victimization.

ADVERTISING

Advertising uses explicit images of physical and sexual violence against women, particularly to promote the sales of clothing and record albums. Recently this theme has become more common and explicit, especially in the entertainment industry. In June 1976, Atlantic Records placed a large billboard overlooking Sunset Strip in Los Angeles depicting a bruised woman with handcuffed wrists straddling a record album. The printed message was, "I'm black and blue from the Rolling Stones and I love it." The cover of a record album entitled "Jump on It" depicts a floodlit closeup of a woman's crotch. Another album shows a woman being abducted by a monster, and the cover of the album "Cut the Cake" portrays a slice of cake cutting through a woman's buttocks. A series of albums by the Ohio Players entitled "Pain," "Pleasure," "Ecstasy," and "Climax" show women being chained, hanged, and trussed in leather. "Wild Angel," by Nelson Slater, pictures a woman wearing a chain gag, and Bloodstone's "Do You Wanna Do A Thing?" shows a gang rape (Van Gelder, 1977:32).

Fashion magazines have also used themes of violence and female abuse in clothing displays. The May 1975 issue of *Vogue* contained a series of photographs featuring, among other things, a man ramming his hand into a woman's breast. The same photographer has done a series that includes a picture of a woman's head being forced into a toilet bowl. A particularly successful ad campaign was created for a Los Angeles pants company named Cheeks in 1976 by advertising executive Loren Miles and photographer Todd Gray. A woman is shown screaming while a man paddles her. Miles explained, "We decided to develop a campaign men could really identify with. We really wanted to give it to women." (*Time*, 1977).

The female abuse theme has recently been used by stores to display and sell their merchandise. A fall 1976 window at Bonwit Teller in Boston showed a woman dragging a female body wrapped in a rug. A boutique in Cambridge, Massachusetts, has shown a mannequin as a dead woman, blood coming from her mouth, placed in a trash can. Men's shoes were placed on her head and neck, with the caption, "We'd kill for these." Picturing the victimization of women has long been found effective and profitable. It has now become a principal technique in advertising campaigns, even those geared to a predominantly female market.

PORNOGRAPHY AND PROSTITUTION

Pornography has traditionally used images linking sex, violence, and female submission. Recent years have seen an increase in the supply of such materials easily available on the newsstand, and the success of magazines such as *Hustler* has shown this combination of images to be lucrative. "Soft porn" movies such as "The Story of O" have profitably pursued themes of female bondage and torture. A

Latin American film, "Snuff," allegedly shows the actual murder of a woman—the actress appearing in the film—who is killed and dismembered on camera during the filming of a pornographic sequence (Balliett, 1977:7). As in advertising, business interests have a stake in the continued portrayal of women as helpless and/or willing victims.

Films, photographs, and record covers are ways of profiting from the vicarious or depicted victimization of women. Prostitution, on the other hand, involves direct or actual victimization for profit. While it can be argued that prostitution is not unequivocally or in every instance a form of victimization, the economic forces at work in this business sector make it difficult for prostitutes to be classifed simply as enterprising businesswomen. In the first place, poor options in the job market tend to push women into prostitution. This has been pointed out by James (Chapter 7) and others. The median income for women ($6,957) employed full time, year round in 1974 was 57% of the median for comparable men ($12,152) (U.S. Census Bureau, 1976:45). Compared with unemployment or employment at the minimum wage, the income offered by prostitution might well appear attractive.

Earlier centuries have been no kinder. In discussing the plight of mid-19th century working women, Barbara Wertheimer (1977:2) says:

> It is small wonder that many turned to prostitution. Where the wages of women reduced them to starvation levels, prostitution sometimes appeared the only alternative.

A survey of 2,000 prostitutes in New York in 1858 found that over half had average earnings of only $1 a week before turning to prostitution.

Until women have access to all occupations and are not confined to a few low-paying jobs, it cannot be fairly said that they choose prostitution of their free will, any more than it can be said that they "choose" to be secretaries. But, regardless of why women enter prostitution, when they get there they find—as in other sectors of the economy—that the capital and management are controlled by men. Male "middlemen" such as pimps and hotel owners all too often control and profit from women's work in this field.

ECONOMIC ASSISTANCE FOR THE VICTIM

The introduction and previous chapters have established that the view of women as victims and their victimization by various methods are reinforced by society—through the media, childrearing, literature, education, and other practices. One cumulative message of the book is that, while women are encouraged by all these insitutions and practices to be passive, dependent, and vulnerable, there is little assistance available to them when victimization—the logical result of these traits—takes place. Del Martin (1976a:6) has described the economic vulnerability of the married woman persuasively:

it is not that women are naturally dependent—economic dependency is forced upon them when they marry, and it is reinforced by social expectations, family law, discriminatory practices in education and employment, credit regulations, etc. Once married the woman finds that every institution of society is geared to keep her in that marriage and to keep her dependent and powerless. When she becomes a victim of marital violence, society turns a deaf ear. To do otherwise would be to upset the economy.

The notion that the female victim deserves what she gets is by no means unheard of. But the idea that the victim of assault or other crime is deserving of assistance is becoming somewhat more common. Some prosecutors' offices and police departments have developed programs designed to ease the victim's progress through the criminal justice system. In addition, there are now community-based rape crisis centers in most cities, and shelters for battered women have been set up in a number of communities. These programs draw upon limited resources. Some do not address the *economic* problems of victims, and those that do, such as victim compensation, seldom reach the female victim. Thus the institutional framework for providing economic assistance to women is further developed than the actual capability and resources to deliver such assistance. The remainder of this section reviews the economic aspects of existing victim assistance programs and identifies major gaps in that programming.

VICTIM COMPENSATION

Compensation to crime victims is a growing practice, and at least 25 states now have laws providing for programs that reimburse victims for medical or other losses incurred as the result of a crime (Olson, 1975). Some states have enacted such laws but are waiting for passage of the federal Victims of Crime Act (HR 3686) before activating them. This bill would provide federal money to the states for their victim compensation programs. It is likely that additional states would also pass compensation statutes should the federal money become available.

As it now stands, only a small proportion of crime victims are reimbursed through these laws, and payments to individuals have been small. Most state statutes are alike in that they severely limit the maximum claim allowable. Payments are commonly allowed for medical expenses, loss of earnings, out of pocket expenses, and a funeral or death benefit (Knudten, 1977).

The chances of a female victim receiving compensation are reduced even further because of limitations in the laws regarding victims of rape and intrafamily abuse. Rape victims cannot be compensated unless they have suffered physical harm or injury. Compensation laws seldom provide benefits to cover psychological trauma so the cost of mental health care necessitated by the attack cannot be reimbursed. Even pregnancy-related medical expenses resulting from rape—prenatal care, delivery, abortion, and loss of earnings due to maternity—are not compensable in most states. Passage of HR 3686 would eliminate some of the ambiguity of those state laws that tend to eliminate rape victims from eligibility.

Current laws also effectively exclude victims of intrafamily offenses. The stipulation of most laws, that a victim cannot receive an award if he or she is related to his or her attacker, makes it impossible for battered women or incest victims to utilize victim compensation programs.

CIVIL DAMAGES

Another approach to ameliorating a victim's losses is a civil suit for damages. Such law suits have been undertaken against third parties, for example, when rape victims sue an apartment house

owner or motel operator for negligence. Suits claiming third party
liability are based on the theory that the action or negligence of the
third party in some way contributed to the victimization. If the risk
of assault could have been significantly reduced through reasonable
measures on the part of the third party, then a case can be made for
payment of damages to the plaintiff (victim). Legal research indicates
that there are currently no clear-cut principles covering third party
liability for rape cases. But generally, the litigant must show that the
interest of society in protecting individuals from assault is greater
than the economic burden such protection places upon third parties.
A precedent-setting decision in Washington, D.C., in 1977, ordered
the defendent (a motel owner) to pay the victims' psychiatric costs
for several years on the theory that the mental distress of two
women who were raped was a direct result of the motel owner's
negligence (*Washington Post,* September 10, 1977). A higher court
has since upheld the decision. While the theory of third party
liability has been of only limited use to rape victims thus far, there
have been some awards, and it remains a victim assistance concept
that could be further developed.

Another potential means of helping female victims of violence is
payment from the offender through a formal restitution program.
Offender restitution programs initiated in some jurisdictions have not
found special application to victims of rape or intrafamily violence.
They are used primarily for repayment of property losses (*National
Observer,* 1977). If the concept of compensation could be applied to
the rape victim, the offender might be required to repay medical
costs, mental health care costs, and the costs of replacing personal
property which was stolen or damaged. The limited capability of
most offenders to render restitution might reduce the chance that
victim payment for "pain and suffering" could ever be included in
offender restitution programs. An additional barrier is the low
number of rapists actually convicted and thus accessible to victim
restitution processes.

MEDICAL AND SOCIAL SERVICES

In a limited number of cities, the police department covers the
cost of the rape victim's medical examination at the hospital.
Although this practice is not yet widespread, it is justifiable because

the examination is forensic in nature and provides the evidence necessary for the state to prosecute. In Berkeley, California, for example, the police department pays the charge if the police have brought the victim to the hospital (Brodyaga et al., 1975).

It is more common, however, for free social services to be available than free medical services. But the availability of social services is likely to be limited by (a) their short-term, crisis-intervention nature, (b) limitation to low-income clients, or (c) overcrowding of facilities. Rape crisis centers provide short-term counseling and referrals. Some hospitals and police departments have sexual assault units that provide services without charge, and community mental health centers provide psychological counseling at low or no cost to low-income victims. However, community mental health programs are frequently overcrowded and preoccupied with clients with extremely serious disorders, and the rape victim may have low priority for treatment (Brodyaga et al., 1975). Thus, it is not uncommon for a rape victim to underwrite the cost of psychiatric care.

DOMESTIC LAW REFORM

Power within a family derives to an extent from the same economic factors that give power outside the family—money, paid employment, financial security, legal sanctions. As it now stands, the combined effect of legal disability, financial dependence, and stereotyped marital roles leaves most women in a subordinate position vis-à-vis their husbands. It has been suggested that a more equal distribution of power and assets between spouses—i.e., sex equality—could in the long run lead to a reduction in marital violence (Straus, 1977). At least with a more equal share of the family's economic assets, more abused women might marshal the resources to leave violent homes.

The economic disadvantages of wives are widespread and emanate from nonenforcement of support laws, sex differentiation in inheritance laws, and a circumscribed role in the control and sale of family assets. The secondary status of wives has been documented by a group of papers published by the National Commission on the Observance of International Women's Year (1976, 1977), which examined laws and judicial practices in the various states.

Domestic laws are the province of each state and must be reformed by action of the state legislature. The concept of "partnership marriage" has been put forth as a model for legal reform (Krauskopf, 1977) and would provide for equal or joint authority for wives with their husbands. Some states, such as Washington, have revised their codes in conformity with this concept; most have not.

DISPLACED HOMEMAKER

The woman who leaves an abusive situation may need long-term assistance in order to accomplish the transition to economic independence. Depending on her work experience and her psychological state, she may need job counseling, training, and help in applying for assistance programs such as food stamps, welfare, or public housing. These needs may be experienced by any woman who terminates a marriage, particularly if she has spent a number of years out of the labor force. Legislation now before Congress would address these needs. The Displaced Homemakers Act (1977) would establish service programs for people who have been dependent homemakers and face a transition to independence. In addition to establishing new services, the bill would make displaced homemakers eligible for some existing programs, such as federally funded training.

THE SOCIAL COST OF FEMALE VICTIMIZATION

While advertisers and the pornography industry may find exploitation of sexual violence to be profitable, society pays a heavy price for the victimization of women. Relatively few rapists, wife beaters, and child molesters are prosecuted, and even fewer are convicted. However, criminal litigation and incarceration of even a few such offenders are carried out at great public expense. Furthermore, a large proportion of law enforcement resources is devoted to family violence cases. It is estimated that in Atlanta, 60% of night calls to police are domestic disturbance cases; in San Francisco, 50% of all calls in 1974 were for such cases. One of the goals of improved treatment for victims of sex assault and wife abuse is more effective criminal justice intervention from initial police response to prosecution, conviction, and sentencing. Accomplishing this goal could lead to an even greater commitment of public money.

Crime prevention may cost less than prosecuting and imprisoning offenders and treating victims. Setting aside the humane considerations of victims' rights and needs, effective prevention programs could be justified in public policy on a cost-benefit basis alone. As for long-term victimization—as in the case of wife abuse or incest—early intervention could prevent some of the expensive consequences to society. Children of violent husbands are often beaten, either by the father or by the abused mother. They grow up to engage in delinquent behavior and later are abusive to their own children and spouses, or are prone to other violent acts. It would no doubt cost less to treat a violent family than to pay for the antisocial behavior of children raised in such an environment.

The girl involved with a male adult member of her family in an incestuous relationship frequently turns to self-abuse later in life—drug addiction and prostitution are common. One program treating mothers who abuse their children reports that nearly 70% of the mothers report sex abuse in their own childhood. If the victims of these practices were either treated when they were children or monitored for problems surfacing later in adolescence, the social costs of treating addicts and dealing with their crime and other destructive actions would surely be reduced.

Some kinds of public assistance for victimized women should be undertaken on humane grounds. Among these kinds of reforms are the sympathetic treatment of victims by hospitals and police, and the provision of emergency housing for women and children in need of refuge. Provision of these kinds of services and reforms often bogs down in debate about which institution or group is best suited to provide them or what the source or level of funding will be.

A larger view of the problem reveals that victimization is linked to the status of women in society; such a conclusion is reinforced by each of the other chapters in this volume. Society thus supports a system that is not only costly to the individual victims, but also to the general public. If society and its major institutions could make a commitment to equalizing the legal and economic status of women, it is well within reason to expect that the heavy social costs of the status quo might be reduced.

Economic dependency and limited political clout seem appropriate characteristics (even prerequisites) for a victim class, but not for influential members of the population. It would be hard to imagine the problem of wife abuse, for example, if most women supported themselves and substantial numbers of judges, legislators, and business executives were women. It would be almost inconceivable that in an egalitarian society, where half the U.S. Senate was female, as well as half the surgeons and corporate heads, that large numbers of them would return home at night to be beaten by their husbands. Victimization is made possible by powerlessness, and a victim class is made possible by chronic powerlessness. Equality and economic equity for women could make their victimization at the hands of men much less inevitable.

REFERENCES

ARNOLD, M. (1977). "Making the criminal pay back his victim." National Observer, 16(14):1.

BALLIETT, B. (1977). "Selling the pain of women." Casa, the Newsletter for the Center Against Sexual Assault, 4(7).

BRODYAGA, L. et al. (1975). Rape and its victims: A report for citizens, health facilities, and criminal justice agencies. Washington, D.C.: U.S. Government Printing Office.

CHAPMAN, J.R. (1976). Economic independence for women: The foundation for civil rights. Beverly Hills, Calif.: Sage.

Displaced Homemakers Act (1977). HR 28. 95th Congress, 1st Session, introduced January 4.

GELLES, R. (1976). "Abused wives, why do they stay?" Paper delivered at the Eastern Sociological Society, March, Boston.

JOHNSON, B., and HAYGHE, H. (1977). Monthly Labor Review, 100(9):32.

JONES, C., GORDON, N., and SAWHILL, I. (1977). Child support payments in the United States. Washington, D.C.: Urban Institute.

KNUDTEN, R.D. (1977). Victims and witnesses: Their experiences with crime and the criminal justice system. Washington, D.C.: U.S. Government Printing Office.

KRAUSKOPF, J.M. (1977). "Partnership marriage: Legal reforms needed." Pp. 93-121 in J.R. Chapman and M. Gates (eds.), Women into wives: The legal and economic impact of marriage. Beverly Hills, Calif.: Sage.

LAMBORN, L. (1976). "Crime victim compensation: Theory and practice in the second decade." Victimology: An International Journal, 1(4):503.

MARTIN, D. (1976a). "The economics of wifebeating." Paper presented at the Marital Violence Session of the American Sociological Association Conference, New York, August.

––– (1976b). Battered wives. San Francisco: Glide.

National Commission on Observance of International Women's Year (1976-1977). "The legal status of homemakers." (A paper has been published for each state and the District of Columbia.) Washington, D.C.: U.S. Government Printing Office.

New York Times (1977). "Child pornograpny called big business." May 28.

O'BRIEN, K. (n.d.). Third party liability in civil actions for rape. Unpublished paper.

OLSON, L. (1975). Briefing paper on victim compensation. National League of Cities/ Conference of Mayors, Washington, D.C. Unpublished paper.

PIZZEY, E. (1974). Scream quietly or the neighbors will hear. Middlesex, England: Penguin.

QUENSTEDT, U. (1965). Survey of 575 domestic relations court judges, friends of the court, and commissioners of domestic relations (Monograph no. 1). Washington, D.C.: Family Law Section, American Bar Association.

REAGE, P. (1973). Story of O. New York: Ballantine.

STEIN, J. (1977). Assisting crime victims and witnesses. Unpublished report.

STEINMETZ, S., and STRAUS, M. (1974). Violence in the family. New York: Harper and Row.

STRAUS, M.A. (1977). "Sexual inequality, cultural norms, and wife-beating." Pp. 59-77 in J.R. Chapman and M. Gates (eds.), Women into wives: The legal and economic impact of marriage. Beverly Hills, Calif.: Sage.

Time (1977). "Really socking it to women." February 7, pp. 58-59.

U.S. Bureau of the Census (1976). "A statistical portrait of women." Current Population Reports, Series P-23, no. 58, Washington, D.C.: U.S. Government Printing Office.

U.S. Congress, House of Representatives, Subcommittee on Criminal Justice (1976). Victims of crime compensation legislation. Washington, D.C.: U.S. Government Printing Office.

U.S. Department of Labor, Women's Bureau (1975). 1975 Handbook on women workers (Bulletin 297). Washington, D.C.: U.S. Government Printing Office.

VAN GELDER, L. (1977). "Women's war on LP cover violence." Rolling Stone, 237:32-33.

VIANO, E. (ed., 1975). Victims and society. Washington, D.C.: Visage Press.

Victims of Crime Act (1977). HR3686. 95th Congress, 1st Session, introduced February 17.

WERTHEIMER, B.M. (1977). We were there. New York: Pantheon.

11

WOMEN AND VICTIMIZATION:
THE AFTERMATH

KATHERINE SALTZMAN

The preceding chapters have described in detail the many forms of victimization of women, from subtle exploitation and discrimination to severe forms of aggression. Until the recent establishment of women's advocacy and feminist groups, singular reports of women's victimization were ignored, ridiculed, or dismissed as unimportant. The victimization of women has been acceptable and in some ways encouraged. Ironically, and bitterly so for many women, the society that has made widespread female victimization an acceptable practice, blames the woman for provoking assault, for encouraging exploitation, and for enjoying the role of masochist.

The solutions and suggestions offered in this book are necessary to mitigate the effects of physical and emotional trauma that frequently result from victimization. The work that has been done to promote change within the criminal justice system, to provide more economic alternatives, and to assure adequate medical care has created some of the first major breakthroughs toward changing societal attitudes to female victimization. Despite the importance of these changes and the impact that they may ultimately have upon individual women, the feeling remains that such efforts are only binding the wounds that are inevitably inflicted.

THE ORIGINS OF VICTIMIZATION

The reemergence of the feminist movement in the 1960s has resulted in widespread efforts to bring attention to the seriousness of female victimization and has raised some interesting issues for consideration. From a political point of view, women can be viewed as an oppressed subculture even in societies that purport to have established the individual freedoms of democracy. The struggle is to attain equality with men, to overcome institutionalized sexism, and to establish that women are inherently as capable as men, subject to similar human failings and successes.

An overview of the literature on victimization reveals that several elements tend to predispose a group of individuals to repeated victimization. These elements include (1) dominant cultural attitudes and myths about the victimized class, (2) the perceived characteristics of the victimized class, and (3) the perceptions and attitudes of the victimized class itself. Perhaps the most significant concept to consider regarding the predisposition of groups to repeated victimization is that of unequal status.

The failure of most cultures to view women as equals has several origins that are perpetuated in traditional belief systems. Judeo-Christian heritage has played a major role in perpetuating the belief that women are innately evil and inferior to men. The dominant Judeo-Christian themes regarding women are that they were created by God for man's pleasure and entertainment, that woman's sexuality is a source of temptation and evil, and that woman's role is naturally limited and inferior because of her biology. Brownmiller (1975) described how the church has promulgated the virgin/whore dichotomy, encouraged the double standard of morality, and attempted to control woman by banning birth control and binding her to her biology. As part of the Western belief system, Judeo-Christian doctrine has convinced women as well as men that in the natural order of things women are inferior beings whose major function is the propagation of the species.

The structure of the family, whether extended or nuclear, has also placed limitations on women's status and freedom that tend to encourage victimization (Straus, 1976). With the family viewed as a mini-government in which there are hierarchical powers, the woman has acquired only those freedoms that have been granted her by the male authority figure. Traditionally considered a possession owned by the father, she is passed from his authority and control to that of her husband at the time of marriage, thus perpetuating her dependency on men and denying her the opportunity to develop personal autonomy. Convinced from an early age that marriage and motherhood are the highest calling and first priority of the fulfilled woman, the female child not only accepts her destiny of dependency but looks forward to it as the achievement of her highest goal in life (Martin, 1976). Her sense of identity and self-worth become identical with her functions as mother and wife, and her other talents and potentials remain latent and beyond her conscious awareness. Thus, in an environment seemingly of her own choosing, the woman submits to an inferior status in her closest relationships. The children of the relationship, observing the unequal state of affairs, in turn grow up believing that male dominance and female submission are natural and even desirable.

Limited expectations for women are futher shown by the fact that equal educational opportunity has been largely denied them as superfluous (Fasteau, 1975). Female children are subtly discouraged, if not blatantly banned, from engaging in fields of study considered appropriate for the male. Traditional textbooks indicate that men only were involved in activities of historical, artistic, or educational importance, while women maintained the home. The low expectations set for women in the educational system serve to reinforce the vicious circle that guarantees the perceived inferiority of the female and the necessity for female dependency on the male.

Even though some women have managed to attain high levels of educational and professional status, they tend to remain rare exceptions and in that sense do not serve as role models for the majority of females. In 1972, 90% of women between the ages of 30 and 44 had no college degree (U.S. Department of Commerce, 1973). Thus the primary model for the female child continues to be that of homemaker, a relatively easy goal to attain and one which fits the self-concept of the child who has learned that she is not capable of studying organic chemistry and algebra even before she has had an opportunity to try. Women who do attain high professional status are not accorded the same respect as males, especially when they also attempt to fulfill the female role.

Thus, as a result of the influence of the three major institutions on which Western culture is based (Judeo-Christian morality, family structure, and the education system), the first condition for the victimization of women as a class is fulfilled: the woman is an inferior being.

Other conditions that seem to be required to justify dominance and oppression of one group by another also pertain to the victimization of women. For example, oppressed groups must be perceived as being different from the dominant group, and individuals within the oppressed group must be easily identified as belonging to that group. Ethnicity, racial characteristics, secondary sex characteristics, and other obvious differences provide a superficial basis for positive as well as negative identification: black as distinguished from white, old as distinguished from young, male as distinguished from female. Such obvious differences may provide a foundation for many judgments regarding the superiority of one group over another. Imagined or real characteristics of the group are then applied to the individual, and the characteristics of a specific individual may be applied to the group—both result in unfounded generalizations. Alienation, depersonalization, and prejudice then prevail, making up the second condition necessary for victimization and serving to legitimize the acts of the oppressor (Fattah, 1976).

It has been observed that women as an oppressed minority have a scapegoat status not unlike that suffered by Jews, blacks, religious heretics, homosexuals, and other so-called deviant members of the community. Szasz (1970) asserts that the scapegoat is made to appear different so that she or he may be alienated and destroyed to perpetuate the aggrandizement of the oppressor and to ventilate his frustration and rage about his own human condition.

The final condition necessary for the occurrence and continuation of victimization is that of acceptance of victimization by the victims themselves. At first it would seem that this acceptance is the most frustrating aspect of victimization, but it is also the aspect from which hope for change may obtain. A person who is convinced that the groups with which she or he identifies is inferior must also believe the self to be inferior. She or he thus shares the same beliefs and biases about self that the oppressor holds, and these beliefs and biases, of course, include the justification for the victimization. The history of the civil rights movement in the United States has shown